The Spirit of Rooster

How Winning Is Done

Hans Keith Oldham

The Spirit of Rooster

Copyright © 2019 Hans Keith Oldham

All rights reserved.

ISBN: 9781073075621

DEDICATION

This book is dedicated to my beloved Andrea who stayed the distance and became my wife. I'm not sure what was tougher for her during my cancer treatment, caring for me or marrying me!

It also pays tribute to all those who have cared for cancer victims, whether by profession or by unfortunate circumstance. You are giants.

THE PROLOGUE
CANCER SUCKS

Cancer sucks.

This is not an uncommon point of view. It's a word that strikes fear; especially into those who have never suffered it themselves and have only felt the blessed naivety of witnessing cancer, and its treatment, in others. "Nobody really survives cancer, do they?"

I'm not so sure; it only ever affects others, not me.

Recent studies claim that one in two people will be diagnosed with cancer in their lifetime. Most of us know someone who has suffered, or possibly died, as a result of cancer. Family and friends of cancer patients also face hardships watching and caring for a loved one struggling with this horrible disease. GPs, surgeons, nurses, oncologists, scientists, researchers, carers, pharmacists, funeral directors and many other professions face the problems of cancer in others, daily. Altogether, that's a lot of people, right?

Do some research and you will find that there are many different types of cancer. It attacks all areas of the body. Sufferers of each type will be diagnosed at different stages. Each stage will come with its own unique challenges.

Treatment can involve, surgery, chemotherapy, radiotherapy, hormone therapy, immunotherapy, targeted therapy, any number of emerging new trials, a change of diet or even doing nothing (always an option). There are many variables in type, diagnosis, treatment and impact on individuals.

My very wise oncologist once said to me that it's more important to treat the person than to treat the disease. This strategy introduces numerous other variables, as those affected face the impact of cancer on finances, work, relationships, exercise, hobbies, sex, intellect, emotional stability… on life itself.

It's normal enough to want things in life and to work hard to get them: a new house, a car, a holiday, a career, to pass exams, to get married or to lose weight. Someone battling cancer wants just one thing; to win the battle. Nothing else matters.

Every individual, once diagnosed with cancer, will start their very own, very personal and unique adventure. It's an inescapable adventure of pain, triumph, exhaustion, inspiration, sadness, wonderment, suffering, courage, tears and laughter. An emotional roller-coaster. Some may survive, others will not.

This book is a record of my very own cancer caper. I should caution you that it is a very real, diarised and honest account. It is graphic and detailed in describing both medical procedures and bodily functions, so it is not for the faint-hearted.

Society tends to shy away from talking openly about the things it fears, or is uncertain about. Cancer, and the emotion it provokes, is often swept away under the carpet rather than analysed, discussed and publicly portrayed. Read on and you will find that the determination to be candid and the refusal to be dismissive, minimises stigma and fear.

Humour sustained me throughout intense sadness and so these two emotions are served up in equal measure, throughout this book. It is not intended to be self-indulgent, far from it as it's brutally self-deprecating and forthright. But writing it has been self-cleansing, even cathartic. The cancer demon has been well and truly exorcised in the writing of these pages.

Everything happened precisely as written. Read with caution and at your own risk. You have been warned.

Welcome to *The Spirit of Rooster.*

1
HAPPIER TIMES

I've heard it said that a person needs three things to be truly happy; someone to love, something to do and something to hope for. I have found this to be true, particularly when enjoying good physical health. Cancer can be a risk to life, it kills. With cancer; having someone to love becomes vital, doing things becomes harder and hope can be all there is.

Surviving cancer restores the balance in such a way that a return to happier times becomes profound and thoroughly gratifying. Life and happiness are never again taken for granted.

"Count your age by friends, not years. Count your life by smiles, not tears."
– John Lennon

December 2016

Sometimes, in life, all the stars seem to be aligned with the gods smiling down on you. Every aspect of life is fulfilling and enjoyable. This is such a time for me.

I live with Andrea, increasingly the love of my life. She brings so much fun and laughter into our lives. I feel loved by her, supported in everything I do, encouraged to be me, validated. The different interests we have seem to strengthen the time we have together. With two difficult divorces behind me I feel happy and free. We have lived together for just over two years but our relationship is still developing, so it isn't without its difficulties. Nevertheless, we have trust, love and a future together. The bedrock foundations we are laying will soon prove to be so very, very important.

My three sons, Luke, Max and Cyrus are all at university. Each of them following their own dream. My boys have become strong, caring, independent men. During their formative years I had been a scout leader, football coach and rugby dad. I had immersed myself in their passions: theatre, martial arts, team sports and holidays. Their friends were always made welcome at our home and my taxi service was readily available. The *Bank of Dad* invested heavily in their upbringing. I love them and tell them so often. I feel such pride for the men they have become. I wonder where life will take them once they have graduated, secure in the knowledge that they are each well equipped to forge happy, independent and successful futures for themselves. I constantly glow at the thought of them.

A source of immense pride was seeing my daughter, Alyssa, enter the world, grow up and graduate from Aberystwyth University. I also spent many years involving myself in her passions; horse riding, sleep-overs, parties, travel and school life to name but a few. Although, currently, there is distance between us she is never far from my thoughts and my heart. The feeling of being Lys' father is wonderful and the many memories I have of her always make me smile. Like her brothers, I love her. She too, is successfully adulting in a very challenging world.

I am an IT contractor by trade. I have worked in senior IT management roles across a number of different industries as an interim leader for over eight years. I have been the interim Head of IT Service and Operations for Co-Op Food Retail in Manchester for about a year. I am thoroughly enjoying my time here as an IT professional and through the many relationships I have worked hard to establish.

My CIO, Cheryl Marshall, is amongst the very best I have worked for: tough, challenging but enormously supportive. She is the epitome of the ethical and people-centric culture of the organisation. My income is very good. It enables me to take holidays and invest in home improvements which I would not otherwise be able to do. I am able to afford a new Range Rover Vogue, a beautiful car and a joy to drive.

My passion in life is the theatre, more specifically the Macclesfield Amateur Dramatic Society (MADS). Luke, my eldest son, had introduced me to MADS some three years earlier. My first acting role was a two-hander with him. Since then I've been cast in a number of supporting roles. I enjoy acting. Whether I am any good I leave to the opinion of others. Occasionally the critics seemed to like my performances and I continue to be cast in plays in the open, competitive auditions. I am lucky enough to be cast as Johnny 'Rooster' Byron in Jez Butterworth's acclaimed *Jerusalem*. It is the lead role of a brilliant play. I am both ecstatic and nervous about it but acting is what I enjoy doing. My first lead role and… Rooster… let rehearsals begin!

As well as the many friendships I have cultivated at MADS, I have many others. In particular, are a group of fellow golfers. Although I have not played a round of golf for a couple of years I am a member of The Considerably Biggar Golf Society (CBGS). So-called because of the annual meeting held each year at The Crown in Biggar. It's a traditional watering hole en route to Edinburgh for a long weekend of drunken laddish behaviour, distracted only by the occasional round of competitive golf. Once you join this motley crew you never really leave. The society was formed by like-minded individuals some time at the end of the last millennium. I have an ambition to join these rascals on tour once again, something to hope for.

By extension, Andrea's friends have become my friends and I continue to enjoy my time with those I have known for many years. If I count my age by friends rather than years, Methuselah would be my contemporary.

I am living in a perfect storm of happy times.

Happy except for one thing, my bowel habits have changed. I didn't really notice it at first but I have started going for a poo more frequently each day and it is taking more time than normal to squeeze out less with each visit. I thought nothing of it until a few weeks had passed and pooing had started to be uncomfortable too.

At the moment, I am far too busy to go to the doctor. However, my contract at work is due to expire at the end of the year so I resolve to visit my GP in the new year if the problem hasn't gone away by then.

January 2017

It hasn't, if anything, my bowel struggle has intensified. Cheryl has asked me to extend my contract until the end of February 2017. Dave Robertson has been recruited to do my job on a permanent basis. I am required to hand over the role to him before departing. Of course I oblige. This means that the visit to my GP will have to wait until the beginning of March.

March 2017

A time to change my priorities. My IT contract has ended but *Jerusalem* rehearsals are becoming busier and more intense. Occasionally I get the urge to poo during rehearsals and disappear to the toilet for a few minutes, much, I suspect, to the annoyance of my exceptionally talented but stressed director, Cameron Chandler. Opening night is the 24 April and there is much work to do. I start to worry about the potential for poo urges and bottom discomfort during a live performance. That would be a tad awkward! The thought motivates me to finally visit my GP.

During my first visit, I answer lots of questions about my bowel movements, diet and general well-being. No clear diagnosis is offered. The most likely theory is that I have developed an intolerance to a food type. It will take a number of weeks to establish exactly what that might be.

I try cutting out dairy, wheat and gluten. I monitor the results. I have a blood test. The only thing that changes is that the symptoms worsen as time progresses... more pooing urges, more pain and producing less with each visit to the toilet.

The final throw of the dice; a stool sample. Now I don't mean to sound ungrateful but anyone who has provided such a sample will know that it isn't as easy as it sounds. The container I am given is tiny. Handling poo and pushing it into small places is not in my skillset. Neither does the process come with instructions.

But help is at hand. There is actually a government website with a press release called *Poo pots: how do you fill them?*. It documents a seven-step process of how to collect a stool sample. It advises the use of a spatula. I wasn't given one but I improvise. After some sticky trial and error the poo pot is filled, the improvised spatula (an ice lolly stick) is consigned to the bin (the wheelie bin at the bottom of the drive) and my hands are thoroughly washed and scrubbed.

I marvel at my success! Looking back I would never have believed at how adept I would eventually become at poo management.

I join the line of embarrassed poo pot purveyors at my GP's clinic and shuffle forward. When I get to the receptionist I do the typically British thing of smiling awkwardly, shrugging my shoulders and looking around in order to share the embarrassment with anyone close enough to see my faeces being handed over.

A few days pass and the GP's receptionist phones me with the results.

"It's okay Mr Oldham, there's nothing wrong with your poo, you'll be fine now."

"Well thank goodness for that; a miracle cure, and from a doctor's receptionist too!"

I'm thinking that it takes about seven years to train a Doctor and two minutes for the receptionist to think she's one as well, but I don't quite feel brave enough to share that opinion with her.

However, my sarcastic response is abrupt because I am presently perched on the loo in considerable pain, trying my best to pass the tiniest poo and failing.

The receptionist is initially taken aback. I am in no mood to be polite as I reply through gritted teeth, straining until my face reddens, the veins on my forehead bulge as I collapse back into the bowl with an:

"oomph argh!"

"I…er…no need to be like that Mr Oldham."

"I'm sorry, but there is every need to be *like that*."

And then, quite out of character, I blurt out:

"It fucking hurts!"

She really has caught me at a bad moment. I immediately regret my profanity sensing that it is likely to result in my lifeline to medical help being disconnected.

"Please, can I speak to a doctor… I'm sorry, really I am."

"I'll arrange for our locum to call you this afternoon."

Silence.

I'm doomed!

The locum phones later in the day and arrangements are made for her to examine me the following day as an emergency case. My first thoughts are "examine" - what does that entail? I imagine a slightly built lady doctor with slender hands and small fingers. At least "emergency" suggests they are taking me seriously.

As I step into the locums' clinic the slightly built lady doctor stands smiling to greet me. She towers over six feet tall. Her hand extends to greet mine. My hand, the size of a child's in hers, is enveloped by her large sausage fingers. She lets her vice-like grip go as I tremble at the thought of the examination. We both sit and she methodically reviews my notes. After a brief discussion of events so far she snaps on her surgical gloves and utters the dreaded words.

"If you could hop onto the bed behind the curtain Mr Oldham and pull your pants down. I'd like to give you a rectal examination."

The cold gel she massages into my anus is, I have to confess, at first rather pleasant. Then the searing pain hits me. My whole body clenches. My teeth grit. Tears trickle out of the corners of my eyes. One of her sausage fingers has forced its way into my rectum, the largest middle finger, up to the knuckle.

"That's right Mr Oldham, if you could just relax."

"RELAX?" I scream inside my head whilst recognising that she has an overwhelming advantage in requesting co-operation from me.

Many months later I was informed of two things which brought this moment back into sharp focus. First, a man's anus is surrounded by strong muscles making the entrance to it tight. Second, I have a cluster of tumours quite low down in my anus causing painful constriction.

How I am supposed to relax as the sausage finger spins and gropes its way around inside my infected ring piece is beyond me. A ring piece that, given the additional constriction of tumours, struggled to pass a turd the size of a finger nail.

I am beginning to think she might get stuck. After what seems like an eternity, but in truth is probably only about ten seconds, the greased finger slides out. Followed, I'm ashamed to say, by a loud noise and a small, but not inconspicuous, poop. The propelled faecal matter is easily caught in the baseball-glove hand of my colossus.

Whilst the way in was painful, the way out offered an anxious, but welcome, relief. I didn't know it at the time but this will not be the last time that the medical profession will wipe my backside for me.

Examination complete, the Babe Ruth gargantuan offers me her pearls of wisdom.

"I'm just not sure," she deliberates, "so I'm going to refer you for a colonoscopy at Macclesfield Hospital."

A colonoscopy, she explains, is a medical procedure that allows the examiner to view the inside of the colon. The colonoscope is a long flexible tube, about the thickness of a finger, with a camera and a light at its tip. It enters the colon via the anus and will travel the full length of the colon. The colon is also known as the large bowel and is part of the digestive system. Therein lies the problem that needs investigating.

"Thickness of a finger? Please not yours!" I sincerely and secretly pray.

I leave the GP's surgery feeling disappointed at not having a diagnosis despite the fisting I had just received. I also wish I had been able to show more gratitude. The locum had done her professional best in very trying circumstances.

A week later a letter arrives confirming that my colonoscopy has been arranged for the morning of Tuesday 18 April.

Damn it! Run-up week for *Jerusalem*.

2
A DIAGNOSIS

A medical diagnosis is the process of determining which disease or condition explains a person's symptoms. Information is collected from a physical examination, various medical procedures and the patient's medical history. Diagnosing can be challenging because many symptoms are nonspecific and don't therefore always provide a pathway to the correct condition. Speed and an early diagnosis of cancer are essential for the right treatment and the best chance of survival. If your body is telling you that something is wrong, get yourself diagnosed without delay.

"You don't drown by falling in the water. You drown by staying there."
– Edwin Louis Cole

17 April 2017

After many weeks of rehearsals, *Jerusalem* run-up week finally commences. This involves rehearsing the full play every evening, in full costume, on set, under lights and with props. Everything designed to trip you up, find you out, fine tune and perfect the play. One of those evenings is a tech run. The actors become pawns on a chess-board for the light and sound engineers to move around the stage as they wish. To ensure all technical cues are defined and recorded. Tonight, Monday, is the tech run.

In preparation for my colonoscopy tomorrow I have to clear out my colon this evening. The camera needs to be able to move freely inside me and have full sight of my inner colon wall. Under the circumstances, I have been granted a leave of absence from the tech run and somebody will stand in for me. Clearing out my colon is not an activity to be shared with others at the theatre.

Moviprep is the means by which my colon shall be cleansed. It comes in powder form and is mixed into a litre of water. The victim then drinks the liquid over the course of an hour. The next two hours is spent sitting on the toilet while a world of poo fires out of your bottom.

It's powerful jet-propelled stuff. It is also the devil's brew with a syrupy consistency and a sweet lemon flavour. The more you drink, the harder it becomes to swallow it. The final glass is almost impossible to ingest. The after-taste is foul, clings to your tongue and lingers for an age. I cringe at the thought of it. It comes from the same menu as the eating challenge in *I'm A Celebrity. Get Me Out of Here!*

Simply put, I'm not a fan of Moviprep; nobody is. But it's a necessary evil brew and after months of constriction I am glad to be having a good clear out.

I am not disappointed. I must lose a stone in weight in those two hours.

18 April 2017

This is going to be a long day. I set the alarm for 6am. The Moviprep process is to be repeated again this morning. Last night was difficult; this morning is doubly so. Thinking there couldn't be much left in my colon, if anything, a two-hour shower of poo gravy comes as a surprise. I feel wafer-thin and hungry as a lion by the end of my ordeal. I haven't eaten anything since midday yesterday.

Andrea drives me to the hospital and we arrive in time for the morning appointment. I am admitted into the Endoscopy and Treatment Unit. Andrea has to remain in the reception waiting area while I am taken into the secure unit and to a changing room opposite the treatment room. I strip and put on a hospital gown as a nurse discusses pain relief with me. As the drug they prescribe can result in prolonged drowsiness, I elect to rely only on Entonox (gas and air). I have a full *Jerusalem* rehearsal scheduled for this evening and will need my wits about me. I will get through the pain with the help of the odd blast of Entonox.

Having established the rules of engagement, I am taken into the treatment room. The high-tech equipment surrounding the treatment bed is impressive. A surgeon, his assistant and a nurse greet me with a warmth, care and humanity that would shame Mother Teresa. The nurse speaks first with the sort of smile used only for an old friend you haven't seen for some time.

"Ah! Mr Oldham you're in a play I believe. Just jump up on the bed, lie on your side and lift your gown please."

"Yes, I, erm… of course… a play yes… but how did you…"

Genius! Showing an apparent genuine interest in my passion as a distraction to the meticulous attention given to surgical preparation going on around me. This nurse is a better actor than me and I'm drawn in by her deception as I arrange myself on the treatment bed without a care. The surgeon joins the conversation and soon banter and laughter fill the room. I am primed and ready, my exposed arse, puckered and pointing toward the hospital chapel in prayer.

The cold gel being massaged into my anus is a stark reminder of what is about to follow. The nurse suggests a few sucks of Entonox. I scrunch my eyes closed and screw up my face. Bracing myself for the assault.

To my relief this fellow seems to have the gentle touch that escaped the Amazonian warrior. As he eases the colonoscope through my anus and into my bowel I feel a little discomfort but nowhere near that of my previous experience. It probably helps that the effects of the Entonox have just hit me. In my bracing panic, I draw long, deep breaths from the Entonox mouthpiece. There is a surge of dizziness coupled with a relaxed, careless attitude that seems to make the pain bearable. As my head clears, I find myself staring up at one of the large monitors and the inside of my colon in full colour and graphic detail.

The challenge for the surgeon is to guide the colonoscope, and hence the camera, right to the end of the colon and back again. Along the way he can pause at anything of note and take a closer look. The challenge for me is to remain calm and do anything that is asked of me. When somebody has you in this position you tend to oblige almost any request. I am quite prepared to hand over my bank card and PIN, if it's asked for. Immediately, the surgeon pauses.

"Interesting!"

I squint to look closely and regret not bringing my reading glasses.

"Tattoo here please." The surgeon demands with authority.

Tattoo complete, to mark the area, he moves on explaining that we will take a closer look at it as we reverse out. We carefully continue our journey. The colon is shaped like a large question mark but with angled corners at the top rather than a curve. As we approach the first and sharpest corner the surgeon advises me to take some deep breaths of Entonox.

"I call this *tricky corner*," he explains. "I'm going to have to use some force to push the colonoscope round it. Are you ready?"

He sees me wide-eyed and drawing deeply on the Entonox so doesn't wait for a reply. I feel very little pain but it is strange to feel my insides being manipulated and pushed around. The instant hit of Entonox has relaxed me back into a careless state. Soon after, we reach the end of the colon. Here the surgeon takes a picture; this is necessary to prove the entire colon has been inspected.

The return journey is much quicker. When we get back to the tattoo the surgeon pauses again.

"Hmm!" This noise conveys so much but says so little.

"What we have here, I suspect, is the cause of your symptoms, Mr Oldham. We will take a biopsy please."

A pincer-like tool extends beyond the camera and snips away some tissue of the damaged colon wall. The colonoscope is then retracted from inside me. With the procedure now complete I am asked to return to the changing room and get dressed. The surgeon will meet me there to discuss findings. Naively thinking of nothing else except that I no longer have an alien inside me trying to burst free I thank my assailants and leave the surgery.

Once I am dressed my Guardian Angel appears.

Karen Rimmer is the mother of our dear MADS friends Cath and Beth. She is a nurse about to end her shift and is aware of my procedure.

"I've arranged for Andrea to join us and the surgeon will be here to explain things in just a moment. How are you feeling?"

Andrea appears just in time to hear me confirm that I am feeling just fine but glad that it's over. She smiles and chuckles in that way she has that always cheers me up. I do the eyes to the ceiling and silly grin thing confirming we are happily on the same wavelength. Then the surgeon enters the room and speaks very plainly and directly to us both.

"I'm afraid there's no easy way to say this, Mr Oldham. You have bowel cancer. A cluster of five malignant tumours very low down in your bowel, just above the anus. Of course, we will have to wait for the biopsy to confirm it, but I don't want you to have any uncertainty at this stage. I have seen enough cases like yours to know. We will have to undertake more tests to understand what stage it's at and determine if the cancer is anywhere else. Then work with you to plan your treatment. We will be in touch with you very soon. Please be assured that now you have been diagnosed and are in the NHS system, you will be provided with the very best care."

He then leaves.

I can honestly say I heard nothing after the words "you have bowel cancer." I am stunned into deafness and silence. Motionless, I have eyes only for Andrea and her for me.

"How do you feel?" Asks my Guardian Angel, seemingly waiting for a reaction.

I have nothing to offer. My cheeks are wet as I sit paralysed, tears rolling down my face. I feel like I have been given a long, slow, painful death sentence. My life is wonderful but this is a show stopper. Then I manage to find the words I want to say to Andrea.

"I'm so sorry sweetheart. You didn't sign up for this."

Andrea throws herself at me and holds on tightly.

"Don't be daft. What have you got to apologise for? We're going to fight this together. I love you so much."

The Guardian Angel calmly watches the highly emotional scene she had anticipated and waits patiently to be brought into it. Her humanity and years of experience tell her we need a few minutes to come to terms with the shock and fear of the diagnosis. Andrea and I hold each other and sob for a brief moment. She holds my face in her hands and smiles right into my soul, full of re-assurance. It is exactly what I need. It is time to be practical.

Sensing this, the Guardian Angel steps in. She knows that the shock of hearing what at first seems like a death sentence causes senses to shut down. We both heard nothing but "bowel cancer, slow painful death."

In this moment she is the rock we now cling to for survival. She repeats the important things that the surgeon had said before he departed. She emphasises that the cancer is in one area in the bowel and that it has been identified early. Cancer treatment is very advanced in the NHS and there is every reason to expect a full recovery.

We hug her with intense gratitude, recognising the role she has played in this game-changing moment in our lives. The smile and warmth she returns is very calming and will never be forgotten.

Despite shock, fear and tears we leave the hospital feeling positive. As we walk back to the car Andrea and I hold hands, not wanting to let go of each other. She confesses that she had expected bad news from the moment she was unexpectedly invited to join me after the procedure. Andrea and I both have a very positive outlook on life and this will prove to be a valuable asset, essential fuel in this moment and for our future survival. The shock is dissipating and our thoughts turn to the need to inform loved ones.

Having braced myself physically earlier in the day I now have to brace myself emotionally. I soon discover that telling your nearest and dearest that you have cancer is considerably harder than hearing it yourself.

As Andrea drives us home, I phone each of my sons in turn. They are all away at university but answer my call immediately. It's in moments like this that the love you share with somebody is crystal clear and shines like a beacon in the darkness. I remain calm and cheery as I tell each of them about my diagnosis. I don't avoid the harsh reality but I do try to focus on the more positive aspects. They each respond by saying they're coming home for a few days. I resist. It's really not necessary at this stage. I don't yet have a full prognosis as more tests need to be done.

"Dad! I get that but I'm not coming home for *you*. I need to be with you for *me*!"

After each call I'm devastated, desperately trying not to sound upset and inflict my sons with my sadness and fear. They are alone and remote. This is hard for them and I am the cause of it. They are my squad and telling each of them feels brutal. I would rather it was in person than on the phone but this is the way it has to be.

Next I call my sister, Jan. No answer. I leave a voice message simply asking her to call me back.

Without doubt my two besties are Paul Bernardi and Paul Horan. Not only is their friendship the result of many years of laughter and childish behaviour but it is rich with good times and bad. I consider them to be brothers. Telling them is therapeutic, it just is.

I am uplifted but exhausted. I can feel the fight rising in me. The cancer diagnosis is cataclysmic. My treatment will be defined by the medical profession but how *I* handle this, fight it and not let it beat me is my choice. It might be that one day cancer will get the better of me physically but I resolve that it will never beat my spirit. Andrea is with me on this. We feel determined to beat this *little fucker* together.

My thoughts turn to rehearsals this evening. My character in the play is the very incarnation of the warrior I have now resolved to become in my battle against cancer. Johnny 'Rooster' Byron is a local waster but with a steely resolve not to be beaten by anything. His closest friend, Ginger, tells of a time that Rooster attempted to jump twenty buses at Flintock Fair in 1981 on his motorbike.

"He fucked it up and he died… St John's Ambulance put a blanket over him… all the mums are crying… when suddenly everyone turns around and he's gone. He's vanished. There's just a blanket with nothing under it. They follow his trail of blood across the field, past the whirler-swirler, into the beer tent, up to the bar where he's stood there finishing a pint of Tally-Ho."

The final scene in the play sees Rooster setting fire to his caravan in a wooded clearing so that the fast-approaching local council officials cannot evict him.

He rhythmically bangs a drum with his hands whilst summoning up ancient, mythical, spiritual giants to help him in his fight.

"COME YOU GIANTS!" He finally bellows to the accelerating beat of the drum… and blackout.

I realise that Rooster's indomitable fighting spirit resonates deep within me. I have rehearsed being this character for so long and so deeply that I can easily reach for his weapons of defiance and invincibility.

"Life imitates Art far more than Art imitates Life."
— *The Decay of Lying*
Oscar Wilde

Paradoxically, my diagnosis also offers me the perfect transition into character in preparation for tonight's rehearsal.

Thank you, cancer. Oh, and fuck you by the way.

Andrea asks if I'm up to going to rehearsals, even questioning if I should be in the play at all under the circumstances.

"Try and stop me." I smile, with steely resolve.

"Good boy." She nods, approvingly.

I arrive at the theatre early and get into costume. I walk the set and run a few scenes on my own, practicing some of the more complicated monologues. Then with a few vocal warm-ups I am ready for the full run, stopping only for the scheduled interval. All thoughts of the day's events are banished from my mind. For two and a half hours I am Rooster and manage to stay in character throughout.

I haven't eaten much since the morning's Moviprep so the evening is not interrupted by dashes to the toilet. It is the best performance I have given so far and I am pleased with myself. I snap back into reality and speak quietly to Cameron, asking that he allows me to address the cast after he has given them his rehearsal notes.

I don't explain why and I don't know if he suspects anything; he knows that I've had a colonoscopy that morning. He is typically discrete and agrees. There are about thirty MADS colleagues at rehearsals: actors, costume, sound and light engineers, stage manager and props are all represented.

I feel it is important to inform the whole cast and production team in one go. Some are aware that I've been unwell, most know I've had a colonoscopy and all are depending on me putting in a strong performance in the lead role of a play they have committed a great deal of time and energy to.

Rehearsal notes complete, I am given the floor. I stand just forward of the front row of seats in the auditorium facing the stage, where most have comfortably settled. I keep my address short and to the point, reinforcing that my part in the play continues. How else do you tell approximately thirty talented theatre colleagues, whom you greatly admire, that you have cancer?

Stunned silence follows. Then the assistant director, the hugely talented Gemma Wilson, jumps up from where she sits, launches herself off the stage and into my arms. Visibly upset, she holds on tight. It triggers an outbreak of emotion. A queue forms behind Gemma. One by one this amazing soup of affection and warmth hugs, holds and kisses me. Bloody hell... gulp... actors!

One in particular, Luke Stevenson, struggles to come to terms with the news. He approaches me, tries to speak, fails to find any words and, frustrated, moves away. He repeats this a few times. Finally, as I move to leave he stands in front of me and blurts out

"It's just not right! It isn't." He is angry. "Of all the people who probably deserve this, why you, Hans?"

I have no answer for him. I smile and hug him. He offers any support Andrea and I need from him and the lovely Kerry, his girlfriend. I accept, but want him, and everyone, to understand that for now cancer changes nothing. When the treatment starts, I will be as determined as Rooster to bang the drum, raise the giants and win.

I leave the Theatre pleased with the way that Andrea and I had faced adversity with strength. From the reaction at MADS I realise that cancer touches almost everyone. The response from Team *Jerusalem* was not limited to their fondness for me but also resulted from their own personal experiences.

Cancer is no stranger to any of them.

19 April 2017

I speak to my sister, Jan. She is older than me by two years. She has had a career in the NHS and more recently was a McMillan nurse. Awarded, in fact, the title of McMillan Nurse of the Year 2012. Her sisterly love for me and the practical advice she gives are both very welcome. I explain how difficult and emotionally draining simply telling people had been the previous day. This will only get worse, she informs me.

Cancer treatment is a tortuous process of diagnosis, information, risk assessment, decision-making and expectation management; an emotional rollercoaster. Keeping others informed is important but repetitive and draining. Jan suggests creating a closed Facebook group, inviting only those to be kept informed and issuing updates to it, when appropriate.

'Great idea' I think but it feels somewhat egotistical and self-important. However, I can see the practical benefit of sending one consistent and instant message to everyone. I agree to think about it.

Luke Stevenson, so troubled by my diagnosis when I announced it to Team *Jerusalem*, is a window cleaner in Macclesfield. Unbelievably he has driven to our home in Congleton and spent the day cleaning our windows. This is no easy task even for Luke. Our home is on three levels and there are many windows, including a conservatory, that have not been cleaned for some time.

It takes him hours and he refuses payment.

This is his way of showing support and, not only that, but he also brings flowers for Andrea. We are both so impressed. Luke is one of the nicest and most genuine men I have ever met. I once described his genius as being a decent human being. "This is his superpower," I had once said to Kerry. Today he proved me right.

> **Puraclean**
> MACCLESFIELD WINDOW CLEANERS
> Do you need a Window cleaner? Call Luke on
> **07847 452 552**

This chapter has been sponsored by Mr Luke Stevenson, window cleaning genius.

20 April 2017

Andrea and I have an appointment with Mr Chris Smart, the surgeon assigned to my case. I am immediately impressed by his bedside manner. He wants first to explore how we are both now feeling about the diagnosis before discussing treatment. He is very tall, six feet five inches at a guess. Every evening this week I've been banging Rooster's drum, summoning up mythical giants to come and help me. One has responded. He's called Mr Chris Smart and he is very real.

The biopsy of the tumours has confirmed the diagnosis. I have five malignant tumours in my lower bowel, just above my anus. My protective giant is confident that they can all be surgically removed. The cancer is unlikely to have travelled but that cannot be discounted at this time. A CT scan and a full body MRI scan will therefore be arranged before surgery. These will help determine if the cancer has spread. A date of Friday the 19 May is agreed for surgery.

Keyhole surgery will be undertaken rather than subjecting me to a single large incision. Three small incisions will be made. One of these will result from the removal and replacement of my belly button. An instrument called a laparoscope will be used. This is a small tube that has a light and a camera which relays images of the bowel to a monitor.

Surgical tools will remove the tumours. There is, therefore, less pain and bleeding after the operation. Full recovery is also faster. A stay in hospital of about a week is expected, although it has been known for patients to go home after five days. This, I decide, is my target.

Mr Smart will want to look at the tumours immediately prior to surgery and proposes to do this by way of a sigmoidoscope. This is a narrow tube with a light and tiny camera used to look inside my rectum. It is not as invasive as a colonoscope. The sigmoidoscopy will help to understand the area being operated on before surgery commences.

All the tests being planned will provide valuable diagnostic information. However, the operation itself will give Mr Smart eyes-on evidence of how aggressive the cancer has become. Seeing the infected tissue and the surrounding area will finally determine my prognosis.

I will start receiving many appointments over the next few days.

My head spins with all the information I'm trying to absorb and commit to memory. Contact details for Mr Smart's team are provided and we are encouraged to use them if we have any concerns or questions. Finally he asks again how we are both feeling, recognising the impact to both patient and carer.

"Lastly I would impress on you both to remember the most important thing. You are now in the NHS system and under my care. I will ensure it is of the highest standard. You, Mr Oldham, are young and I am confident of restoring your full health."

A giant indeed!

22 April 2017

After consulting with family and close friends I create a Facebook group and call it *Winning*. Nobody I speak to thinks it egotistical and all could see the benefits instantly. I muse on the good that social media can provide. There is only one rule, however; before I post any important update I will discuss it first with my sons.

Since being diagnosed my inner strength and determination to beat this disease has grown. I have the mind-set and will-power to defeat it, to come out on top, to win or, as Johnny 'Rooster' Byron advised his son:

"To fight to the death. Don't give up."

Tonight is the closing night for *Jerusalem* and it's been a challenging but thrilling week. I have had to control my diet and carefully time my eating during the day in order to avoid bowel movements during the evening performances. I have had plenty of experience of doing this over the last few months. The performances during the week could not have gone better. Tonight the cast get a final standing ovation.

The fighting spirit of Rooster is strong in me.

4 May 2017

Star Wars Day and I do like to celebrate a good dad-joke. Andrea and I drive to Macclesfield Hospital where I am scheduled for a CT thorax scan and a full body MRI scan. These scans produce different results but form a collection of diagnostic information used by doctors to find evidence of cancer. I am asked to change into a hospital gown and a cannula is placed in my arm.

A *Computed Tomography* (CT) scan of the thorax is a diagnostic imaging test used to aid detection of diseases of the thoracic cavity or chest where the heart and lungs reside, as well as many blood vessels.

Once I am settled horizontally, the machine passes my body in and out of a metal tube. A tannoyed voice asks me to hold deep breaths. A special dye called contrast is then injected into me via the cannula, causing a hot flush. First warmth hits the back of my throat and spreads, from there, to the rest of my body. With the contrast in my system, I am again asked to take a deep breath as I enter and leave the metal tube. The contrast helps highlight the areas of my body being examined. CT scan complete I return to the waiting room for a short while and then on to the MRI scan.

The *Magnetic Resonance Imaging* (MRI) scan uses strong magnetic fields and radio waves to produce detailed images of the inside of the body. I am again asked to lie down on a bed that will move me into a large metal tube. The radiographer explains what will happen. I need to lie as still as possible. MRI scans are very noisy so I am given ear plugs and headphones to wear. The machine moves me into the coffin-like tube. The space is quite small so I close my eyes and relax.

The radiographer controls the scan from a separate room but she can see and hear me throughout. Instructions come through the headphones several times asking me to empty my lungs and then immediately hold my breath. After about thirty minutes I move out of the machine, grateful that I don't suffer from claustrophobia.

Scans completed we return home.

6 May 2017

I post my first update on Winning:

> *I thought that keeping my family up to date with my recovery from cancer via this closed FB group would make communicating quicker and easier. Thanks for the idea Jan. Feel free to add others.*
>
> *To bring you up to speed the day before yesterday I had a thorax scan and a full body MRI scan. This completes the set really. It will finally determine if I have*

> *secondary cancer elsewhere. Evidence so far suggests that it is only in my colon where I have a cluster of 5 malignant tumours. I do not yet have the results of these scans.*
>
> *My next appointment is next Tuesday - a pre-op meeting. I'm hoping to get the scan results during this consultation. The signs are good and I remain positive. I get days of intense pain caused by bowel movement. The tumours are always painful but bowel movement makes it worse.*
>
> *Andrea has been amazing with her support. She knows me so well and has been with me at all hospital visits and consultations. Surgery on the 19th May cannot come soon enough. More updates to come here. Much love and thank you all for your love*

It is seen by 112 people, liked by 41 and attracts 96 supportive comments. They offer love and speak words of inspiration. Most confirm that setting the group up is a great move. I am truly humbled by the response. Feeling humbled is something I realise I will have to get used to.

Amongst my favourite posts is one from my old friend Dave Shaw who is now living in Australia:

> *Dave Shaw - The Shaw Wellness retreat has aired the bedding and your room is all sorted. The suite features Sheffield United TV, English Rugby League, a 20 minute jaunt by ferry to Sydney Theatre Company, year round Soft stone fruit (for the bowels) and outside temp of 22 degrees (This is supposedly Autumn pah!). We look forward to welcoming a fit and well deserved version of you soon. Love D&D.*

Some sports banter follows and Dave reminds me how his easy, big-hearted humour always cheers me up.

8 May 2017

My former work colleagues are worried about me.

Chris Quin and I both reported to the CIO at the Co-Op. Apart from his lovely family Chris' great passion in life is cycling. I'm not just talking about a fun ride out with his two beautiful daughters but serious road racing for the Onimpex Bioracer Racing Team. I've run alongside this Olympian to catch a train. He hardly broke a bead of sweat as he jogged, gazelle like, onto the platform. I eventually caught up with cramps, breathless, crumpled and unable to speak. I would undoubtedly have missed the train had I not followed in his slipstream. The expression that comes to mind is 'fit as a butchers dog'.

Imagine my surprise and horror when, on the 14 April I heard the news that he had gone into cardiac arrest the night before. He was saved by his wonderful wife Helen who gave him CPR until the ambulance arrived and took him into hospital. After two weeks in hospital, being monitored and tested, his life as a bionic man commenced when he was fitted with a pacemaker. But here's the thing about Chris: I know throughout this period he will have worried more about his loved ones than about himself. Top bloke.

Having recovered he has returned to work. He lives locally and visits me on his way home from work. Because of my involvement with *Jerusalem* and my own health issues I have not been able to see Chris until now. I've always enjoyed Chris' company and today is no exception. We swap health horror stories and the time with him also reminds me of the professional life I plan to return to.

9 May 2017

Nurse Neil Jeff completes my pre-operation health screen today. He is very thorough but still finds time for his good-natured sense of humour. This man is a professional medic that I will remember for some time to come.

I post the following on Winning:

> *Today I had my pre-operation meeting at Macc Hospital. This involved a full*

> health screening. The good news is that I am sufficiently fit and healthy for surgery on 19 May. I have come away with lots of info about the operation itself and the post op care process. I have various bowel preps to administer prior to surgery. I also met with my MacMillan nurse who discussed the results of the CT thorax scan and MRI scan that I had last Thursday. Whilst there is no evidence of secondary cancer there is evidence that the cancer has travelled beyond the 5 tumours on the inside of my colon to the outside of my colon wall. The travel is within the area for planned surgical removal. This is a slight concern but not alarming and the planned treatment remains the same.
>
> The next step is on Thursday for a flexible sigmoidoscopy (camera but only as far as the tumours) to gather detailed size/location information in readiness for surgery. Then on Friday I visit the MacMillan Centre for a holistic clinic aimed at anyone undergoing bowel surgery.
>
> Once again my Andrea was with me throughout. Grateful to her beyond words xx. I feel incredibly privileged to be treated by the NHS and to have the support of a loving family and friends. My confidence that I will beat this has increased today but realistically there are still many risks ahead.

It is seen by 113 people, liked by 54 and attracts 41 comments. I make a decision to reply to comments only by exception. As much as I enjoy reading them I'm not sure I will be able to keep replying to everyone. The point of setting this group up was to make informing people easier. Instead I post a heart emoji against each post to signify my gratitude.

All the responses are very positive and encouraging, full of humour and support. Pete Munro was in the cast of *Jerusalem* and offers the following:

> Pete Munro - That surgery sounds like a right pain in the arse. Oh come on, someone had to say it! Seriously HK, thoughts, hugs, love and whatever else we can throw at you. Stay strong! Come, Gog and Magog!

I am tickled. The reference to Gog and Magog, two of the Giants that Rooster summons up in the final scene as Council Officials charge toward his woodland home to evict him, make me chuckle.

I'm going to beat this.

11 May 2017

Another visit to Macclesfield Hospital to visit my surgeon, Mr Chris Smart, and another Winning post:

> *A digital rectal examination was today's treat. The sigmoidoscope (camera) achieved its objective of precisely measuring the 5 tumours and ensuring there are no surprises on the 19 May. On the up side there is enough clearance in the colon above and below the tumours to remove only colon and to leave my rectum untouched. On the downside the cancer has travelled beyond the colon walls and into fatty tissue. However the amazing Mr Christopher Smart is confident he can remove it in one surgical procedure. The tumours are growing and the stricturing therefore worsening. However that is manageable until the operation.*
>
> *As I looked at the tumours on the monitor Rooster Byron came to me and despite the pain I smiled and thought…*
>
> *"I was minding my own business when there's a finger up my bum hole. Sitting inside are all 5 birds off Girls Aloud with a case of super T, 200 rothmans and 5 mars bars. I tried to clench my buttocks but they bum rushed me clean across the colon and on to the bed pan. Nicky guards the rectum while Kimberley, Nadine, what's-her-name and the other one go to work. Months of unspeakable acts. Finally they managed to biopsy Cherry Cole. Now they're fucking furious. They're taking in turns to piss me right off………".*
>
> *Not convinced? Pftt … well it amused me. They don't stand a chance next Friday.*

It is seen by 111 people, liked by 50 and attracts 25 comments. Despite the horror of the treatment I have had and the major operation that lies ahead, there is much mirth.

To laugh in the face of adversity is quintessentially British and Rooster typifies St George. I've taken a Rooster monologue from *Jerusalem* and modified it to describe my treatment.

The humour is contagious and appreciated:

> Suzanne Copeland – You show those Girls Aloud who's boss
> Jane Evanson-Horan – Nicola being the scouser needs more of a lead role!! Would love to see girls aloud faces if they knew who they are replicating. All sounds positive everything is crossed bring on the 19th!! What a fab way to think "what would Rooster Byron say". Think I might use that for future challenges in life xx
> David Shaw – What about a list of tracks the "girls" could cover on a compilation album. Obvious one is "We gotta get out of this place" The Animals.
> Paul Bernardi - "Into the Valley" by the skids.
> David Shaw – "All things must pass" George Harrison.

12 May 2017

The day of the operation draws near. A day of final preparation at the Hospital.

I post another Winning update:

> I met with my amazing MacMillan team today. Discussed the journey so far and the risks of what lies ahead. If I need a colostomy bag then X marks the spot just above the top of my trousers so that the bag will tuck into my pants. I also signed up for HART - a trial for a new type of stitching. It's being sponsored by my surgeon so how could I refuse. About a week in hospital post-surgery followed by a month of self-injection to avoid blood clots.
>
> I feel a mixture of emotions so intensely - humbled by all the fuss and support - love for those near to me - excitement that this fucker inside me will be removed next Friday - inspired by my NHS team. Because of all that I have no time for fear or apprehension and I will not waste a moment feeling negative.

So you little fucker you are outnumbered. I have you surrounded. For at my back is every human being that e're was born a carer. We are numberless. Next Friday you are screwed.

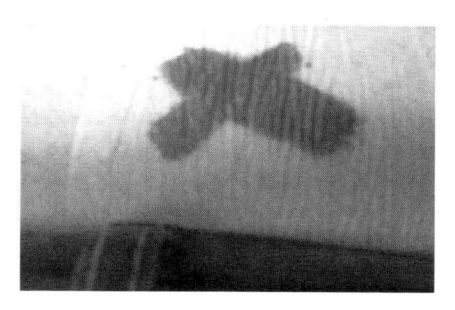

Stoma or no Stoma? X marks the spot

It is seen by 113 people, liked by 50 and attracts 27 comments. The final paragraph is another Rooster monologue modified to illustrate my fighting spirit. I feel I'm preparing to get into the boxing ring for twelve rounds with a monster.

The responses to my post encourage my fight with lots of "go get the little bastard", "beat the shit out of it" and "kick its arse". One comment, however, simply said:

> *Richard Probyn – Thank goodness for that………I thought you'd had a shit tattoo.*

With friends like this!

18 May 2017

An evening of Bowel Prep medication for tomorrow's show down. In order to dance with the devil, I have to empty my bowel. Sadly, it means I will miss my weekly social evening at the Theatre. Tonight, they are hosting the debrief for *Jerusalem*. It will be an opportunity to place on record what went well, what didn't go so well and, where necessary, change things for the better.

The three adjudicators who watched the play have sent in their reports. They are exceptionally good. I could not have praised the production more highly if I'd written their reports myself. I'm sad to be missing the debrief. However, as I sit on my throne for the evening, I receive many messages of support from those who do.

The talented Kayleigh Smith posts this picture confirming that the whole of MADS is behind me. The usual stream of online banter follows and I chuckle as poo is jet-propelled through my constricted anus. If those faces were peering into my bathroom window right now their smiling expressions would undoubtedly change, except maybe for that of Cameron Chandler at the bottom of the picture.

My Promotional head shot and some of the wonderful MADS folk.

3
BOWEL SURGERY
THEIR KNIFE IN MY GLANDS

Your life, is indeed, in their hands.

"Surgeons must be very careful when they take the knife! Underneath their fine incisions stirs the culprit, life!"

– Emily Dickinson

Surgery is the most definitive cancer treatment but not always possible or appropriate. It carries significant risks which, however, are mostly mitigated by the correct preparation before surgery.

Major surgery is any invasive operation in which a more extensive resection is performed. For example a body cavity is entered, organs are removed or normal anatomy is altered. In general, if a mesenchymal barrier (connective tissue layer) is opened, the surgery is considered major.

There are many variables to consider in analysing the risks of major surgery, such as the type of operation and health, age or condition of the patient. A mortality rate of just less than 1% is generally accepted by most studies.

19 May 2017

I'm awoken at 7am by a call from the hospital. We've been asked to come in earlier than planned due to a scheduling error. I agree, but the unexpected request increases the anxiety and tension in both Andrea and I. We take a moment to dwell on the day ahead.

Months of bowel discomfort will end today, but only after the significant risks of a major operation. The moment passes, negative thoughts are quickly banished and we are both keen to get moving. I shower using the liquid antiseptic soap wash provided by the hospital.

We arrive at the Pre-Op suite at about 8am and are welcomed by the nurse who called and is expecting us. The suite is busy with other patients being made ready. I am asked to get undressed and put on a rather fetching hospital gown. The nurse asks me my name, date of birth and address in order to correctly identify me.

This is often repeated throughout the morning to mitigate the risk of undergoing the wrong operation, procedure or medication. What are the chances, I wonder, to be prepped for a bowel operation and then, by accident, have the major heart surgery planned for another patient! Having established that I am who I am, the nurse secures an identity bracelet on my left wrist.

Whilst the nurse repeats the risks of the operation I am about to undergo, I pull on my surgical stockings. These are designed to compress my legs and thereby help prevent the occurrence of venous disorders such as edema, phlebitis and thrombosis. The stockings get my vote; I really don't want any more disorders.

"What's this?" I ask, as I hold up a sort of bag made from gauze.

"Ah!" Exclaims the nurse pulling the curtain around me. "Surgical underwear, you'll need to put those on too."

"Really! How? It looks like something I'd store caught fish in."

After stretching the fish bag into shape, I pull it up my legs and tuck my manhood safely inside. I strike a Mr Universe pose, much to Andrea's amusement.

"You're not the first to do that." Giggles the nurse suddenly appearing through the curtain.

The stoma nurse also checks that the location of the stoma I may need is still marked with an X. There is a risk I will need a stoma bag either temporarily or permanently. A stoma is an opening on the front of my abdomen which may be made during surgery. It will allow faeces or urine to be collected in a bag on the outside of my body.

All risks have to be explained again, including the risk of death. Andrea squeezes my hand tightly and I respond in kind. No words are needed between us. I sign the consent forms, confident that I am in the best possible hands. We are visited by the anaesthetist and consultant who introduce themselves to answer any questions we may have.

Finally the nurse inserts a cannula, a thin plastic tube, in a vein in the back of my left hand. Tape is used to hold the cannula in place. This venous access allows sampling of blood, as well as administration of fluids and medications.

I am ready. This feels like the lull before the storm, seconds before the actor walks onto the stage or the fighter gets into the ring. It's a moment of quiet contemplation for what lies ahead. I steal myself, thinking:

"Come on Rooster, you can do this."

We have both received so many messages of support this morning. Phone calls, text messages and social media posts remind us of the giants that have our backs. It's humbling and helps enormously.

About 10:30am:

"They're ready for you now, Mr Oldham. Could you both follow me please?"

Andrea and I walk hand-in-hand and follow the nurse to the Operating Theatre. We raise a cheer at my expense. I am dressed in a hospital gown, wearing surgical stockings, netty underpants, and my beloved Crocs. Facing adversity, we turn to the refuge of humour and my appearance provides plenty. We are still giggling when we reach a set of double-doors at the end of another corridor and the nurse says:

"I'm sorry, Andrea, but this is as far as you can go. The operating theatre is just down there on the right."

Andrea and I turn and face each other. Big smiles of re-assurance beam across our faces. Hugs, kisses and 'I love you's. We are ready, turn and move away from each other to go our separate ways, letting go of hands then finger tips with arms outstretched. As I walk through the double-doors, I turn to find Andrea one last time. Big mistake! I see her about ten yards away leaning on a wall, shaking, sobbing... alone! There's nothing I can do. Fuck you, cancer!

I'm led into a small room annexed to the operating theatre and invited to lie down on a treatment bed. The nurse leaves me with the anaesthetist who attaches a drip to the cannula in the back of my hand. He's busy paying clinical attention to his work.

I'm vaguely aware of some noise emanating from the next room as the surgical team is preparing for my entrance. Then just as I'm about to ask "what next?"... blackout.

During surgery Andrea posts an update on Winning:

> *Keith has now gone down to surgery. He is feeling very positive and relaxed about it all, as you can imagine with this fab guy. A little bit of a shock this morning when the hospital called to say come in now as they'd made an error with the letter that they'd sent out to him. To be honest it was better this way I suppose as everyone has been rushing around him doing bloods, anaesthetist, consultant, surgical stocking fitter, stoma bag marker pen lady etc. I will update as and when I have news but thank you all for your support Xxx*

Many comments, likes and heart emoji's follow. Then a few hours later:

> *I rang at 2pm and then again at 3:30pm and he is still in surgery. As soon as I know more I will let you know.*

After six hours in surgery Andrea is finally able to post the following:

> *The surgeon, Mr Smart, has just telephoned me to say that the surgery has gone very well indeed and that they found that the tumours were relatively larger than they first thought. They've cut the cancer out and they've joined him back up well. He is now in recovery so he should be back in an hour or so. No stoma bag so Keith will be pleased about that. It's now vital that we just need to get him better and through the next few days xx*

As before, a flood of supportive messages arrive like a love tsunami. I'm still out cold, but I know the response will have helped Andrea.

Under anaesthetic there is nothing. No feeling, no thinking and no dreaming. It must be what being dead is like, a void. I start to think again, like in a dream state. I can hear giggling. I'm being re-born. Warmth on my lips. Light! Whiteness coming for me in the dark. Voices and more giggling, now laughter. I squeeze one eye open and immediately close it... too bright, groggy. Who, where am I? My consciousness re-introduces itself to my physical being. I am slowly awakening and trying to make sense of things. Then soft warmth on my lips again. A kiss! What? Open my eyes again. I keep them squinted open and shapes materialise. So tired. Big beaming smile, most beautiful sight ever. My Andrea. My sister Jan and her wife Ali are with her. I am becoming more compos mentis.

"Go on, Andrea, kiss him again," chuckles Jan.

Another kiss. "Hello sweetheart. How are you feeling?" The soft whisper of an angel close to my ear.

I smile and nod. It's all I can give in answer to her question. Consciousness feels so good once you get past its brutal awakening. There's a surge of happiness as I realise I've survived. It's done. I'm still alive.

"No Stoma. You clever boy."

"Argh! Wibble jabber."

My first, unintelligible words were meant to be served up as:

"Brilliant, no stoma."

But the grogginess got the better of me. My inability to speak and the dribble on my chin causes me to chuckle.

Humour, the heartbeat of life, encourages me to attempt another try.

"Cancer?" Is the best I can manage.

"All gone. You, my love, are cancer free."

I shut my eyes for what seems like the briefest moment to let those words sink in. I take a sudden, deep and emotional breath. A tremor follows and a tear trickles out of the corner of one eye. I hear my sister tell Andrea how happy she is that I am alright and that they will go home now. I fall asleep, unable to resist its appeal.

I wake an hour later. Andrea is holding my hand. I feel anchored to the living world. The grip of her hand is my umbilical cord to reality. I squeeze open my watery eyes and smile, elated to be able to see, smell, touch, taste and hear. Andrea returns my smile.

"I'm fine. Glad it's over." I mutter weakly, before she asks.

Beaming, she reminds me that Mr Chris Smart successfully removed the cluster of tumours during six hours of surgery. His hero status has significantly increased for us both. Following surgery I had spent two hours in the recovery room vomiting, a reaction to the anaesthetic. Thankfully, I have no memory of the recovery room.

I glance around me. I'm in a six-bed male ward. All the beds are occupied. The curtains on either side of me are pulled part way down my bed so I'm unable to see all the other occupants. Time for that later.

I swiftly assess myself. I feel little pain due to the effects of the anaesthetic and painkillers in my system. I have a cannula in the back of my hand hooked up to a saline drip, a vital fluid feed. There is a catheter in my penis to drain away my urine. The catheter is a plastic tube placed into my bladder through my urethra and is held in place by an inflated balloon in my bladder. My urine is slowly draining into a large plastic bag.

I am wearing a nasal cannula to provide me with an increased airflow. This is a lightweight tube, hooked around my ears and which splits into two tubes placed up the nostrils. The lower half of my legs feel compressed by the surgical stockings that I am still wearing.

I'm not yet ready to look at my surgical wounds. That requires movement that I don't yet feel confident committing to. I lie still and listen to Andrea giggling as she tells me how she first woke me when I arrived on the ward.

Her instinct was to kiss me on the lips as Jan and Ali watched. My sad and drained face immediately broke out into a lopsided grin that lasted for no more than a second. In fits of giggles Andrea was encouraged to repeat the kiss and again my wretched face flashed a smile. She did this several times; it became a game. One in which I was the easy prey, the happy victim.

I snigger at the memory of being woken up, the soft warm lips on mine bringing me back to consciousness.

"No wonder I smiled stupidly, I knew it was you." I ruse cheekily.

Seeing that I am awake, the senior duty nurse introduces herself to us as she pulls the curtains fully around us. She efficiently records my observations and checks all the equipment I am connected to. She hands me two devices, explaining that pressing the button in my left hand will provide an IV feed of morphine via the cannula in the back of my hand. I am encouraged to press it whenever I feel pain. I cannot overdose as the feed is limited to a safe dose.

However, the number of presses are recorded to provide valuable pain management data. In my right hand is the button I press to call a member of the nursing staff if I require help.

It is way past visiting hours, but the ward staff are relaxed about Andrea's presence at my bedside. Exhaustion is starting to get the better of both of us. We discuss her planned visit tomorrow afternoon and what to bring. A final kiss and a look that needs no words, pure love.

I fall asleep before she reaches the entrance to the ward.

20 May 2017

It is 3am and I'm awoken by Michael, the nurse taking my observations. As I open my eyes, he is stood at the bottom of my bed scribbling down notes on my record card. The curtains are drawn around me. Realising he has disturbed me he offers an apology and introduces himself.

"You've been in the wars then? Is there anything I can do for you to make you feel more comfortable?"

"A Caribbean holiday, a large bottle of malt, world peace and feed the starving masses." I chortle.

"A bottle of Jura when you go home maybe, but you're on your own with the rest!" He retorts as he pulls my languid body up the bed and plumps my pillows.

I like Michael. I like him hugely. This is a man who loves his job. He is in his mid-fifties and recently re-trained as a nurse having been a plumber all his previous working life. His good, quick humour and calm manner are perfect nursing attributes to couple with his natural instinct as a carer.

Tonight he has started a duty of three consecutive nights. I have instant faith in his clinical ability and his humanity. I am vulnerable and unable to care for myself in the most basic way. Michael understands this and will not only provide for my essential physical needs, much like a baby depends upon its parent, but will do so with the utmost compassion.

"I'll pop round to see you before I leave, Keith. Now you sir, need to rest."

"Thank you, Michael." I yawn.

He pulls the curtains around my bed and goes to check the last patient in the bed to my left. The remarkable Rob Gregory. During my discussion with Michael I found myself pressing the morphine button frequently. It gave me the pain relief I badly needed, sufficient to allow me to fall asleep for a few hours.

I'm awoken at 7am by the day nurse doing my observations. I'm aching and sore. I immediately feel the need for a shot of morphine. I press the button several times.

"Hello… I thought Michael… "

"Michael's shift has finished. He's just left." Smiles his replacement as she finishes scribbling on my record sheet.

"No, I haven't." His grinning face appears through the curtain. "Before I go, let me formally welcome you to Room 4, Ward 1."

He pulls back the curtains in a flourish to reveal the general hubbub on the ward. There are six beds, three opposite me. Mine is the middle bed on the right as you enter the room.

There is a large upright food trolley from which breakfast is being served by a cheerful dinner lady. Nurses are rushing around carrying the things they need to undertake various tasks. Some patients are out of bed, shuffling around gingerly, attached to saline drips and catheters.

I notice that on the bed to my left a thin, bald man is curled up, eyes closed with ear-phones in his ears. He's tapping his hand to music I presume he's listening to.

"Right I'm off. I'll see you tonight. I'm back on at 7pm. Cheerio!"

"Good bye Michael." I salute dramatically.

The cheerful dinner lady asks me if I'd like anything to eat or drink then notices the *nil by mouth* on the white board above my bed. She withdraws her kind offer.

The nurse explains that the sooner I start moving around, the sooner I will recover. I should be aiming to get out of bed and be walking around by tomorrow morning.

I have lots of questions about my operation and recovery which the nurse cannot answer. However, she informs me that there is a doctors' round this afternoon and Mr Chris Smart will discuss everything with me then. I will need to be a patient patient.

I post the following on Winning:

> *WON!*
>
> *The op went well and all the cancer removed. I'm in very good hands and feeling positive. The recovery begins and I've managed to raise myself in my bed a little.*
>
> *A massive thank you to all you wonderful people and your amazing support. I feel humbled and inspired. Andrea as always has been my angel. Doctors round in a while so may know more later.*

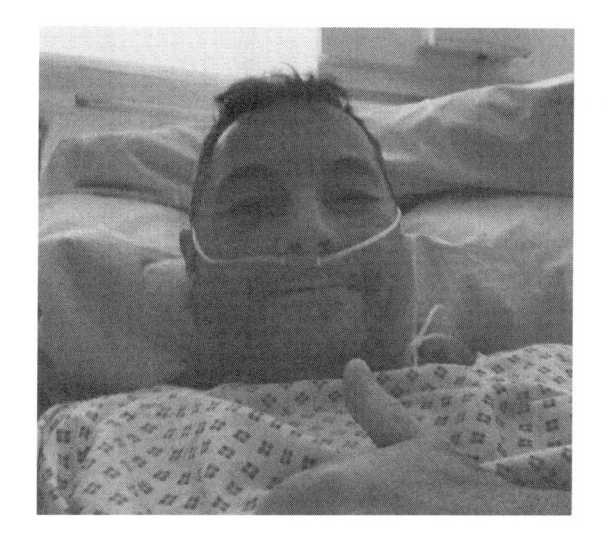

A Winning smile!

The good wishes come thick and fast. This one from fashion guru Dave Clayton is one of my favourites as it encourages golf buddy banter and is a reminder of the healthy life I'm eager to return to:

Dave Clayton - Yes Keithy! Great to see you looking about as chipper as anyone could look after major surgery. Top Stuff / balls of steel. Rest rest etc. Hmm… your choice of robe is forcing me to question this golf top I purchased in Orlando..!!

Dave Clayton with the style and fashion sense of an NHS hospital gown!

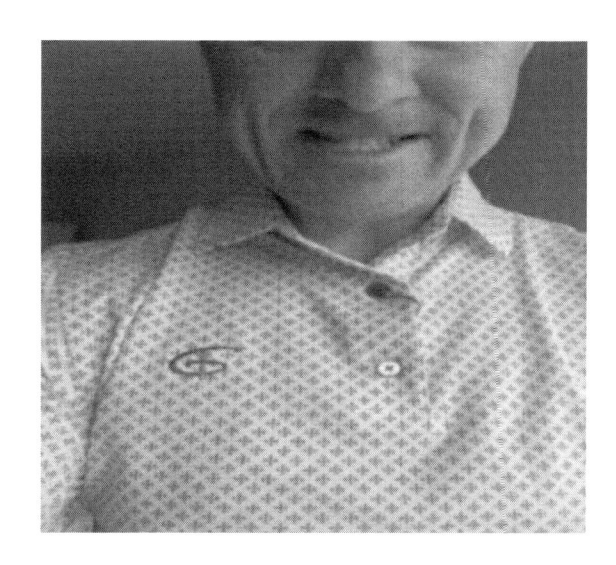

The thing I most admire about DC is his sense of humour, there are few boundaries. His natural, easy-going charm allows him to joke, in the face of adversity, about subjects most would think but not dare to talk about.

The thin bald man to my left sits up from his fetal position and takes off his headset. I notice for the first time that he is not burdened with any plastic tubes or catheters. He's a free man apart from the cannula in his hand, a badge of honour that all patients on the ward carry. His freedom makes me wonder why he is here. His movements are very slow and deliberate. He is clearly unwell but has no obvious signs of treatment.

As he climbs off his bed he plants his feet on the floor with painstaking accuracy. He doesn't straighten up completely but instead remains slightly crouched as he slowly trudges towards the toilet. There is no eye contact with anyone else, he focuses only on the floor in front of him. He pauses momentarily to rest against the nurses desk. A nurse links his arm and helps him the rest of the way to the toilet.

I'm curious. This man doesn't fit.

He returns ten minutes later at the same slow pace. Then sits on the edge of his bed and with great effort slides his legs up, shuffling backwards on his bottom. Before he can return to his isolated world of fetal position and music I speak.

"Hi there, I'm Keith. What's your name?"

"Pardon… Oh… Rob, Rob Gregory." Soft and faint. Hardly audible.

A smile breaks out across his gaunt features. He nods, puts on his headset and returns to 'Rob World', closed off from those around him. Well I got a name and a smile, I suppose.

I spend the morning dozing, falling in and out of sleep. It hurts whenever I move but the button in my left hand brings instant relief. I hardly notice how busy and noisy the ward is nor the occasional interruption to my slumber by a nurse doing my observations. The dinner trolley comes and goes at lunch time. I feel rejuvenated enough to take a first look at my war wounds.

I lift my gown, chuckling at the sight of my man junk nestling comfortably in the netty surgical underpants I am still wearing. I partially remove the dressing, enough to scrutinize the incisions. I have three puncture wounds. My belly button is bloodied and held together by stitches and gauze; this is where it hurts the most. On either side, and slightly lower, are two smaller wounds.

As I inspect my newly formed navel I applaud the surgeon's skill. It's not exactly going to be admired on the beach this summer but it's pretty good given the battering it's taken. As I slowly cover myself up and regain my modesty I realise that the curtains are open and I have exposed myself to the busy ward, ill-prepared for my brazen display. Ho hum, there is no dignity in recovery from cancer! Why should I care? I doubt it constitutes indecent exposure in here. I'm more likely to have engendered pity than offence.

Andrea and Max arrive just before afternoon visiting hours. I am overjoyed to see them, although disappointed that the doctors' round hasn't yet made it to my ward so I have no real news to tell them. They have brought grapes, various nibbles, books, puzzles and get well cards, but most importantly good cheer and banter.

I reach for the grapes and go for one of my best dad jokes, certain that outrageous laughter will follow:

"I've started telling everyone about the benefits of eating dried grapes. It's all about raisin awareness… *raisin* awareness?"

Not even a titter, so I continue:

"If you're here for the yodeling lessons please form an *orderly orderly orderly orderly* queue."

The collective groan, with eyes pointed at the ceiling, comes somewhat as a surprise to me. I gave it my best shot and, unbelievably, I'm left chuckling to myself. Pfft! Go figure.

Andrea posts the following on Winning:

> *Visiting Keith with Max Oldham for the afternoon and he is really cheery and positive. He is happy to see any visitors now for short visits. Visiting times are 2pm-4pm and 7pm-8pm every day. He is in Ward 1 Room 4 at Macclesfield Hospital.......form an orderly queue!!*

The usual wave of positive comments that follow remind us how fortunate we are to have such kind and loving family and friends. I anticipate an orderly queue forming soon.

Visiting time comes to an end and my spirits have been lifted. As Andrea and Max get up to leave I am pleased to note that Rob has two visiting ladies fussing over him. One older than the other.

With the ward now clear of visitors I take the opportunity to speak to Rob before he retreats.

"So what are you in here for?" I ask.

"Life!" He grins mischievously. "Cancer. It's a life sentence."

"Me too. They've just cut mine out. Bowel." I point at my midriff, as if my bowel could possibly be anywhere else.

"Ah! Let's hope you're one of the lucky ones."

With that he puts on his headset and curls up on his bed. I feel dismissed. He has gone straight back to Rob World without any transitional conversation. No hesitation. He just went. Yet it isn't rude, just controlled, that's where he wants to be. He is a deeply troubled man. Sadness penetrates his every pore. Yet he is able to be at peace, stay in control and occasionally flash the most beautiful smile with twinkling light blue eyes. I start to wonder what his prognosis is. My eyes feel heavy so I close them, pressing the button in my left hand repeatedly.

Suddenly there is noise. I snap my eyes open to see my protective mythical giant leading the charge into Room 4. The doctors' round has arrived.

Hospital curtains are magic, every bit as real as magic carpets. The thin lightweight fabric can create a barrier that sound cannot penetrate in much the same way that some carpets can fly! Words cannot be spoken by medical staff until the curtains are drawn closed, when anything can be said, safe in the knowledge that no one else can hear. This, it seems, is the mistaken belief upon which the doctors' round is executed. I don't mind. Why should I? Cancer is not dignified.

Chris Smart eventually gets to my bed and I'm alert, ready to hear his opinion about my surgery directly from him. The curtains are pulled around me. He is very pleased with his work and its outcome, confident that all the cancer has been removed. A sizeable piece of my bowel and the top of my anus was cut away. However, the need for a stoma was avoided. His only concern is that one side of the tumours were too close to bone structure. This meant he was unable to cut away a safe margin of good tissue on that side. It's a minor concern.

My bowel has effectively gone to sleep and now needs waking up. Bowel movement is an essential part of my recovery. I will need to fart and I will need to poo. For this I must have a light, easy to digest dinner of soup and yoghurt this evening, as well as trying to get out of bed and move around. The IV stand is on wheels and the catheter bag can be carried.

In my head, I hear Rooster shouting:

"get out of bed you lazy sod, bed rest is for wimps. A pint of tally-ho and a bag of pork scratching's for you my boy!"

As the doctors' round moves to the bed on my left the relief I feel is overwhelming. The emotion rises in me and I allow a little sob. I've fucking made it this far, it's downhill from here! Hang on a minute the curtain monitor has failed in his magic duties. I can hear the medical staff talking to Rob behind his curtain.

What I hear crushes me. Rob has been fighting cancer for two years. He has been on the receiving end of some horrific, but necessary, treatment. He recently collapsed at home and was admitted into hospital. Tests have revealed that the cancer is now in his liver and his kidneys. I'm no expert and can't hear every word but I think they are still waiting for some test results. It doesn't sound promising. When they pull the curtain back Rob is curled up on his bed and listening to music. He's actually smiling, nodding his head, tapping his hand and mouthing the lyrics. I can relate to him. Cancer is breaking him physically but his spirit continues to bloom and flower. I will try to add some fertilizer.

I doze on and off for a while. The same cheery dinner lady suddenly appears at the foot of my bed.

"No longer nil by mouth then. What can I get you?"

"To start I'll have the fried Calamari with a marinara sauce. For my main course I'll have the buttered lobster thermidor served with roast mushrooms and a light avocado salad. If I have room I'd like profiterole served with salted toffee ice cream. All washed down with a bottle of champagne, the 1959 Dom Perignon is rather good, if you have it on your trolley."

Peals of laughter echo around the ward from my fellow inmates as the cheery one replies.

"So it's soup and yogurt then, all washed down with a bottle of orange juice?"

"That'll do nicely thank you and yum yum." I reply, rubbing my belly.

She collects my hot vegetable soup from her trolley and, as I watch her walk back to my bed, I am reminded of Julie Walters playing Mrs Overall in the *Two Soups* sketch. As she gets close I realise she has an uncanny likeness and movement of Mrs Overall. The bowl is carefully placed on the table that straddles my bed. The cheeky grin and finger shake she gives me signifies she has enjoyed our impromptu outbreak of mirth. I'm feeling courageous enough to ask:

"I'm hoping for a fart today. Do you think this will do the trick?"

"One-hundred percent, satisfaction guaranteed." She fires back immediately, much to the amusement of our audience.

Do not underestimate how good hospital vegetable soup tastes to a starving man. The emptiness inside me combined with the hot, fibrous, salty, liquid causes my tummy to stir. It rumbles loudly and I've never quite looked forward to breaking wind as much as I do now. It'll be an important milestone on my route home.

Meal time complete and visiting hour begins. Andrea arrives with more goodies to keep me entertained and amused. As usual I am delighted to see her and bring her up to speed with my recovery and news from the doctors' round.

Having met my eating challenge I decide it's time for me to get out of bed. I sit up and swing my legs over the side of the bed. Andrea helps to clear my path, moving the IV stand and curtain. I slide off the bed and onto my feet. With one hand on the bed I take a couple of steps. I feel light-headed but energised.

With encouragement from Andrea I walk the short distance that I'm able to without moving the IV stand I'm connected to. I look left and Rob is giving me a thumbs up to cheer me on. Enough is enough and I climb back into bed desperately feeling the need to repeatedly press the morphine button.

A small group of MADS well-wishers arrive shortly afterwards. As visiting hour comes to an end, I feel my eyes getting heavy and my head nodding. Sensing this, my visitors leave with a flurry of air kisses. Andrea remains for a short while, but I'm not great company as I feel exhausted. Realising this, she too leaves, promising to visit tomorrow afternoon.

I'm not sure how long I sleep for but I'm woken by faint cries for help. The curtains are closed around me and the lights are dimmed.

"Help, help is anyone there?"

It's Rob.

"Rob, what's wrong?"

"I can't get up. I've got out of bed to get something out of the bottom of my locker. I'm on the floor and can't get up. I can't reach my emergency button to call a nurse."

"Hang on. I'll press mine… crap!"

"What?"

"Mine has dropped down behind my locker and I can't reach it. Right. I'm coming to get you. It might take a while. Don't go anywhere."

"I can't fecking go anywhere, fool, that's the point." He starts to giggle, as do I.

The giggling becomes contagious and it doesn't help because it causes paralysis which, of course, makes us giggle even more. I struggle to sit up. I had practiced getting out of bed earlier so I am familiar with the routine. As I land on my feet, I steady myself and pull back the curtain between us.

Rob is shaking with laughter, a crumpled heap on the floor. I am nervously stood over him wondering what to do next. My uncontrolled chuckling is causing internal pain.

"Well, I made it. I'm here, to save the day!" I exclaim, as I strike the Usain 'lightening' Bolt pose over the top of him.

He looks up at me. "For all the sodding good you are."

I have to steady myself by leaning on his bed. We are both still in fits of laughter, unable to stop. He is struggling to get up and I am struggling to stay up. I bend down towards him and, careful not to disturb any of the tubes connected to me, place my hands under his arms. Rob shifts his weight to move his feet underneath himself.

"Right, ya fecker, on the count of three we stand together and onto your bed. Are you ready?"

"No!... hang on... okay ready."

"One, two, three... and... heave!"

With superhuman effort we both stand and fall onto Rob's bed. Him on his face, me on my side, trying to avoid hurting my wounds. A few seconds of silence pass whilst we each contemplate any physical damage to ourselves. I was surprised at how light Rob had been to lift even in my weak and emaciated state.

"What now genius?" Rob bursts into a muffled laughter as he lay face down on a pillow.

"How the feck should I know?" I snort.

Unbeknown to us the old gentleman in the bed opposite us had been watching our ridiculous behaviour unfolding and had managed to press his emergency button.

A couple of nurses soon arrive on the ward and immediately run towards us. One of them is Michael. Just in time too as I realise that my catheter bag is swinging freely over the side of the bed and pulling at my penis and the retaining balloon inside my bladder. It is causing considerable discomfort. I reach down to grab it. Michael's hand gets there first and he replaces the catheter bag on its stand.

"Well gentlemen, aren't we a pair of wrestling comedians?"

"It was his fault!"

Rob and I both blurt out at the same time like naughty school boys, each pointing accusingly at the other.

The two nurses tuck us both back into bed. Great care is taken to check us over and record observations. We explain what had happened. It is heart-warming to hear my new bestie laugh so much despite the pain it's left me in. As Rob recoils into Rob World I ask Michael about my catheter. It is really uncomfortable to live with and I'd like it removed.

"Tomorrow, maybe. Now get some rest."

Some more shots of morphine and sleep.

21 May 2017

3am and I'm awake. My curtain is drawn and I'm lying on my back staring at the ceiling. My left hand instinctively calls for pain relief and it is duly delivered. Michael appears and records my observations. I'm feeling fretful but he is a calming influence. I hear him have the same impact on other patients as he moves around the ward recording observations and offering re-assurance.

I doze on and off until Mrs Overall appears with the breakfast trolley. Always bright and cheery, she asks if I'm going to order Quails eggs on lightly buttered toast or smoked salmon in muffins.

"How about a Full English?" I retort.

"How about jam on toast?" She is ready for me.

"Strawberry?"

"Blackcurrant!"

"Perfect. With a drink of your finest loose leaf herbal tea, served in a fine bone-china teacup and saucer please."

"How about a PG Tips tea bag in a blue builder's mug?"

"Excellent. Milk, no sugar."

Our morning routine complete I tackle breakfast. There is one thing I didn't realise about my operation that becomes readily apparent soon after I quaff my breakfast - the surgeon fills the bowel with harmless gas to expand it. This makes movement around the bowel easier during the operation. Pockets of this gas can remain until they are disposed of naturally.

Before Mrs Overall disappears she approaches me to ask if I'd like anything else. I lean forward to hand her my blue builder's mug intent on a second cup of her refreshing brew. As I shift my weight a long, deafening and unexpected noise emanates from my back passage.

My bed shakes and everyone in the room stops and looks at me. Having secured everyone's attention, a repeat fart. There is no smell, just a noisy, long drawn out bottom burp. The world around me stops and looks on in wonder.

"Excuse you!" Exclaims Mrs Overall, turning away from me, facing her audience and waving her hand mischievously in front of her nose.

"YES!" I shout, punching the air. "I've trumped. Come on. Back of the net!" Full of self-congratulation.

I have never since repeated these words in a public place and to an assembly of relative strangers. The day nurse has witnessed this momentous event and, impressed by it, writes it up on my record card.

Whilst I have her attention she informs me that it's time to release me from my IV drip, morphine feed and oxygen tube. This will free me up to be more mobile. It also means that my pain medication will change to tablet form. These are prescribed and administered. The dressings on my wounds are also removed. Wounds are cleaned and aired.

Encouraged by this I venture to the bathroom, carrying only my catheter bag, for my first post-op wash and shave. I inspect my naked body. I've lost so much weight and it shows. The surgical wounds are clean and dry but the stitching and gauze are surrounded by bruising. The line to the catheter bag hangs limply from the end of my sore penis.

When I return to my bed I post the following on Winning:

> *Good progress made so far. Had some soup and yoghurt last night. Today I managed a little walk round the ward and to wash myself. The IV and oxygen tube have been removed and the catheter gets removed later today. Also I farted which usually gets blamed on someone else but I am owning that fart and proud to do so. It's my colons way of saying "you sir are doing well". Still having to manage the pain and general tiredness but that's as expected. Happy days.*

As I suspect most of the responses focus on the fart:

> *Paul Bernardi – Hope it cleared the ward. Do I need a HazMat suit if I pop in later?*
> *Neil Burrows – Never has the expression "Keep passing open windows" been more apt*
> *Luke Stevenson – You've said it now. I'm going to be blaming all future farts on you whether you happen to be in the same town as me or not* ☺ *"No not me, I think it was Hans Keith"*
> *Pete Munroe – Great to hear Hans. No literally…..*
> *Roy Hammond – More tea Vicar?*

Is it me or is fart humour just a male preserve? They've turned a trump into an event reminiscent of the Chernobyl disaster.

I feast on sandwiches, fruit and yoghurt at lunch time. I even start snacking on some of the chocolate goodies brought to me by Andrea and other visitors. I really feel like I'm getting back into my stride again.

I've taken it upon myself to share some of my spoils with Rob. He particularly enjoys nibbling on Toblerone, which is, fortunately, in plentiful supply. I'm moving around the ward more frequently but walking draws more of my attention to the catheter which I'm finding increasingly disturbing and uncomfortable.

Afternoon visiting time and Andrea arrives early as usual. It's so fabulous to see her. I fill her in on my eating, farting and medical progress. She's congratulatory. My spiritual brother, Paul Bernardi, arrives with his lovely wife, Julie. Their company cheers me up, as it always does. Other visitors come and go and before I know it visiting comes to an end. I get a big hug from my Andrea; she'll visit again tonight.

I really do need this damn catheter to be removed. I'm perfectly capable of getting to the toilet so I can't understand why it's still necessary. I discuss it with Michael again. He agrees that it's time to take it out. He disappears to double check with the ward sister and comes back nodding, pulling the curtain around me.

"Right, let's take a look, Keith." He affirms snapping on his surgical gloves.

I hesitate. Then stand and lift my gown.

"What's wrong?" He asks.

"To be honest, I'm a bit nervous. It feels sore and a bit sensitive. I want it out but… it's going to hurt isn't it?"

"Okay. Look me in the eyes so you know I'm telling you the truth. I'm going to tell you exactly what I'm going to do then I'm going to do it. It won't hurt. All I'm going to do is let the air out of the balloon in your bladder that's holding it in place. Then I'll give it a little tug and it will simply fall out. No pain. Are you ready?"

I continue to stare deeply into his eyes, grit my teeth, take a deep breath and prepare myself for the searing pain that I am expecting down the inside length of my appendage.

"Okay, ready!" I whimper.

"I've already done it." He shoots back.

"What? Done what?" Surprised. Confused.

"Done it. Your catheter is now out. You are a free man."

"But I didn't feel anything!" I shriek looking down.

"I know. I hate to say I told you so but… I told you so."

I'm overjoyed. It's a massive step forward. However, I feel the need for a wee, but I'm thinking it will be like pissing broken glass. Michael explains that there will be no pain but that it is quite common to develop a psychological barrier to urinating immediately after a catheter has been removed. He recommends I stand in front of the toilet and tell my todger to just let it go.

"Let it go and relax. Don't let me tell you I told you so for a second time."

I must confess I feel a bit ridiculous chatting to the limp and wrinkled awd fella. But there I stand locked in the toilet telling him to relax and just let it go.

"Let it go me awd mucka. Just let it go."

I've never been so happy to see a stream of piss. Michael was right again; no discomfort at all. Hmm, I wonder. I take a seat and YES! A poo, I'm having a poo. Not much of one. Only a small one but it eases its way out and plop! I haven't had such an easy and quick discharge for six months. This reminder of a normal bodily function comes as a huge relief.

I feel a bit daft but as I slowly make my way back to my bed I give Michael a thumbs up from across the ward. He smiles, shrugs, raises his hands and silently claps in my direction. I like Michael.

Feeling inspired I post the following on Winning:

> *And finally…….not a single needle, tube or cannula inside me. My nurse Michael called me a free man. Also my fart has promoted itself to a shit. Progress indeed. Just a couple more targets to hit then home*

Happy poo comments all round:

> *Kayleigh Smith – Me: (reading Facebook) oh good. My mum: what? Me: Keith's had a poo*
> *Paul Bernardi – Not so full of shit now are you?*
> *Tony Chadwick – There will be golf courses all over Scotland trembling at the thought that you will be back, bolder, stronger and now also on target. Good to hear you're on the mend!*

I am on oral medication and the routine observations taken by the nursing staff now also include the prescription of strong painkillers. The evening meal is not served by Mrs Overall but, I conclude, by her miserable alter ego. There's no banter and the food is delivered efficiently but without feeling. I was ready to place my order of steamed mussels in a white wine sauce with a frisee salad in the expectation of being served with beans on toast.

Andrea visits in the evening and we swap news. She has her own local dog walking business called Paws Tours. It's extremely successful not least because Andrea intuitively understands and speaks 'dog'. Her human clients love her because their four legged pets instantly fall in love with her. The care she gives them goes far beyond a good run, out in the countryside.

She's had a busy day. My chats with Andrea remind me of the normal life I'm looking forward to returning to. I miss being at home, in our own surroundings and pain free. Melancholy rises in me, tiredness doesn't help. Once Andrea departs I close my eyes and daydream about happier times. It's what Rooster would do.

It's late, dark outside. I look to my left and Rob is sat up on his bed reading a magazine. I take advantage of his presence in the real world and strike up a conversation with him. I quickly tell him some basic facts about my life; work in IT, live with Andrea, have a daughter and three sons, love the Theatre, etc. I find out that he also lives in Congleton.

He's been living with his mum for the last couple of years whilst battling cancer. It was his mum and sister who I noticed fussing over him during visiting hours yesterday. He has had a lifelong love of motorbikes, specifically Ducati's. His own Ducati is locked up in his mum's garage. The happy place he goes to in his mind sees him riding out through the countryside. Something he says he would love to do one last time.

"One last time?" I enquire.

It's a question that I instinctively feel needs to be asked. It may open up a subject Rob wants to explore, if not, he will shut it down quickly enough. My instinct is right. He is losing his battle against the demonic disease, cancer.

The medical profession in all its glory has thrown every possible, conceivable treatment at him over the last two years. There is little more they can do for him. It's secondary, in his vital organs and very advanced.

I remain silently attentive, listening to every word. He has accepted his fate and has come to terms with it, not afraid of death but curious to meet it. The surgeons have not lost hope completely, however. He is waiting to see if recent test results make him a candidate for a new cancer treatment being trialed.

I realise that had we met in ordinary life we probably wouldn't have been friends; our interests and lifestyles are poles apart. But in here, invaded by cancer, we are brothers in arms, the very best of pals. We know very few facts about each other and yet we know each other so well. Cancer has given me the gift of meeting this remarkable man.

Thank you, cancer. Oh, and fuck you by the way!

"Alright, you can sod off now," titters Rob. "I'm knackered. I've only had fourteen hours' sleep today. My body runs a marathon every day fighting this fucker inside me. I need more sleep."

"Goodnight matey." I blow him a theatrical kiss.

He lies down and, right on cue, the stern, efficient and fearful ward sister appears beside him. She carefully covers him up and holds his hand bending over to whisper in his ear. I'm puzzled, so strain to listen.

"Goodnight, my beautiful man. Sleep well, my Robbie. Remember you are loved. Sweet dreams. Enjoy your happy place riding out on your motorbike."

Hushed, lyrical and angelic. Like a mother softly singing her child to sleep. Planting the seed of a Ducati dream at the very moment he loses consciousness, in the hope that he avoids the nightmare of his frightful condition. She holds onto his hand for a few minutes as he falls asleep, ensuring he doesn't feel alone. This kindness from such an unexpected source is enchanting to witness. I am spellbound, watching humanity at its splendid, glorious best.

She knows his fate and is prepared to reach beyond her professional training to somewhere deep inside her. To offer him a love and compassion that will help sustain him through his darkest hours.

How does she find the emotional strength to do this?

The ward has fallen silent except for the low rumble of distant snoring. I feel a tinge of guilt at having been an unseen voyeur to the tender and personal gift from the stern ward sister to *My Robbie*. More importantly I'm grateful, honoured and humbled by the spectacle.

Exhausted, I also close my eyes.

22 May 2017

I'm woken at 3am by Michael recording observations and administering my medication. Michael congratulates me on my pissing, farting and shitting. I can imagine no other circumstance where that would be relevant but in here and at this time, it's an easy conversation.

I can't sleep and decide to get up and walk the ward. I plan a route that takes me to the main corridor of the hospital. It brings me close to the feeling of departure and home. How I miss home.

After a couple of circuits I return to my bed. I couldn't be bothered to tie up the drawstrings on the back of my gown, it's a painful process to stretch my arms behind me. I've walked the ward with my backside on full display to the few medical staff on duty. I'm not bothered. I climb back into bed and doze restlessly.

The early morning routine of shift handover and the breakfast trolley brings me to my senses. Mrs Overall is absent again so breakfast is merely transactional and humourless. My hunger has returned and I add cereal to my usual two rounds of toast.

A young man in his late teens has been admitted in the early hours with a hernia resulting from a Colts rugby match yesterday afternoon. He is in pain and fretting because he didn't bring a phone charger with him and his phone is about to power down. He looks pretty hopeless so I take my spare charger to him and plug it in, offering him the end of the lead to connect to his phone in order to re-charge it.

"Ah mate, that's sick. Thanks."

"We're all sick in here so get used to it."

I smile at him but my little dad joke has fallen on deaf ears as he immediately starts typing a message on his iPhone. Having solved his problem I have been silently dismissed, like any modern day parent, by the importance of technology. Nothing else matters to him except for the gadget in his hand. This now has his complete focus.

The larger meals I have been eating recently are finally having the desired effect. It's taken time but, feeling the urge to poo, I walk to the bathroom and settle down for the inevitable. Miraculously, the first heave results in the smooth delivery of a couple of stools. I'm not used to such an easy undertaking. Pleased with myself, I happily whistle a made-up tune whilst I wash and shave.

When I return to my bed I share the love by posting the following on Winning:

> *2 of the most enormous bowel movements since my Moviprep days. Well proud of myself. Twins as well!!*

Poo banter ensues:

> *Neil Burrows – Photos or it didn't happen*
> *Luke Stevenson – Haha have you thought of names yet?*
> *Chris Quin – Can we change the name of the group to Keith's bowel movements*
> *Toby Danger – I have never been prouder of you*
> *Suzanne Copeland – Well, I certainly won't be the one to poo poo that!*
> *Paul Horan – The twins names were they Wayne and Phil or Zlatan and Paul all big poos*
> *David Shaw – Paul beat me to it! Red Devils would pay millions for them in the transfer market.*
> *Ally Burrows – That was a really shit update!*

Determined to keep encouraging an active bowel I eat as much fibre as I can from the lunch trolley. Mrs Overall has returned and I explain my challenge to her. She recommends the chicken soup to start with, followed by the pot of vegetables and a pear from the fruit basket. She also fills my water jug.

"If that lot don't get you going, nothing will." She bawls.

Lunch leaves me feeling bloated and I pray it has the desired impact. Andrea visits after lunch and is happy with my progress and determination to recover. Whilst she is with me the doctors' round arrives. Mr Chris Smart is also pleased with me when I tell him I'm a free man, able to walk and poo. As always, he asks Andrea how she is coping. He looks at my wounds and asks about my pain level.

"Excellent progress. I think we should aim to let you go home the day after tomorrow. I would like to monitor your progress over the next 48 hours. Keep up the exercise and the eating and make sure you drink plenty of water. You're doing well, Keith."

When he's gone Andrea and I smile at each other, happy with the surgeons conclusions. Andrea takes a picture of me and posts it on Winning:

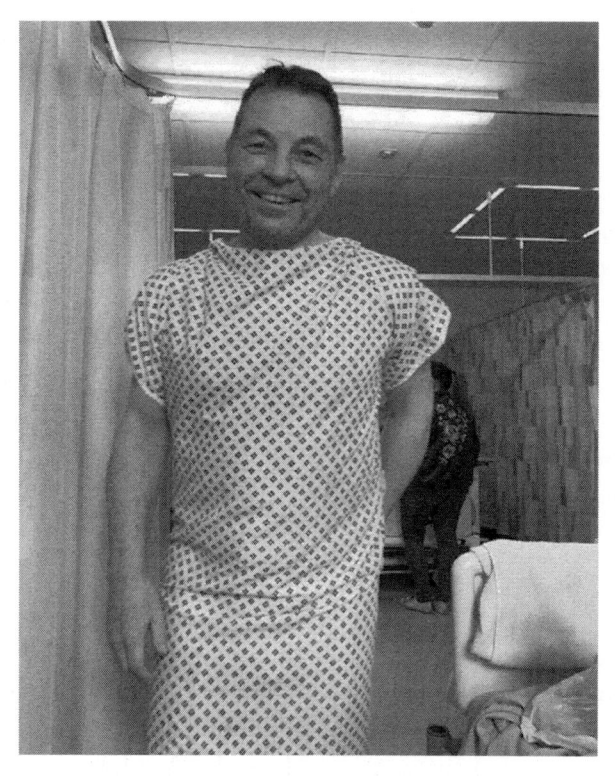

Homeward bound with flaps held firmly in place

She adds the following comment:

> *Just visiting Keith and he is now walking about really well and there has been a suggestion by the surgeon of him coming home on Wednesday.*
>
> *It's hard work getting his bowel working properly again but that's the criteria for coming home so he is working hard at this task!!!*

This is the happiest I've felt with myself during my short stay with the NHS. The culmination and progress of many small recovery steps is starting to pay off.

The responses to Andrea's post lift me further:

> *Paul Bernardi – Glad he's holding his flaps together – in every sense. Come on Keith – need you home on Weds so we can watch the footie and kick Andrea's soaps off the telly box.*
> *Jane Evanson-Horan – Witwoo xxxx*
> *Pele Johnson – I got a nice vindaloo will help in getting the ali puckering up. Looking good Hans Keith Oldham. Role model for us all!*
> *Neil Burrows – Does it come in pink to match your cheeks?*
> *Ally Burrows – How do you know his cheeks are pink?*
> *Pete Munroe – 'Ere, it's a bloke in a dress! Each to their own. Here's hoping for a speedy recovery*
> *Suzanne Copeland – Tremendous news! Looking forward to seeing you with some clothes on*
> *Kayleigh Smith – I'm running over quickly before that happens*
> *Tony Collier – You look as good as me in my Alice outfit lol*

Chortle, chortle, chortle!

The rest of the day on the ward is reasonably uneventful. There is no TV so news from the outside world comes in via the visitors or smart phones. Yes we have Wi-Fi, or Rob's radio, but only when he joins me in the real world. Mrs Overall serves up a sumptuous evening meal full of fibre. She's on my case and quite prepared to force-feed me if necessary.

Visiting time is cheerful as usual. Andrea sits with me chatting about her busy day. There is more to feel excited about given my targeted release date. Some other friends call in for a brief time. Chairs are always in short supply during visiting hours and a couple of my friends perch on the edge of my bed.

Rob is visited by his mum and sister. They too have spent two years worrying about Rob and supporting him through various treatments. I sense that their collective energy is deteriorating.

It's been an exciting day. The prospect of going home the day after tomorrow has rejuvenated me. The ward has gone quiet and most of my fellow inmates have pulled their curtains round themselves and have gone to sleep.

I'm on my iPhone reading the news. I'm horrified to read about an emerging and tragic event. A bomb has been detonated tonight at the MEN Arena after an Ariana Grande concert. The death toll is rising and many of the victims are teenagers. It's horrific and so very sad. *Why?* I ask, but I can't find the answer.

Sometimes life just sucks!

23 May 2017

3am and it's time to wake up for pain relief and my circuit training around the ward. I reach the exit door to the main hospital corridor and pause. I can't wait to walk through that door, fully dressed, get in my car and be driven home. It comes to me that if I am released tomorrow I will have been in hospital for five days, the target I set myself when I first met Chris Smart. Awesome! On that note, and after another circuit, I return to bed and doze until breakfast time.

The ward becomes very busy at 7am with a shift change and the arrival of the breakfast trolley. I wake as my curtains are pulled fully open by the day nurse. My observations are recorded and my medication administered. Toast, cereal and a mug of tea for breakfast. So begins another day.

I'm bored. Worse than bored, because I'm tired and in pain too. At mid-morning I take myself off for more circuit training. As I return to my bed two men are pulling the curtain around Rob. One doctor speaks and, in a very matter of fact tone, informs Rob that the test results are not good. He is not a match for the new trial. There is nothing more that can be done to treat him. His cancer is at a very advanced stage, it is considered terminal. The other doctor then speaks. He is a psychiatrist:

"Rob, I know this is very difficult for you but do you understand what you've just been told?"

"Yes." And then, silence.

The silence drifts. I'm guessing the psychiatrist is letting Rob think about what he has heard.

"How are you feeling? Is there any one thing that's worrying you more than anything else?" The silence is eventually broken.

"Can you tell me, please," comes Rob's reply, "have they caught the man who blew up the MEN Arena yet?"

I choke and bite down on my hand to remain quiet. He's just been told that his cancer will soon kill him and he's more worried about last night's bomb blast in Manchester.

I want to scream:

"FUCKING CANCER. FUCK OFF AND DIE YOURSELF!"

He is either in denial or acceptance. I reckon it's the latter. I'm pretty sure he has come to terms with his death. The psychiatrist calmly informs Rob of the current news headlines concerning the MEN Arena, then returns to the subject of terminal cancer.

"I've thought of little else for the last few months," explains Rob. "I've known for some time that it'll get me in the end. How will it happen?"

The medical doctor explains how Rob's liver and kidneys will fail and how that will make him feel. The medications they can use to help him and how those will make him feel. It's going to be a very confusing time for him and he should think about how he wants to be remembered. They can help him with this too.

It's important that Rob understands that he is nearing death, so he also has the opportunity to re-evaluate and fulfill his hopes and his final wishes. The plan is to discuss the process with him each day to help him think it through. It also means that when the end comes and Rob is confused and on drugs the medical team will be more aware of his needs and can care for him accordingly.

I really don't want to hear any more. I'm devastated. I roll over onto my bed and bury my head under the covers.

"Fuck you, cancer." I sob.

I'm not sure how long I hide under my bed sheet. Long enough for the doctors to have left and for Rob to have returned to Rob World.

Mrs Overall appears with her dinner trolley and heads straight for me.

"Soup followed by beans on toast." She bellows at me. "Beans, beans they're good for your heart, the more you eat the more you fart! Well, that's what my grandson tells me and he should know, the little tyke."

I laugh, more than I would usually, because I need the relief from misery that humour provides.

"Do you really think I need encouraging after my performance yesterday

Mrs… I… er… don't even know your name… Mrs?"

"Openshaw. You can call me Julie."

I do the quick translation in my mind… Overall to Openshaw and Julie Walters! I'm in hysterics and poor Julie just cannot understand why. It's uncanny and I just cannot explain it to the perplexed Mrs Overall.

However, I do discover that she is quite correct. Soon after my lunch my bowel is gurgling and firing out pockets of gas. I'm also encouraged to dash to the toilet where I produce a beautifully formed stool.

When I return, Rob is sat up on his bed, frustratedly shaking his radio with both hands then pausing to listen to it. He sees me and tosses the radio to me.

"You work in IT. Fix that, it's broken."

I'm momentarily rooted to the spot. Frozen. I want to explain that I might work in IT but I don't actually fix things. I have trouble turning my own phone on and off. But this radio is Rob's sanctuary, one he desperately relies on to transport him to 'Rob World'. In desperation I look at the device in my hand, hoping for a miracle.

Then one happens. My thumb accidently moves against a button on the side of the radio and I hear faint music coming out of the headset still plugged in to it. Rob must have accidently moved the button turning the radio from digital to analogue, thereby losing the station he was listening to.

"Ah!" I exclaim loudly. "Yes, I see the problem. There you go matey. I don't think you'll have any problem with it now." I hand back the 'fixed' radio.

"You genius." He beams a big-hearted and grateful smile at me.

"No problem. I work in IT me. Fix anything!"

He nods as he puts the headset back on and slips back into Rob World. I lean forward and kiss him on his bald head. He gives me a double thumbs up then curls up onto his side, lost. I've never felt so panicked and self-satisfied at the same moment. It was a good feeling.

Thank you, cancer. Oh, and fuck you by the way!

After finishing another fibrous lunch it's visiting hours. Andrea arrives early followed by three of my old mates. Their company is an antidote to this morning's heartbreak. When I'm alone with Andrea I tell her about Rob's news and about the conversation he will have to repeat each day with the psychiatric doctor. She is deeply saddened and looks at him chatting happily to his mum and sister.

"Acceptance, definitely acceptance." She concludes, holding my hand.

Our shared empathy is broken by the arrival of the Doctors round. After a brief inspection of my wounds and observations we are delighted to hear that I will be released tomorrow. The histology from the tumours and lymph nodes that were removed will take a little longer. But given my steady recovery, bowel movement and stable reliance on medication, I can go home and wait there for the histology.

After all, I have Andrea to look after me, and who better? The rest of the evening passes uneventfully and sleep takes me early.

24 May 2017

When I wake, my first thoughts are of going home. I check the time – 1am! Damn that's early. I'm not tired but I am in pain, so I call for the nurse who checks my observations and is able to prescribe me some analgesic. Once the pain has subsided I set off on my circuit training.

The ward, normally so busy during the day, is a quiet lonely place at 1am. As I stride down the corridor my untied gown occasionally exposes my rear. I'm ready to hold it closed if anyone should appear. Nobody does until I pass the nurses' station on my way back to my bed. I read a book until my eyes start to feel heavy, then lay down and sleep.

I doze for most of the morning until 6:30am, when I decide to give up trying to fall asleep and sit up in bed. The tiredness and pain are immediately conquered by thoughts of home, the sanctuary to which I will return later today. My curtains are soon pulled open by the day staff and the breakfast trolley arrives. No Mrs Overall, but I tuck into my breakfast of toast, cereal, yoghurt and a builder's mug of char.

Andrea arrives about mid-morning expecting to take me home, but I am still waiting for the doctor and pharmacist to sign my release papers. I have spent the morning getting washed, tidying out my locker and packing my bag. Everything is done slowly but meticulously. Andrea has brought me some fresh clothes which I change into. Socks, pants, jeans, a t-shirt and trainers feel so much better than a hospital gown, surgical stockings and Crocs.

We wait. The dinner trolley arrives and I order my food for Andrea as I've grown tired of hospital food. More waiting. Eventually, news arrives that the doctor has signed my release papers but we still have to wait for the pharmacist to authorise my drugs.

I dwell on my time on Ward 1 and post the following on Winning:

> *The doctor has signed my release papers and I'm just waiting for pharmacy to do the same. Then home. I'm still in pain and on medication and there's still work to do to keep my newly formed bowel moving. I have to say it's been one of the most humbling experiences ever. I have met THE most amazing people both patients and NHS staff.*
>
> *The memory of physical pain will go but my memory of my comrades never will. There is so much that the NHS gets just right. It will be a few weeks yet before I can swing a golf club or tread the boards but the reality of those things is within reach. Daily contact with the hospital will continue for a while and the histology from the tumours will take another week. This will prove absolutely that the*

cancer has gone completely. For now the surgeon is pretty damn sure I am now cancer free.

It's a good day. Come on United. Let's win for Manchester

The congratulatory replies are immediate and plentiful. The final line is a reference to the UEFA Europa League cup final that Manchester United are playing in tonight and a shout out for Manchester, in mourning as a result of the suicide bombing at the MEN Arena. It's difficult to respond to my post with humour but the opportunity is not lost on some deviants:

Dave Shaw – get on the sofa with your feet on a stool
Hans Keith Oldham – I'll have to form one first
Paul Bernardi – Love a good poo joke me

To our relief the pharmacist finally signs for my drugs which are then made up. I need the toilet and leave Andrea sitting on my bed as I make my way slowly to the ward bathroom for one final heave. Job done, I return. Andrea is distraught, tears rolling down her face. She points towards Rob's bed, curtains drawn around him.

"He's having that conversation." She weeps. "I've heard it for myself. It's so hard sweetheart. He is just so humble and resigned to it."

As I put my arms around her to comfort her my bag of medication arrives and we are free to go. The moment I've been waiting for and I can't bring myself to walk out, not yet.

"Go and say goodbye. You need to and he will thank you for it. Go on!"

Andrea insists, waving the back of her hand towards me. I hesitate and then pop my head round Rob's curtain.

"I'm really sorry to interrupt," I bumble, "I know this is important but I just couldn't leave without saying goodbye."

Rob looks up from where he sits on his bed with his big crooked smile, piercing light blue eyes. I lean forward and kiss him on his bald head, hold it in my hands for a moment. The doctor smiles graciously. His silence permits this interruption.

"Good luck, buddy, and for fuck sake don't go falling out of bed again. Here's some Toblerone. I've got to pop back on Friday, so I'll swing by and make sure you're behaving yourself."

We fist bump and drop the mic, as a final parting.

I apologise to the psychiatrist once more, turn and leave, pulling the curtain closed behind me.

"Who was that?" Asks the doctor.

"The idiot from the next bed." Chuckles Rob.

I pause to allow myself a moment of sadness but Rob's final chuckle stiffens my resolve and I swallow my sob with a smile.

Andrea and I make our way to the nurses' station and collect my bag of medication. I have drugs for pain relief, diarrhoea, constipation, various creams and needles to self-inject an anticoagulant or blood thinner. I'm at risk of a deep vein thrombosis as a result of the surgery I've had.

We take the route of my early morning circuit training, but rather than turning back at the doors to the main corridor I burst through them, punching the air in celebration.

We walk slowly to the end of the corridor and through the door that takes us down some stairs and to the exit by the car park. Andrea walks in front of me as I gingerly make my way down the stairs. A uniformed lady is coming up the stairs towards me.

Our eyes meet briefly as we draw level. It's my ex-wife, she works here. The mother of my four children. Someone I was married to for over twenty years. She doesn't speak. She's aware I have had cancer and major life saving surgery to remove it. I stop, grip the hand rail and smile, ready to greet her. She looks away, as if to deny my existence and continues her journey. She has seen me but is unable to bring herself to offer sympathy or ask me how I am. Am I naïve to think that the serious illness of the father of her children would elicit some sort of interest?

The place in life that she inhabits, that encourages such behaviour, must be terribly lonely and woeful. It's a shame for her. Our separation and divorce was not an easy one. Both of us, perhaps, have much to forgive. Yet forgiveness is central to the religion she follows. I simply fail to understand her perspective. *"Life is too short"* I think, as I sadly watch her walk away. Unfortunately, there is nothing I can do or say, even though I wish there was. Andrea is as bemused and dumbstruck as I am.

Home is warm, familiar, cosy and with Andrea. Home cooked food, the TV and my own toilet. For the record Manchester United win the final beating Ajax 2-0. It is a magical evening.

My brother Paul Bernardi calls round to watch the match with me. The cheeky so-and-so posts the following on Facebook:

> *At chez Hans Keith Oldham watching Utd. Lazy sod is just lying there – not got me a drink or owt!*

He knows where the beer fridge is!

4
RECUPERATION

The human body has amazing powers of recuperation. It was designed to heal itself. If you cut your finger it bleeds, forms a scab and, in a short time, it heals.

The body makes 2.5 million red blood cells and 250,000 white blood cells every second. Your liver performs over 657 known functions simultaneously without you being aware of them. The human brain has a memory capacity which is equivalent to more than four terabytes on a hard drive. Nerve impulses sent from the brain move at a speed of 274 km/h.

There are nearly one hundred trillion cells in a human body all controlled by the nervous system. Yet each of us started out as only two single cells, one from mum and one from dad.

Digestion involves the breakdown of food into smaller and smaller components until they can be absorbed and assimilated into the body.

Finally, a bowel movement is the last stop in the movement of food through your digestive tract. It is necessary for the elimination of toxins from the body. The stool or faeces passes out of the body through the rectum. Any damage to tissue in this area can disrupt this bodily function.

It can take time for the body to heal itself naturally from major colonic surgery before returning to properly functioning bowel movements. If necessary, a stoma can be temporarily fitted.

"A champion is defined, not by their wins, but by how they can recover when they fall."

– Serena Williams

26 May 2017

We return to Ward 1 for my check-up and notice a sign on the wall as we enter the main entrance to the hospital. It states:

NHS
The 6 Cs
Our Culture of Compassionate Care
Care
Compassion
Competence
Communication
Courage
Commitment

We have both witnessed this culture, all six C's, at very close quarters. The sign gets our vote for sure.

On arrival at Ward 1 we are met by a junior doctor who inspects my surgical wounds and confirms that I am healing as expected. My stitches should be ready for removal at my next appointment.

Check-up complete we sit with Rob chatting for a while. He is distant and doesn't have much to say. I sense that he craves the sanctuary of Rob World, so we leave promising to pester him with another visit next week, after my scheduled check-up.

31 May 2017

Over the weekend Andrea has bought lots of biking magazines, mostly about Ducati's. I have an appointment at the hospital this morning to have my stitches removed, so the plan is to visit Rob afterwards armed with reading material he is sure to enjoy.

Approaching the ward we are met by the same junior doctor who attended to me last week. He tells us he will remove the stitches in the treatment room just by the six-bed room I was in. Andrea sits in a waiting area while I follow the doctor.

As I approach the treatment room, I see the senior ward nurse whom I had heard whispering in Rob's ear so lovingly and I greet her with a hug.

As I do so I glance over her shoulder and notice that Rob's bed is empty.

"Where's Rob?" I ask, "I've got these for him."

"Oh… Rob… he's not with us anymore."

"He's gone home?" I start to enquire.

Suddenly, Mr Chris Smart appears by my side and gently but purposefully man-handles me into the treatment room.

"I heard you asking about Rob Gregory, Keith." He explains. "I'm really sorry to tell you but he passed away over the weekend, he's gone from us now."

Stunned. Unable to comprehend the words as quickly as they are spoken. Confused. 'Gone' has to be the saddest word ever spoken.

"I… he?... no!" Is all I can manage.

"I don't tell you these things to intentionally upset you, Keith. I tell you because I think you should know. I will always tell you the truth, no matter how painful. He died very peacefully in a hospice with his mother and sister beside him."

"Yes!" I blub, dropping my arm full of magazines onto a chair. Nostrils flaring, lips quivering and trying to suppress my tears.

"But understand that he is not you. Your prognosis is completely different from his. His was a sad case, yours is not."

I hardly notice the sharp stabbing pain to my wounds as the stitches are removed, lost in the memory of a best friend I hardly knew. He deserved better and I was privileged to have known him.

Thank you, cancer. Oh, and fuck you by the way.

Stitches out and check-up complete Andrea is asked to join us. Seeing that I am upset she is immediately concerned, suspecting something sinister. I relay the news about Rob.

No words, just a big, warm hug and then we depart.

2 June 2017

We have two Jack Russell's. Alfie, old and wise and Stanley, young and playful. It is said that dogs have a sixth sense about the human condition and that they can smell disease. That is certainly the case in Alfie.

Before I was diagnosed with bowel cancer Alfie would occasionally lie next to me on the sofa as I watched TV in the evening. He would rest his chin on my tummy and lovingly look up at me. This was unusual as he normally sat with Andrea, whom he adores.

Since I have come home from hospital he has regularly repeated this, but now it makes sense. The old fella knows and is looking after me, comforting me. His generous and calming influence is very welcome.

Our friends Paul and Jane Horan visit for the evening and stay overnight. I have known them both for many years and they are both hugely supportive of me in my current state of health. I am grateful to them beyond words.

As I languish on the sofa Stanley spies his tennis ball on the other side of me and leaps for it. His front paws land right in my midriff. As he pushes against me to take off, his claws dig deep into my navel.

It all happens very quickly and it feels like I have been shot, as I double up in pain. Alfie springs to my rescue and chastises the young pup with an angry growl, returning to lick me as I come up for a gasp of air with a howl of my own.

3 June 2017

I have known Jeff Rosser as a friend since I first met him in Exeter in 1980. Jeff and his closest friend, Pete Beaven, remind me of Ant and Dec; short in stature, in tune with each other and extremely quick-witted and good-natured. Whilst watching Ant and Dec present on the TV I often wondered if, early on in their TV careers, the comedy duo had ever met Jeff and Pete and thought:

"Now those two guys have got something, maybe, just maybe, we should be more like them!"

Both J and P (how else do you shorten their names?) still live in Devon, a place I have moved away from some twenty years ago. Jeff and I are Facebook friends. He has followed my progress on Winning and phones me for a chat, to offer support.

It is fabulous catching up with him, that is, right up to the point he informs me that he too has cancer.

Sadly, it is primarily in his brain but is also appearing in his lung and arm. His cancer is very different from mine, as is his treatment for it. However, we each feel very positive about our own prognosis, but also devastated for the other. It's a bitter paradox. We agree to keep in contact and call each other at least once a week.

After the call I send him a message:

"Hi Jeff. Thank you so much for your call. Your positive attitude is inspiring and is perfect. You are absolutely going to beat this. Phone me anytime 24x7. I'm so here for you old friend xx. Much love xx".

MADS is a member of three drama academies – North Stafford Drama Academy, Greater Manchester Drama Federation and Cheshire Theatre Guild. *Jerusalem* was every bit as successful as the adjudicators' reports suggested.

The awards season has commenced and the MADS production of *Jerusalem* has received a host of nominations across many different categories.

For my own efforts all three academies have nominated me in the Best Male Actor in a Lead Role category. Judging one's own performance is difficult. Reading the adjudicators' reports can help with personal acting development and receiving a nomination is a clear indication that MADS got something right in a particular category. However, the number of nominations for *Jerusalem* is unprecedented and thrilling.

Tonight is the NSDA Awards Evening. A number of the *Jerusalem* cast are in attendance with the director. I am amazed and proud to win my category, particularly in spite of my health problems during show week. Something, I recall, using as motivation to stay in character during my performances.

Absurdly and conversely, Johnny 'Rooster' Byron is now motivating me to face my extreme health problems.

Yes Rooster!

North Staffs Drama Academy

Best Male Actor in a Lead Role

5 June 2017

Since leaving the hospital my health and general well-being have continued to improve. I have done everything asked of me; taken my medication, kept my wound cleaned and aired, continued to wear surgical stockings, maintained a nutritional diet and injected the anticoagulant into my fatty tissue each day. This, coupled with daily light exercise, has revived me. I am gaining strength and ready to face almost any challenge. However, I do not feel ready for the phone call that comes from my MacMillan nurse this morning.

The histology results have come through and the nurse discusses them with me. They show evidence that the cancer had travelled to surrounding lymph nodes before the operation. There is, therefore, a high risk that seedlings of cancer still remain in my system. She strongly recommends chemotherapy as a treatment to wash away these seedlings before they take hold. An appointment is made with Mr Chris Smart and the MacMillan nurse for 7

June to discuss the recommended treatment in more detail with me. There are some additional treatment variables to consider.

To describe this as disappointing after major surgery is a huge understatement. I feel a sharp downward trajectory on the emotional rollercoaster that is cancer treatment. By the time Andrea and I have talked it through, however, the Rooster in me has taken hold again and my determination to come out on top has returned.

As promised I call each of my sons to let them know. I'm in a positive mood about what lies ahead and, whilst they too are disappointed, they join me in my fighting spirit.

Later in the day I post the following in Winning:

> *My Macmillan nurse has phoned me with the histology results. When the surgeon removed the cancerous section of my colon they also removed 28 lymph nodes in the immediate area. They have found cancerous tissue in 3 of them.*
>
> *So the recommendation is a 6 month treatment of chemotherapy to ensure the cancer does not return. I will have a cannula in my arm for the duration of the treatment so that the chemotherapy can be easily given intravenously once a fortnight.*
>
> *There will be side effects - loss of hair is not one of them. This is obviously not the news I was hoping for but it has not dented my determination and positive outlook one bit. If it takes 6 months of chemo to nail this then I say "bring it on".*
>
> *I meet with my surgeon on Wednesday to discuss the details. My recovery from surgery continues to go well and today I feel better than I have felt for some time. I am genuinely humbled by the love and friendship you have given me - thank you xx. My beloved Andrea continues to be my rock*

Rooster's fighting spirit is contagious in the messages of support that respond. Theses typify the fifty comments posted:

Craig Tweedie – Another chance to give the evil bitch a slap!!
Dave Clayton – Round 6 of a 12 round bout and you're ahead on points Keithy. Keep your hands up, feet moving and keep throwing your jab. You will win pal and probably by KO! Not sure where the boxing metaphor came from but I've just been training and it felt apt
Elizabeth Sarah – On the bright side you get to keep your hair! X
Kayleigh Smith – Wish the world would stop chucking stuff at you and just accept you're a hard bastard that can't be broken. Lots of love to you both, still behind you xx

7 June 2017

Andrea and I meet with Mr Chris Smart and my MacMillan nurse at Macclesfield Hospital. The histology results are discussed. There is a risk that the cancer has travelled and that needs to be tackled with a treatment of chemotherapy. This can be administered at Macclesfield Hospital.

Once complete a treatment of radiotherapy administered at The Christie Hospital will provide belt and braces.

Chemotherapy is a cancer treatment whereby chemical medication is administered to kill cancer cells. There are many different types of chemotherapy medications but they all work to stop cancerous cells from reproducing, growing and spreading throughout the body.

However, chemotherapy also attacks healthy cells resulting in a range of side effects. Too little chemotherapy and cancer cells will survive, whilst too much chemotherapy may cause permanent damage to good cells. A medical oncologist endeavours to ensure that the right dose of the right type of chemotherapy is administered.

The term "chemotherapy" was first used by Paul Ehrlich in the early 1900's. He was a famous German chemist who set about developing drugs to treat infectious diseases. However, it wasn't until World War Two that it was discovered that people exposed to mustard gas developed significantly reduced white blood cells. The era of cancer chemotherapy began with the first use of nitrogen mustard drugs.

Radiotherapy is a cancer treatment that uses high doses of radiation to kill cancer cells and shrink tumours. An external beam directed by a machine delivers the radiation to the affected area with pin-point accuracy. The treatment is delivered daily and each session lasts for a few minutes only. It is not painful but can have some side effects. Its use, to treat cancer, can be traced back to experiments made soon after the discovery of x-rays in 1895 by Wilhelm Rontgen.

The MacMillan suite at Macclesfield Hospital is a satellite unit of The Christie Hospital which specialises in cancer treatment. Arrangements are made for us to meet a Christie's oncologist on 12 June to plan the type of chemotherapy best suited for my condition. There are options and I have a choice to make. Once again the bed-side manner of Chris Smart and his team is outstanding.

I really do feel in safe hands.

10 June 2017

Today marks the first anniversary of the death of the great and humble Robin Williams. He is a man I admired both for his performing talent and his humanity. I am reminded of something he once said.

"In the end, none of us have very long on this earth. Life is fleeting."

11 June 2017

I've been thinking about Jeff since he made contact with his devastating news. I call him for a chat. One of the fabulous things about Jeff is his ability to laugh off adversity and, despite his condition, he has not lost his mischievous sense of humour.

He tells me about CBD brothers, a recent discovery of his. They produce cannabis oil products using an organic growing process, without the use of pesticides or artificial fertilizers, on small artisanal farms across Europe.

Their products are freely available via the internet. They do not claim to cure diseases but Jeff is hopeful their products will help his pain management. I express my doubts and so Jeff agrees to be my stooge, to try it and give me the benefit of his experience.

"Yeah right! You just want to get high." I giggle.

"Ha ha… I hadn't thought of that but now you come to mention it… yeah… ha ha!"

"I've got your number but yeah let me know how you get on… ha ha."

Jeff just has that ability to lighten anyone's load. He is a remarkable, cheerful man.

12 June 2017

Andrea and I meet my oncologist at the MacMillan suite in Macclesfield Hospital. I am presented with a couple of chemotherapy options. One which involves having a cannula permanently fitted throughout the treatment process, the other to take medication orally in tablet form. This is an easy choice for me; it's a no to the cannula.

On completing the chemotherapy treatment, arrangements will then be made for me to have radiotherapy at The Christie. The radiotherapy will be focused on the area of my bowel that had surgery. I will have one session per day, excluding Saturday and Sunday, over a five-week period, twenty-five sessions in total.

This is going to be a long haul. I think about Rob Gregory. I am treatable, so bring it on! Or as Rooster said, "Bring the ruckus!" When we get home

I post the following on Winning:

> This morning I discussed my further treatment options with my Chemo doctor. There are many variables to consider but we have settled on a plan for my condition. The plan comes in 3 stages.
>
> First is a 3 month cycle of chemotherapy. This will involve an initial 2-3 hour intravenous feed followed by an oral (tablet) feed every day for 2 weeks. Week 3 is my week off. This 3 week cycle is repeated for 3 months. It starts 2 weeks today on 26 June.
>
> The second stage is a transition stage - a 3 week period of scans etc to prepare me for stage 3.
>
> The third and final stage is 5 weeks in duration and is a combination of chemotherapy and radiotherapy. The daily chemo dose will be less than that administered in stage 1.
>
> The daily radiotherapy will be administered at Christies. Chemotherapy infuses my whole system to destroy any seedlings of cancer that may remain undetected by scans. Radiotherapy is a blast of gamma rays aimed at the previously infected area to ensure it no longer can exist there. The alarmists amongst you should note that diarrhoea is a common side effect of chemo so getting caught in traffic en route to Christies will be interesting!!
>
> I remain positive about my planned treatment and have resolved to fully embrace it. Why wouldn't I? It's going to be my saviour. Many thanks to all for your support and kind wishes. They are much appreciated.
>
> As always Andrea Barker is at my side to pick me up when I stumble. Without her things would be so much more difficult. On a more positive note my recovery from the operation continues to go well and I am confident of achieving my ambition of being pain and drug free for at least one day before my Chemo treatment commences. Wishing you all a merry Xmas.

So many positive, supportive messages in response, not to mention one or two funnies:

> *Paul Bernardi – Blasted with gamma rays? I for one will definitely not be making you angry for a while! Good to have a clear plan of attack laid out though.*
> *Suzanne Copeland – Ensure no small insects accompany you. We've all seen the films!*
> *Tony Chadwick – Hope all goes well for you. I never thought I would see the day when your bottom caused you more trouble than your slack Bladder!*
> *Jeff Rosser – With you all the way as you well know x*

18 June 2017

It's Father's Day and all my sons are at university. However they phone and have sent cards. I am particularly moved by this one:

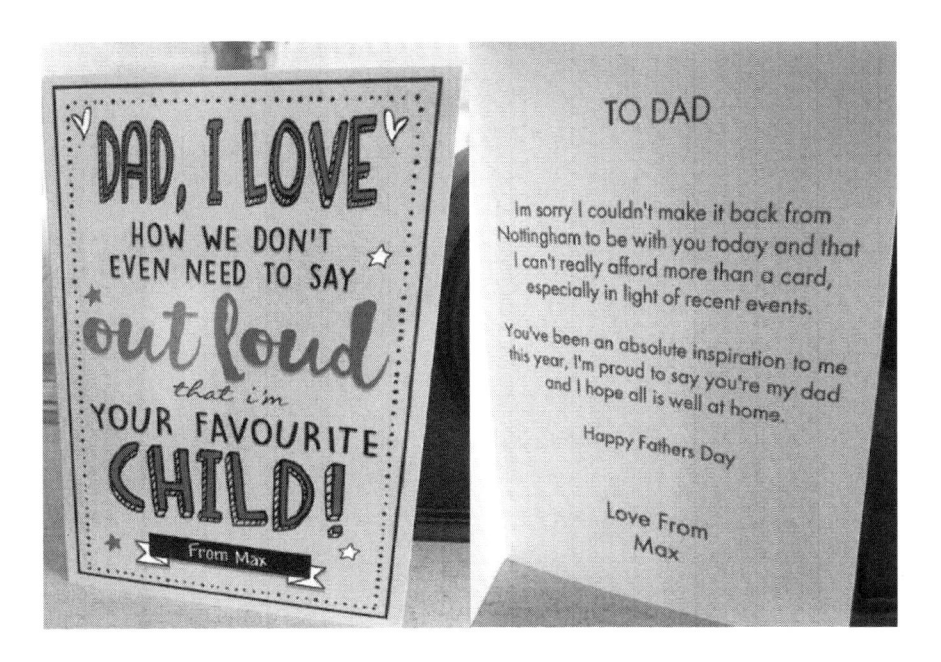

20 June 2017

Andrea and I had our first date on this day three years ago. We eat out to celebrate and before chemotherapy starts next week. It's wonderful to enjoy the simple, good things in life without a care.

21 June 2017

For the first time this year I am pain free, as long as I remain still and don't strain myself. It's very liberating and I consider running a marathon and leaping tall buildings. Andrea has gone out in my car for the morning, leaving me to call the RAC to come out and change a flat tyre on her car.

"Nah!" I think, "I'm having that."

I manage to get the spare tyre on and set off to drive her car to the garage to repair the main tyre, now in the boot. Half way to the garage the spare goes flat. Refusing to give up, I walk home and get Andrea's business van and then pick up the main car tyre, from the boot of her abandoned car, on the way to the garage.

Tyre repaired I return to the car in order to remove the spare and replace it. Unfortunately, the thread on the locking wheel nut has worn to the point of making the removal of the spare impossible with the limited tools I have. It is in this moment that I discover the limit of my physical condition.

As I sit on the side of the road, sweating profusely and cursing my aching wounds, I call the RAC. I explain my predicament and, I'm ashamed to say, call on the *cancer card,* informing them of my recent major surgery. They sympathise and offer the next available mechanic.

What made me think that changing even one tyre was a good idea?

22 June 2017

Chris Quin visits on his way home from work. He's in good shape following his heart attack scare. I'm delighted to hear he's getting back to his cycling best again.

25 June 2017

I receive a text message from Jeff, a man of his word and a fellow warrior.

> My thoughts and best wishes will be with you tomorrow. stay strong and positive, you're going to beat this, we're both going to beat this. Will ring you later on on the week. If you're not up to it when I ring, just tell me. I won't take it personally. X

> Thank old friend. Damn right we will both beat this. Chemo is just a thing. It's going to help save me so bring it on. Hope you're doing well. Love you loads bud x

27 Jun 2017, 09:52

5
CHEMO FOG

Chemotherapy is an aggressive form of chemical drug therapy used to destroy rapidly growing cells in the body. Cancer cells grow and divide faster than other cells.

Victims of this chemical poison respond differently with various symptoms. Almost all experience *chemo fog*, a complete, constant and unrelenting exhaustion, coupled with cognitive impairment. Confused sufferers have difficulty concentrating for any length of time and finding the right word. Feelings of depression, anxiety and emotional instability are also common symptoms. Coping mechanisms do exist but there is no real antidote for *chemo fog*.

"In the theatre of confusion, knowing the location of the exit is what counts."
— Mason Cooley

26 June 2017

So begins the endless months of *chemo fog*. Andrea and I are ready for this period in our lives. Whatever lies ahead we are determined to live life to the full and enjoy every opportunity it brings. This, in the knowledge that there is an exit, we will create happy memories in spite of the continued treatment.

I read a number of fighting posts on Winning this morning. This one from an ex-army chum of mine is typical:

> *Dave Carson – Starting today, fighting mode re-engaged, lasers set to "kill the mo-fo" and away we go Captain. Best of British with the treatment mate.*

Andrea and I arrive at the hospital and are able to park for free, one of the many small benefits of cancer treatment. We make our way to the MacMillan suite for my first IV feed of oxaliplatin.

Following a brief chat with my oncologist we are introduced to Charlotte, the senior nurse, and the day room where the chemotherapy is administered. Here eight large comfortable armchairs are arranged in a semi-circle. Each chair has a small table on one side and an IV drip stand on the other. We select my armchair and Andrea pulls up another chair to sit with me.

As we wait for the nurse to prepare my drugs we chat with the older married couple sat next to us. The gentleman is receiving IV oxaliplatin.

Shortly after retiring, five years ago, he had been diagnosed with bowel cancer. After his operation to remove the tumours the surgeon had recommended a follow-up treatment of chemotherapy. He had managed one session of oxaliplatin and found the symptoms too severe to live with, so he decided to stop further treatment. Five years later the cancer had returned with a vengeance. He is incurable. The oxaliplatin he now receives is to keep him alive for as long as possible. He is hoping to see one last Christmas with his family. His wife clutches his hand and stares at him lovingly as he speaks.

Andrea and I are speechless.

Although I eventually mutter, "I'm so very sorry to hear that," it feels inadequate. There is a familiar calmness in him; he has accepted his fate and the daily suffering he couldn't tolerate five years ago. I resolve to remember him as I face months of treatment that this man could not endure. He is a sad lesson to me. He inspires me to feel more determined to power through and take whatever, whenever the medical profession throws at me.

Charlotte approaches pushing a trolley. She parks it next to the IV stand to my left, blocking my view of the elderly couple. Andrea continues to chat with them whilst I am being attended to. They don't sound unhappy or tormented as you might expect, only weary and resigned.

Charlotte has my attention as she informs me of the procedure about to be administered. She pats the back of my hand looking for a vein, an entry point. When satisfied she inserts a cannula and tapes it down. A bag of clear liquid, the oxaliplatin, is hung up from the top of the IV stand. It's going to take about three hours to drip into my system. It is possible to use a pump but, although this may make the procedure quicker, it is more painful.

There is a common quality in doctors and nurses that I have come to recognise and respect. It's more obvious in the more dedicated and I see it in Charlotte in abundance. The attention to clinical detail, to stay absorbed, to meticulously concentrate and correctly administer treatment whilst at the same time deliver comfort, humanity and reassurance to the patient. To do both well, and concurrently, is rather like patting your head with one hand and rubbing your tummy with the other. Actions that are at odds with each other. It truly is a remarkable skill, all the more so given the dismal condition of some patients.

"Wherever the art of medicine is loved, there is also a love of humanity."
– Hippocrates

I watch the very start of oxaliplatin travel down the IV line and into the back of my hand.

"Poison! Do your worst. I'm ready for you." I mutter under my breath with all the fortitude I can muster.

Before Charlotte leaves to attend to other patients she advises me to sit still and relax. If I need to go to the loo I can do so, as the IV stand is on wheels and can be taken with me.

After about thirty minutes I can feel the icy cold pain rising up my arm and into my chest and across the rest of my body. This continues to intensify and the last twenty minutes are disturbingly painful. I close my eyes, grit my teeth and breathe rhythmically. Andrea grips my right hand sensing my discomfort. Charlotte periodically checks on my progress and asks me how I am.

A dinner lady appears, sadly, not Mrs Overall. She has a trolley of various sandwiches, fruit, yoghurts, tea and a pot of vegetable soup. Both Andrea and I are offered nourishment, another free perk.

After two hours and fifty-three minutes the bag of clear liquid is empty. I have been poisoned by oxaliplatin for my own good, for my own survival. At first I don't feel so bad, apart from the pain in my left arm. Then I stand. My head spins. Hmm, a little nauseous and listless. I can deal with that, no problem.

I am given a record book with an entry against today's date for the treatment I've received. It also illustrates a plan for the treatment to come. I look at the future dates stretching out in the months ahead. "Just one day at a time," I contemplate. The book also contains emergency phone numbers, including The Christie Hospital which provides 'round the clock' advice. We both also have access to free reflexology and various other holistic therapies. If required, financial help and advice are available.

Charlotte gives me a bag and hands my medications to me, one at a time, carefully explaining each. The capecitabine comes first, two weeks' worth of tablets to be taken twice daily, after breakfast and after an evening meal, starting tomorrow morning. It's the largest and most important box.

I am at risk of a variety of symptoms – fatigue, infection, nausea, vomiting, constipation, diarrhoea, painful nerve endings, loss of concentration or *chemo fog,* mood changes, loss of libido and a significant loss of appetite. Charlotte has a drug for most of these, many of which I will have to take regularly starting tomorrow and the others only when required. They will help, she assures me with a smile. Andrea gives me her *'please just do as you're told'* look. As I watch the elderly couple leave I concede, promising to take everything as prescribed.

We leave with an armful of helpful literature, my record card and enough drugs to stock a pharmacy. As we walk back to the car the length of my left arm feels sore right into my chest. I feel heavy and can only manage a slow pace. The worst of the nausea has passed, but climbing into the car requires effort and I laboriously close the door on my leg before I can drag it into the car. The shape of things to come!

By the time Andrea has driven us home the nausea has returned; probably triggered by the car journey.

I collapse on the sofa and post the following on Winning:

> *Just got home from receiving my first intravenous feed of chemotherapy. Multiple symptoms so far but nothing too extreme. I have enough drugs to stock a pharmacy. I'm confident I can handle this.*
>
> *As usual Andrea was with me. I am grateful beyond words for the humour and comfort she gives me. Chemo tablets for the next two weeks then a week of rest. That 3 week pattern is repeated for about 6 months. Bring it on.*

My brother Paul Horan posts a picture of Superman in response. I feel more like Rancidman!

It's a lovely, warm summer day. As I lay on the sofa the back door and windows are opened to create a nice cooling breeze. As the day turns to dusk the nausea passes but I've grown increasingly tired. I become aware of pins and needles in my hands and fingers so I sit up, clench and unclench my fists and wriggle my fingers. A light breeze drifts through the room and swirls around me. Suddenly, pain hits me and I cry out. My hands are crippled and sore. The pins and needles have instantly magnified into an acute stabbing, forcing my hands into a claw-like shape. It's tortuous and I'm traumatised. Andrea and Max both appear having heard my screams.

"What's the matter? Your hands? What's wrong with them?"

"I don't know. It's agony. Get Christies on the phone, quick. Please just hurry!" I plead, unable to handle the phone myself.

Andrea calls The Christie help-line immediately and is put through to a member of the medical support team. She puts the phone on speaker and places it on the small table in front of me. By now my hands feel like they're on fire and, through gritted teeth, I describe my agonizing condition into the phone.

"I understand, Mr Oldham. How are your feet?"

"My feet? Did you say my feet?" My breathing is getting heavy. "My feet are fine, why?"

"Do you have socks and shoes on?"

"Yes, yes I do. Argh!"

The pain has ramped up.

"Right. Wrap your hands up warm. Get some gloves on quickly."

Andrea has already left the room as I try to understand what is being said. Seconds later she stands over me forcing a pair of thick ski mittens over my debilitated hands. The impact is incredible.

Within five seconds the pain starts to subside as my hands warm up, no longer exposed to the light breeze. Within twenty seconds the pain has gone completely. The Christie's help-line medic explains that oxaliplatin seeks to destroy nerve endings and the impact is particularly felt in the hands and feet. Any attempt to pick up, say, metal or get something out of the fridge will have the same effect.

To test the theory I go to the fridge, take off one glove and open the door. As I touch the door handle I feel a shock of pain. By the time the fridge door is open my exposed hand is crippled once more. I recoil immediately and quickly pull my glove back on.

"Yeah! I'm an idiot. I won't be doing that too often." I announce to the tittering duo watching on.

27 June 2017

After breakfast I swallow my first two capecitabine tablets. They are quite large and initially tasteless but with a faintly bitter after-taste. Four other pills follow to prevent various symptoms that I may otherwise suffer. I also have constipation and diarrhoea pills should I need them. I plan to follow the advice I've been given and do some light work in the mornings and rest up in the afternoon. That means gardening and then couch surfing whilst binging Netflix.

The postman knocks on the door, with a parcel I need to sign for. I wearily sway, slur my words and sign for the parcel wearing my large ski gloves. I wonder what he makes of me. I feel the vague urge to explain, but just don't have the energy. Maybe next time.

I get a text message from Jeff Rosser which simply says:

"Hoping things aren't too bad for you today x."

Despite his own illness he still has time to check in with me at this difficult time. Knowing this warrior is in my corner helps. I reply:-

"Some interesting and challenging symptoms bro but Christies are on hand with advice to deal with it all. They'll tune my dose to the symptoms I'm getting so things should settle down. Thanks bud x."

29 Jun 2017

Another message from Jeff Rosser:

"Hi Bud. How are you feeling today? Hope things have settled down for you a little bit. Just got the tablets/drugs from CBD Brothers. Taken 1 already. Will let you know in a few days what effect they have on me!! I know you won't be able to take them with the chemo but you might benefit from them after treatment. Take care of yourself. J x"

I am exhausted and in pain. The best I can do is reply with a heart emoji. Jeff will know my suffering well enough to understand my brief response. I am grateful for his message but need to rest.

30 June 2017

The pain caused to my left arm from the oxaliplatin IV feed is now minimal. However, I am exhausted, over-emotional and unable to concentrate on anything. In addition, I have suffered from diarrhoea several times a day. It's urgent and painful.

Whilst trimming the hedges in the front garden this morning I suddenly feel the need and run indoors. When I say "run", it's more of a drunken plod, bumping into things and tripping up along the way, desperate to make haste. I just about make it on this occasion.

However, just as I set off I notice the same postman starting to walk up the drive. He will have seen the same mad resident in shorts and ski gloves turn and run from him. Not only that but he got no answer to the door when he knocked.

I am sat on the toilet painfully relieving myself whilst the kind postman knocks several times on the front door in the certain knowledge that the barking mad householder is indoors. I start to giggle at the situation wondering if I should shout an apology out of the bathroom window just above the front door. My suppressed laughter needlessly turns to tears. I am shaking with emotion, weeping inconsolably. Why? I'm confused. What has become of me? Get a grip, Keith!

The postman leaves a note to say the parcel requires a signature and can be collected from the local parcel depot.

2 July 2017

Chemo Keith is born on this day. I consider the real, normal me to be reasonably tough, emotionally strong and rational. But today this is not me. I have a complete emotional meltdown.

"That child of Hell had nothing human; nothing lived in him but fear and hatred."
— *The Strange Case of Dr Jekyll and Mr Hyde*
Robert Louis Stevenson,

At midday I find myself sitting on the lounge floor repeatedly screaming to be left alone, bawling my eyes out! I have no idea what triggers this uncontrolled, irrational outburst. It's completely opposed to my usual nature. Never have I behaved so appallingly.

To make it worse my extreme anxiety is aimed directly at Andrea, the person who has cared for me the most. It is shameful. I am full of the poison that is chemotherapy mixed wth a cocktail of other toxic drugs. The impact of this reveals itself in a vile rant that I am unable to control, instead, it controls me. I am left to stew until, debilitated, I crawl back to something like my normal self.

There is no pride in my uncharacteristic flare-up. Andrea, not normally blessed with patience, has had to dig deep to cope with my alter ego. It fuels remorse and self-pity in me. I feel broken, bereft of dignity, uncertain that I will be able to keep *Chemo Keith* at bay. There are many months of treatment ahead of me. The exit now seems impossible to find.

As I silently eat the evening meal that Andrea has lovingly prepared, the magnitude of my earlier conduct starts to weigh heavy and my chest begins to tighten. Sharp stabbing pains cause me to reach for the phone and I call The Christie Hospital. Tearfully, I describe the events of the day and the pains in my chest.

"Chest pains?" Comes the immediate response.

I am advised to get to Macclesfield Hospital A&E department as quickly as possible. The Christie medic will phone ahead so that we are expected. Chest pains are a very serious matter, more so when being treated with chemotherapy. The thought of spending a Saturday evening waiting to be treated in a busy A&E department is not very appealing, but nonetheless, we set off with a sense of urgency.

On arriving, we are met at the entrance by a receptionist who asks me to confirm my name. We are then led through a very busy waiting area directly to a treatment room and a doctor. The waiting room is full of patients with visible injuries.

To look at me, nothing would appear wrong and the questioning gazes I get from apparently more deserving patients is palpable. I can only respond with sheepish apologies as we are whisked past broken limbs, head injuries and vomiting drunks.

I am immediately hooked up to an electrocardiogram (ECG) machine and a cannula is put into the back of my hand. The ECG machine is used to check the rhythm of my heart via sensors attached to numerous parts of my body. The cannula is used to take my blood for tests and to administer any potential IV medication.

I remain in hospital for a couple of hours being monitored. My heart rate is found to be abnormal but my condition is not at risk so I am discharged. However, to be safe, I am advised to postpone my capecitabine prescription by twenty-four hours, giving time to re-assess my treatment with my oncologist tomorrow.

We return home and I am exhausted and over-emotional. Chemotherapy is full of nasty surprises and I resolve to toughen up and, somehow, keep *Chemo Keith* at arm's length.

"It was no longer the fear of the gallows; it was the horror of being Hyde that racked me."

— *The Strange Case of Dr Jekyll and Mr Hyde.*
Robert Louis Stevenson,

I post the following on Winning:

> *Christies told me that chest pains are not a good thing to get with the chemotherapy I'm on. Rushed into A&E by my lovely Andrea Barker. Hooked up to an ECG monitor and bloods taken. All fine now just waiting for blood results. The diarrhoea was a minor distraction to an eventful evening. All this is fairly common. The good news is I get 24 hours off chemotherapy.*

It's been a highly emotional day. I don't know whether to laugh or cry at the responses:

> *Paul Bernardi — Rooting for ya buddy. Take it easy.*
> *Suzanne Copeland — Well that all sucks! Hope they get you sorted quick smart. Big hugs to you both xxx*
> *Jane Evanson-Horan — Thanks for the update big man keep the faith xx onwards and upwards xxx sending you big hugs*
> *Fran Dykes — Bugger!*
> *Peter George — Keep drinking (not alcohol) and eating Keith thinking of you keep calm and carry on.*
> *Chris Quin — Nothing on telly tonight anyway. Probably good to get out. Keep at it mate. Rooting for you*
> *Pete Munro — Kick it in the pips*
> *Lizzie Bloor — Bloody hell man! You need a break! X*
> *Gordon Hamlin — I prescribe Girls Aloud and five mars bars! That'll get you off your back! Oh. Wait. Hang on....*

It seems the gents want to fist bump me and the ladies want to hug me. I'll take that.

3 July 2017

We meet with my oncologist and discuss the events of yesterday. I am to complete my capecitabine tablets for this session which will shorten my rest week. This is a good outcome as it doesn't delay the end of my treatment. I want to get through treatment on schedule.

Encouraged, I post the following on Winning:

> *My oncologist has put me back on the same chemotherapy treatment but with more drugs to deal with the side effects.*
>
> *I consider this to be a great result because it doesn't delay the treatment. I have invested massively in this first week of treatment and it's good to know it hasn't been wasted.*
>
> *So it's back to the chemo fog….happy days. In other news the blocked drain causing sewerage to flood my drive every time I flush the loo or have a shower is being attended to. Progress!!*

Readers respond to both the treatment and the poo update:

> *Paul Bernardi – I assumed it was a capacity issue. Onwards and upwards.*
> *Julie Bernardi – Those are two great results*
> *Peter George – Good to hear both bits of news. Win win.*
> *David Clayton – Good result…make enough noise and you get more bandwidth. Am sure the neighbours will be pleased too. Good to see you in fine bullish mood keef.*

A problem with our drains has occurred, or should I say erupted!

Whenever the shower is used or a toilet is flushed sewerage emerges from the drains onto the drive. Our drains have become blocked. It is within acceptable bounds of humour to blame me due to the high frequency with which I use the toilet.

When it first happens I blame myself and others soon jump on the bandwagon. This has the potential to be an incontinence and diarrhoea disaster. I discover that there's nothing that gives you more a sense of urgency than being denied the use of a toilet.

Fortunately, a friend of Andrea's has a family firm of drainage engineers. The mighty hero known as Scott arrives in the afternoon to rescue us from our predicament.

When he carefully lifts the manhole cover on the drive even I, now somewhat of an expert in managing my own waste product, take a step back and gag repeatedly. A small amount of sick appears in my mouth resulting in a choking cough as well as a gag.

Scott calmly takes everything in his stride. He connects a couple of rods together into one piece and rams it into the drainage system submerged by the putrid brown lumpy gravy. After a few forcible thrusts of his rod there's a loud suction noise from the surrounding drainage holes and the rank fluid quickly runs away.

The end of the rod has a camera on it. Scott is able to extend the rod further and guide the camera to the very end of the drain on our property, rather like a homestead colonoscopy, I muse. Inspecting the full length of the drain on a black and white monitor, surgeon Scott confirms the all clear and then power washes the drive clean.

He explains that a small amount of rubble had loosened in the drain. This together with a large amount of tissue paper and a low flushing pressure from one of our toilets had caused the blockage. My fault indeed, guilty as charged! Scott had gone to a great deal of trouble.

With very little notice, he had gone out of his way to prioritise and complete the job (no pun intended) today and do it thoroughly. The most amazing part is that, aware of my condition, he refuses payment. I am struck by his compassion and kindness. As I am now prone to bouts of extreme emotion, I have to choke back tears and insist on making a payment which he eventually accepts.

8 July 2017

Almost two weeks into my chemotherapy treatment and I'm beginning to learn from the experience. It feels rank, noxious, putrid, fetid and downright loathsome. It undermines you physically, emotionally and intellectually. It takes away so much of you as a human being. To truly understand it you have to experience it. It's an experience I wouldn't want to burden anyone with.

But, I feel like I'm getting the measure of it and learning how to cope. I can understand why the elderly terminal gentleman we met in the MacMillan treatment room had decided to stop his treatment five years ago. Sod that, I'm not for quitting; Rooster style.

This evening is the annual Greater Manchester Drama Federation Awards ceremony. An event when all the drama societies across Greater Manchester converge on the Last Drop Village Inn in Bolton, particularly those who have received a nomination for a role in their theatre's production. It's a grand affair and attended by about four to five-hundred local amateur theatre members.

I have been nominated in the category *Best Male Actor in a Lead Role* for my part in *Jerusalem*, the part of Johnny 'Rooster' Byron. The play has also been nominated in several other categories.

Myself, Andrea and Cameron Chandler are in attendance. Little Macclesfield is up against some stiff opposition, but does extraordinarily well. I win my category and the play wins the most prestigious award of all, Best Overall Production. We also leave with an armful of awards for other categories and it takes the three of us to carry all the trophies to the car.

The Rooster

Greater Manchester
Drama Federation

Best Male Actor in a
Lead Role

Jerusalem

Greater Manchester
Drama Federation

Best Overall
Production

Before we set off Cameron ensures that the big, bad-boy shield, pictured, is wearing a seatbelt. We drive home in a jubilant mood. The memory of Rooster and his fighting spirit renews my determination to rid myself of cancer by whatever means necessary, even chemotherapy. To win!

10 July 2017

Jeff Rosser phones in the afternoon and we chat for an hour or so. Talking with him is therapeutic. We are both very positive about our conditions and determined to return to full health. Because of his own cancer he understands my suffering completely and he knows he has a friend in me that will support and love him throughout his recovery and beyond. The misery of cancer has renewed our friendship beyond anything we thought possible.

He's enjoying the CBD Brothers products. They don't give him the high he was hoping for but they are relaxing and do help with his pain management. He makes it clear there is so much to laugh about and to live for. His love for his wife Di, his daughter Sammi and son Jed run deep. We talk about his passion for music and Welsh rugby. There is much to admire in him. His lust for life inspires me.

11 July 2017

I take my final capecitabine tablets today to complete my first treatment cycle. The large box that was full of tablets two weeks ago is now empty. I screw the box up into a ball, open the bin, stand on the other side of the kitchen and take aim.

I'm a shadow of my former self and I'm wearing ski gloves so I miss by a mile of course, dammit! Refusing to give in to this man-against-cancer tournament, I keep trying until the confounded screwed up cancer box flies into the bin. An underarm toss finally consigns it to the rubbish heap.

I hear a knock at the front door. Elated with my triumph and completely absorbed by it I open the door and without care shout:

"YES! Get in, back of the net!" Slightly crouched and punching the air with both fists.

My postman stands before me. He takes a step backwards and, with furrowed brow and outstretched arms, hands a parcel to the lunatic in shorts, thick woollen socks and over-sized ski gloves; appearing to be practicing the All Blacks Haka, a traditional Maori war dance.

"Er……sign here, please." He, quite rightly, looks perplexed.

"Ah, yes, you, hello! Please let me explain."

I'm in full *I've got cancer* mode as I describe my condition, treatment and numerous symptoms whilst clumsily signing for the parcel in large ski mittens. I apologise for my erratic behavior
with a promise of much more to come.

The postman has a sense of humour and laughs in all the right places. Feeling more relaxed now, he responds:

"Don't worry mate, we see all sorts on our rounds…."

I think he is going to tell me about some of the "all sorts" he has seen on his round but I cut him off with a ski-gloved facepalm and "sorry," shut the door in his face, turn and run. I just about make it to the toilet in time.

Well, I did promise him much more whimsy.

12 July 2017

I wake this morning feeling ecstatic. Yesterday I was liberated from the burden of having my life ruled by chemotherapy. It was the delayed start to my first rest week. Not having to eat, shit, stumble, sleep and dance to the tune of capecitabine for the next five days fills me with euphoria. The ski gloves have been replaced with a pair of thin working gloves. I can't wait to show them, and my new found dexterity, off to the postman.

In my jubilation I post the following on Winning:

> *Yesterday I stopped taking chemotherapy and started my rest week. The improvement I felt physically, emotionally and intellectually was significant. Some poison is still in my system but the impact of the many side effects has lessened.*
>
> *The worst physical symptoms were complete exhaustion, crippling pins and needles in hands/feet and diarrhoea. Worse than that however was the impact to my intellect and emotional state. Memory loss and the inability to cope emotionally with some ordinary daily challenges. I had a couple of meltdowns which my amazing Andrea had to deal with. "Chemo Keith" you sir can sod right off! We have certainly learnt from the experience and are better prepared for the next phase which starts on Monday.*

The humour, the love and the support flow in abundance:

> *Fran Dykes – Ah…but what I want to know is…did you glow in the dark? Chemo Keith! But seriously it will be worth it when you can ring the bell and walk away having beaten this because we want you in our lives.*
> *Cath Rimmer – Glad to know that your week off coincides with the important week of the MADS BBQ! On a more serious note, keep going, keep smiling and give 'em hell! We're backing you all the way.*
> *Suzanne Copeland – Sounds utterly shitty – pun completely intended. I know that you'll grit your teeth and power through this. At least you've had some insight into what it's like to be a middle aged woman! As always big love and huge cuddles xxx*
> *Claire Taylor – Chemo Keith! – that's your superhero name! #notallheroswearacape. If you need anything let me know x*
> *Craig Tweedie – Have you considered your superhero costume? Is it one of them hospital night shirts that ties up the back? If so, can I recommend a cape too!!*
> *Simon Waring – Mate, we are with you all the way, and I LOVE Suzi's comments. I had a vision of you in a twin set and pearls.*

15 July 2017

Today is the silliness that is the annual MADS Summer BBQ, an important event in our calendar. Tradition dictates that the adults behave like children. It involves outdoor games like boules and giant Jenga, a bouncy castle, lots of beer and wine, gazebos, wrapping people in cling film and watching them trying to stand up and grazing on BBQ food throughout the day. More important than any of that we get to hang out and laugh with many friends, fellow members of the Theatre.

I am lacking in the high energy required to survive the event, but I'm determined not to miss it. I have learned how to moderate my diet to avoid diarrhoea. However, if the worst should happen, the venue is a safe place and I am amongst understanding friends. I put a change of clothes in the car just in case.

It's a fabulous afternoon and evening. Although I'm not blessed with too much mobility, I do get to hang out with Jessica, the cute, lively, two-year old daughter of Tom and Gemma. Gemma is a very accomplished actress and a hugely talented director. As Assistant Director for *Jerusalem* she helped shape the character of Rooster, to find his spirit. I am forever grateful.

The event is a reminder of what fun life can be, a stark contrast to the misery of the last couple of weeks. It gives me renewed strength for the chemo battle that starts again in two days' time.

17 July 2017

I wake with Rooster steel and determination coursing through my veins, ready to meet chemotherapy head on. Today is day one of my second three-week treatment cycle.

On arrival at the MacMillan suite, Andrea and I meet my oncologist and review the first cycle of treatment. The first cycle always carries with it the risk of uncertainty. There is a good deal of science behind the chemotherapy prescription but patients can react to it in uniquely different ways.

I describe my reaction, particularly the arrival of *Chemo Keith*. The oncologist suggests that *Chemo Keith* may have been a product of those drugs taken, in addition to capecitabine, to control the symptoms. One in particular is a strong steroid to be taken for the first four days only. Coming off steroids can cause uncontrollable mood swings. This, combined with capecitabine and other drugs, can induce a chemical toxicity sufficient to create *Chemo Keith*.

The oncologist also reminds me that whilst I may have felt released from the Chemo Fog for a short time during my drug free third week, this is unlikely to be the case in future treatment cycles. From here on I will build up a reserve of chemotherapy that will stay in my system. Week three will feel just as lousy as weeks one and two.

I decide to stop taking all the drugs prescribed to treat symptoms and to take only the capecitabine. If I suffer a symptom I will either put up with it or consider taking something at the time to treat it. The many drugs prescribed to treat the symptoms of chemotherapy are themselves giving me symptoms I am struggling to tolerate.

This decision establishes a sense of control within me that I thought I had previously lost. I am ready for the oxaliplatin. When we arrive at the treatment room, Charlotte is ready to administer it. We select the same armchair that I sat in previously and Andrea pulls up a chair to sit with me through the three hours of torture that lies ahead. Once again, Charlotte is meticulous yet comforting.

"You must love your job." I remark as she buries the cannula into the back of my hand. "You are saving people's lives every day that you come to work. Patients must love you for what you do for them and the caring manner in which you do it"

"I do love it," she replies, "but you couldn't be further from the truth. I poison patients. They leave here in pain and feeling much worse than when they first arrived. It does save lives but it's a bad experience. One most people would rather forget. In fact I've seen some patients outside the hospital, long after treatment has finished, and they have crossed the road to avoid me."

Horrified to hear this, Andrea and I both screech, "no way!"

"Way!" Charlotte cuts in soberly with a shrug of her shoulders. "I think some people just don't want to be reminded of their time here."

She attaches the IV line to the cannula. As I watch the first drip of poison enter my body I promise that if ever I see her outside the hospital I will go out of my way to greet her. I am not sure she is convinced as she smiles and moves to check on the patient sitting in the next chair.

The next two hours and fifty-six minutes is every bit as gruesome as the first time. But knowledge is power and having experienced it once I feel more in control and able to cope with it. To take my mind off the slow moving cold pain rising up my arm and into my chest, I post the following on Winning with a 'feeling fabulous' emoji:

> *Well hello old friend. It's been a while welcome back. Now we're not going to fall out with each other this time are we? Jolly good!*

The responses are every bit as supportive as they always have been:

> *Suzanne Harrop – Not this week! This week is going to be plain sailing! Fingers crossed that's the case for you. Thinking of you as always and sending lots of positive and good vibes.*
> *David Shaw – Not sure "fall out" is a term you should be bandying around! Make em have it my son.*
> *David Wilkinson – That's the spirit*

Yes, David Wilkinson, it is. It's the Rooster spirit.

Despite the summer temperature outside, once the treatment is complete, I climb into my ski gloves and warm clothing before we leave the MacMillan suite for the car park.

Once home I collapse on the sofa in front of the TV as the *Chemo Fog* continues to take hold of me. We have a busy week ahead and I'll need all my strength, and Andrea, to get through it.

18 July 2017

As much as I hate taking the capecitabine tablets they are so much easier to ingest without the usual concoction of other drugs. Now it's just two in the morning and two in the evening.

I had a good night's sleep but I feel exhausted. Everything I do is in slow motion and my mind is foggy, unable to concentrate or rationalise. Most of the time I have to give into the chemotherapy, to let it have its way with me.

I can find the energy to lift myself out of it a little but only occasionally, when it's necessary. The next couple of days are important and I need to be attentive and at my best. I have learnt how to moderate my diet to be comfortable and how to conserve energy for key moments.

Doing this starts today.

19 July 2017

Today, Luke graduates from Northampton University to become a professional actor. I am hugely proud of his achievements. He has an abundance of talent to take into the world.

I have watched Luke's performances at MADS and, indeed, shared the stage with him. Andrea and I have seen and enjoyed all his curriculum performances during his time as a student. It's a milestone day and one I am looking forward to immensely.

We meet up with Luke before the ceremony and go with him to collect his gown and mortar. Once he's appropriately attired various photographs are taken. During the ceremony we film the moment Luke is on his feet to collect his degree and cheer him with abandonment. It's thoroughly rewarding to see my son get the recognition he has earned. With Andrea's support and my stubborn refusal to let my exhaustion show we return home feeling very smug.

Luke Oldham

graduates in Acting
Northampton University

20 July 2017

If yesterday was tiring, today will be doubly so. We have an early start to drive the three hours it takes to get to Aberystwyth University where my youngest son, Cyrus, will graduate in Mathematics. We have to return in time to attend the MADS AGM in the evening. As membership secretary I have a short presentation to make about membership during the previous season.

The drive to Aberystwyth is on A roads which twist and turn through the Welsh mountains. It is a hard drive but worth it. This day, I am as proud of

Cyrus as I was of Luke yesterday. We meet Cyrus at the University campus and drive into the town for lunch at The Olive Branch, a delightful Italian Restaurant. We are joined by his girlfriend Adele and his friend Jay. It's a very happy occasion, a time to celebrate. Cyrus will spend time with his mum after the ceremony. This suits our plans as we have to leave as soon as Cyrus has collected his degree to ensure we arrive at the AGM in time.

Returning to the University Campus for the ceremony, we have some time to take photographs in the sunshine before taking our seats.

Cyrus Oldham

graduates in Mathematics
Aberystwyth University

The auditorium is packed but our seats are very comfortable. Fortunately, Cyrus is scheduled to collect his Degree soon after the ceremony commences. I shed a tear as he stands and walks onto the stage to shake the Dean's hand. Chemotherapy has made me emotionally unstable but this is about pride for my son; I am happy to own those tears.

Once Cyrus sits down again Andrea and I make our move to leave. I slowly get up and follow Andrea. My head spins with fatigue and I am unsteady on my feet as we jostle past the people on the same row as us, now forced to stand to let us pass. As we reach the end of the row a large, rather rotund gentleman on whose foot I had accidentally stood in my clumsiness to squeeze past him, is clearly irritated. Before I am able to apologies, he pushes me in the back and barks:

"Oh for goodness sake, can't you wait, or at least be more careful?"

"Excuse me!" Calmly replies Andrea, the lioness protecting her cub. "I am sorry to have disturbed you but this man has bowel cancer and is about to shit himself. His final wish is to see his son graduate. Is your rudeness really necessary?"

"Well... I... really...?" The man starts to reply defensively.

In an attempt to rescue him, his wife jumps up to help me down the few steps at the end of the row. I am an amateur actor and Andrea has given me a role to play up to. I take the lady's arm and softly thank her as I pitifully struggle, more than is necessary, to dismount and collapse into Andrea's waiting arms.

Our impromptu performance merits a standing ovation, but the menacing glare that 'Sir Galahad' receives from the watching audience around us is satisfaction enough. In that moment, and for our own amusement, we had played our first ever *cancer card*. It is naughty of us, but it's fun to use my condition so defiantly and to our advantage.

The drive home is interrupted by a road closure and so takes four hours. We arrive home with just enough time to get changed and drive to the Theatre. The MADS AGM is about celebrating the previous season and presenting the season ahead as well as the usual AGM governance formalities required of a well-run organisation.

I am worn out by the time I have to present my report so I elect to deliver it from the auditorium rather than the stage. As the *Chemo Fog* is getting the better of me I simply read it from my notes.

Toward the end of the AGM I am fortunate enough to be presented with the MADS Dawn Sims Award for Acting. This is mainly due to my performance as Rooster in *Jerusalem*. For me, it represents the best of this season's three trophies as I was voted for by my MADS peers, those for whom I have the greatest respect. Given the high acting quality in the company I feel both honoured and humbled. I just about make it from my seat in the auditorium to the stage to collect it.

Despite the cancer, the chemotherapy and the *Chemo Fog*, I have forced myself into the rewards of life over the last couple of days. Without Andrea's support it would not have been possible.

The Rooster

MADS Dawn Sims
Award for Acting

21 July 2017

I have known Andrea's priorities since we first met.

There is her love of dogs and horses, then there is me. That said, her love for me has shone brightly in her support for me since I was diagnosed with cancer. Today is a day to shift the balance back in favour of her equine passion. Her new little lady, Mia, a beautiful cob is safe and sound in her new stable at Woodhouse Farm. Mia is perfect for Andrea in many ways and I'm delighted for them both, particularly as Andrea's other two horses have had to retire and are now considered to be field ornaments.

23 July 2017

Woodhouse Farm hosts a dressage event and I proudly look on as Andrea puts Mia through her paces. It's quite incredible to watch. Neither pony nor rider have had much time to get to know one another and yet they are completely in tune with each other. A very credible score of 66.5% puts them in third place. Superbly done!

Andrea on Mia at the Woodhouse Farm Dressage event

25 July 2017

My dear old mum, Helene, has dementia and lives in a dementia-friendly Care

Home about an hour's drive away. I feel strong enough to drive to her and visit for the afternoon. She suffered from bowel cancer herself about sixteen years ago. She is very confused so I've never told her about my diagnosis and treatment. I'm not sure she would understand and telling her would serve no purpose.

I always feel sad going to see her but she always cheers me up when I'm with her. The picture should say why; the pure love of a mother for her son. One of the sad side effects of my illness is that I am unable to visit as much as I would like.

A mother's love

27 July 2017

Happy birthday to me. Lots of congratulations, cards and gifts. In the evening Andrea and I go out for a meal at Chilli Banana, one of our favourite restaurants. To round the evening off we call in at MADS Theatre for their social evening. This is proof enough that although cancer treatment slows you down it does not mean life can't still be fun and fulfilling.

28 July 2017

Whilst we are out shopping in Matalan, Andrea spots Charlotte, the nurse who had administered the oxaliplatin on those awful Monday mornings. She is with her two very young children. We recall what she said about former patients crossing the road to avoid her. Still finding this hard to understand we go out of our way to greet her warmly.

To make a point I sit on the floor and chat with her children informing them that their mum is a superhero. Her super-power is making people better. I explain that every time I see her she helps to make my illness go away.

"Your mum is amazing, brilliant and awesome and we like her a lot."

They both nod and giggle. I am pleased to be able to give a little something back to this hard-working, lifesaving, NHS employee.

30 July 2017

We live at the very end of a cul-de-sac. At the bottom of our drive is a turning circle that has space for visiting cars. To the left of our drive is a footpath that runs into tree-lined open fields. It is there that planning permission has been granted for the build of a dozen four-bed, high-spec houses. The footpath can only be widened a little, providing space for a single-track entrance to the new estate.

Clearing the wooded area started last year and it caused a rat infestation in our garden as the rats deserted the woods. This year the house build has commenced. The new estate will be called Park Pavilion.

Huge lorries have been arriving daily carrying building material. Various contractors have been parking up in the turning circle and the cul-de-sac has been littered with rubbish by the visiting workmen. The build has created a constant layer of mud on the main road and, unfortunately, driving through this has dirtied our driveway. The disruption to local residents has been significant.

I have taken it upon myself to decorate one of the rooms on our lower ground floor and to then convert it into a bedroom that we may choose to let out. Its position in the house is ideal for this purpose and could provide some useful income. However, it has been slow progress mainly due to my condition. In addition, driving off our property, to get to the local DIY shop, is often hampered by the arrival of a lorry en route to the Park Pavilion.

This morning a van is thoughtlessly parked across the bottom of my drive, blocking my exit. It takes me a while to find its owner and then even more time to encourage him to move it. I complain as strenuously as I am able to the site foreman again, but complaints are now commonplace and little is done about them.

I am fuming about the lack of care from the building firm. This morning I could have been delayed on my way to hospital in an emergency rather than going out to buy paint. As I slowly paint the bedroom I am reminded of the New Estate that Rooster was battling against and daub an expression of my feelings on the wall.

Johnny 'Rooster' Byron.
Fuck the new estate
and the Kennet and Avon Council.

It occurs to me that you should never pick an argument with anyone being treated with chemotherapy. Like me, they are probably full of irrational and uncontrolled fighting spirit. Like the Park Pavilion builders, you'll definitely get more than you bargain for.

2 August 2017

It's my rest week from treatment but because the chemotherapy has built up in my system I feel no different. The *Chemo Fog* is constant and unrelenting. On top of that, the area around my naval is sore and there is a lump just beneath the surface. It is sinister enough for Andrea to drive me to the Hospital to have it inspected.

Our worst fears are averted; it's not a cancerous growth. I am diagnosed with a hernia. Apparently, this is quite normal following the operation I've had. I may have been over-doing things and I'm told to take things easier. My surgeon will monitor it. It's uncomfortable but not too painful. I am scheduled for a CT scan tomorrow providing the opportunity for a closer inspection.

I post the following on Winning:

> *Hello hernia. Have you come to play with your friends diarrhoea, exhaustion, chemo fog and crippling pins and needles? Well do me a favour once you've had some fun just bugger off. There's a good chap! I've got stuff to do.*

I just know that certain rascals will be amused by this turn of events. I am not disappointed:

> *Paul Bernardi – You've not been changing tyres again have you?*
> *David Shaw – Sounds like Mourinho talking to the squad*
> *David Wilkinson – Poke it back in and tell it to f***ing stay there! Do you want to borrow a stapler?*
> *Tim Roskell – What?? Total bum! I've had two hernia ops in the past but not with the crap you've been going thru as well. It sounds as if you've been*

stitched up!! Well u will be. Happy belated bday (perhaps it should read bidet!)
David Clayton – You tell it Keef. No gatecrashers allowed.
Julie Bernardi – that's what looking after Paul Bernardi for a week does to you xxx
Neil Burrows – making Andrea carry the luggage again huh?

3 August 2017

A visit to Macclesfield Hospital and the CT Scan confirms the hernia. Thankfully, nothing more sinister is discovered.

Thursday evenings are a time spent at MADS Theatre socialising with fellow thespians. There's usually something going on; rehearsals, Front of House rota to create for the next show, re-stock the bar, cleaning and any number of other sundry jobs to complete. It all ends up with members congregating in the bar for a few drinks and a late night. Tonight is no exception and it's about midnight when I eventually pull onto my drive at home and park. As I get out of my car, to my surprise, a police car stops immediately behind me and a policeman gets out.

"Good evening, sir." He says, polite but firm.

"That's rather a nice car you have there and I just wanted to make sure you got home safely. I couldn't help but notice that you failed to indicate when you turned right into Windsor Place. I have to warn you that failing to indicate is a punishable traffic offence."

"Is it? I can only apologise." I reply wondering where this conversation is going.

"Yes, it is. A fine and three points I'm afraid, sir. This is your car, isn't it, sir? Can I ask you your name, please?"

"Yes, it's my car. My name is Hans Keith Oldham and I live here. This is my drive."

By now he's on his mobile phone running a check on my car, its owner and my address. The information he gets back proves my honesty and that I am not a car thief.

"Can I ask you where you've been this evening, Mr Oldham?" He continues, hoping, I think, to find something more he can prosecute me for.

"I'm a member of an amateur dramatic society and I've spent the evening at my Theatre, socialising with other members."

"Socialising, Mr Oldham? Have you had anything to drink? I am going to ask you to take a breathalyser test, Mr Oldham."

"I'll be happy to take a breathalyser. I have had plenty to drink but I should tell you that it's only been water. You see, I am being treated for bowel cancer and I can't drink alcohol. It doesn't react too well with the chemotherapy I'm taking, nor the bowel surgery I've had. If you are going to breathalyse me, could I ask you to hurry up as I'm about to shit myself; another side-effect of my condition."

The policeman who, up to this point has been very efficient in the performance of his duty, pauses momentarily to consider what he has just been told. It's all very true but not what he had expected to hear. By now I have placed my hand on my bottom and I'm hopping from one foot to the other, a sort of slow poo dance. This agitating movement may have finally encouraged the policeman's next comment.

"Good evening, Mr Oldham, I'm sorry to have bothered you."

With that he gets into his car and drives away. I have always had the greatest of respect for any of the uniformed services and tonight's exchange, if anything, has increased my respect. The policeman had carried out his duty efficiently and politely. I may well have failed to indicate when turning right, and it is a punishable traffic offence, but that was my only crime. He had the good grace to recognise my condition and make an allowance for it.

I run inside to use the loo and then explain what happened to Andrea. However, I do struggle to convince her that I didn't overplay the *cancer card* on this occasion.

6 August 2017

Jeff Rosser calls to wish me luck with the start of round three tomorrow. He always sounds so positive about life but when he describes his cancer and his treatment I fear the worst for him. I'm truly inspired by my friend and fellow warrior.

7 August 2017

Today is the first day of my third three-week cycle. I sit in silence in the car as Andrea drives me to the hospital. The IV Oxaliplatin is painful, barbaric and inhumane but necessary. I contemplate what has now become a routine procedure with trepidation.

The next couple of days will be awful. My arm will be sore, the ski gloves will be worn to prevent painful pins and needles, there may be diarrhoea and almost certainly nausea.

With all that the *Chemo Fog* will intensify and leave me in a cloud, a shadow of my former self. A bumbling, dribbling, incoherent, dopey buffoon. I cheer myself by thinking of the responses on Winning if I were to post that last sentence.

"So, nothing's changed then?" or,

"Well, there's five of the seven dwarfs right there!"

Charlotte is on hand and with both her care and professionalism administers the poison that is Oxaliplatin. We ask about her children and she smiles. One is about to start school and the other is still in nursery. They had enjoyed meeting us in Matalan.

During the three-hour drip, drip feed of the toxic fluid there is a moment of cheering and celebration for a young lady, very pretty and in her early twenties. Her breast cancer had necessitated a mastectomy followed by months of chemotherapy. This morning she has met her oncologist and her surgeon to be informed that she has been scheduled for reconstructive surgery, news that she is now excitedly sharing with the nursing staff who have gotten to know her.

I am happy for her but can't help thinking what a sad paradox it is to celebrate the onset of such surgery. She should be celebrating a holiday, marriage, promotion at work or the purchase of a new car. She is too young to be inflicted in this way, but cancer has no consideration for age. It is cruel and it is merciless.

Although I am pleased for her, I also have very mixed feelings.

I post the following on Winning during treatment:

> *Ding ding ...... round 3! Two down six more to go. The gloves are off let battle commence.*

Lots of fighting comments stream in but I'm too lost in self-pity to notice. For now I'll just give in to it but tomorrow I'll punch my way back into life.

9 August 2017

John and Shirley Chandler visit this afternoon. They have visited me a couple of times whilst I've been treated with chemotherapy. As usual they message first to make sure I'm up for visitors. I love the fact that when they arrive they make themselves at home, put the kettle on and make us all a cup of tea. They stay for an hour and are fabulous company. The friendship they offer is exactly what the doctor ordered. They recently married late in their years and marriage certainly agrees with them.

10 Aug 2017

Andrea and I post messages on Facebook. They both include heart emojis.

Mine says:

> *She said yes. Happy days.*

Andrea's says:

> *He asked me……..and I said yes!!!*

We have been living together for three years and have discussed marriage. I know it is something we both want but we are in no rush, quite content with the way things are.

However, being diagnosed with cancer and facing mortality changes your perspective. Through adversity our love has flourished. Life has become more precious and, without realising it, our determination to have fun and live for each day has blossomed in us both this year. The time just seems right for a marriage proposal.

I'd like to have come up with some grand scheme, proposing at the top of the Eiffel Tower or with a public declaration of love on a large screen at a concert. Something romantic, magical and memorable. But a big gesture would be difficult to plan with my current poor health. Also, Andrea doesn't like surprises, particularly when she suspects one is being planned. I'm not confident enough in my *Chemo Fog* state to maintain the discretion required of surprise planning.

Having window shopped in jewellers the choice of engagement ring was easy enough. I had purchased it last week during my rest week. I wanted the moment to be impromptu, simple but meaningful.

At lunch time, Andrea returns home from walking dogs. We are alone in the hallway except for Alfie and Stanley as witnesses. I get down on one knee, tell Andrea that I love her, pull the ring box from my pocket and ask her the single most important question I'd ever asked her. She is both surprised and happy.

Thankfully she isn't expecting it and says yes. She fusses over the ring excitedly as I place it on her finger. We have no idea when or where we will marry but eagerly start to discuss some thoughts on the matter. For now, however, they are less important than enjoying this moment. Our Facebook posts receive many congratulatory comments and we are christened 'Hansdrea' by Suzanne Copeland.

In the evening we go out for a celebratory meal and continue to discuss our nuptial plans.

23 August 2017

The current cycle of chemotherapy treatment has become unimportant and customary. The last two weeks have been focused on our wedding. Andrea and I have agreed on everything; no compromise from either of us has been too difficult. Today we book the registrar and the Clonter Opera as a venue. We will marry on the 29 September next year. By then I will be nearing full recovery and back to work.

The Clonter Opera is a Theatre in the Cheshire countryside big enough to cater for up to three-hundred guests. The ceremony is booked for 4pm and will take place on the stage with the guests watching from the auditorium. An evening reception will follow. There is much more to arrange but the foundations are in place to create a memorable event.

I set up a fund-raising page on justgiving.com. We will be asking our wedding guests to not purchase wedding presents but instead to donate the cost of one to our cause. This will be a combination of funding for the surgical ward I was admitted to after my operation and for MacMillan support. The details will need to be worked out in discussion with Mr Chris Smart the next time I meet him.

A t-shirt arrives in the post. Designed and posted by my brother Paul Horan who came to watch *Jerusalem*.

"Bring the ruckus" is an often said Rooster phrase and a reminder of how well I am supported in my on-going battle against cancer.

Rooster, "Bring the Ruckus"

29 August 2017

It's *that* morning again, the start of another three-week cycle. As Andrea drives me to Macclesfield Hospital I feel deeply upset. I've been in *Chemo Fog* for two months now, doing my best to cope with the rank, putrid and rotten symptoms that come with the treatment. It is so tiresome. Some days no amount of support and positive thinking helps and I am forced to accept my despondency. I do so in the knowledge, however, that it won't last, even though it sometimes feels like there's no end to it.

Whilst I am receiving my IV poison I do my best to come to terms with my temporary malaise and post the following on Winning:

> *About to start session 4. Once completed in 3 weeks I will be half way through my chemotherapy treatment. Feeling very positive and loved by my gorgeous Andrea.*

As is normal my post gets lots of positive, supportive messages, but I particularly enjoy this one from my cousin, Peter. It causes me to think about my mum and reminisce about my dear departed superhero-dad:

> *Peter George – Was thinking that I'd not heard from you for a week or so. Good news keep it up. Eat lots and drink lots to keep your strength up, even if you're feeling poorly. Glad you're on positive mode. Your Mum and Dad are and would be proud of you. Thinking of you and yours.*

Chemotherapy has a certain way with me. My lack of physical activity means I think more, my emotional instability means I feel more and my lack of reasoning and intellect means I get confused about what I'm thinking and feeling. Peter's comment brings some clarity. My mum and dad would have been proud of me.

It's a good thought to hang on to.

7 September 2017

The following is posted by Sir Kenneth Branagh on the MADS Theatre Facebook page. The publicity team is on to it immediately encouraging all members to share it and promote our little Theatre:

> *To everyone involved with MADS Theatre, I send huge congratulations on your 70th Birthday. What an amazing achievement to have been providing theatre in this way for a whole lifetime. I salute all members of the company, and I salute*

the good people of Macclesfield. Great theatre survives and thrives with great audiences. Thanks to all for their loyalty, support and (no doubt), passionate opinions! Here's to the continued success of your magnificent anniversary season, on behalf of all of us who have found magical memories in the Great Little Theatres of the UK. We're proud that it's still a MADS world! Warmest wishes, Sir Kenneth Branagh.

I contemplate that it may be some time before I am able to tread the MADS boards again. Until then I will help out at the Theatre in any way I can. Interestingly, this year is also the seventieth year of the NHS. I have become a strong advocate of both organisations.

14 September 2017

The End of The Affair is a play written in 1947 and is of that time. It was selected by MADS not only because it's a well written play but also to celebrate the company's seventieth year. I am the Front of House manager for this evening's performance.

Fortunately, it's my rest week from chemotherapy which helps a little. My symptoms have become easier to cope with and the exhaustion is now a way of life. The performance goes well and my duties are not too taxing. The evening is a welcome break and I feel temporarily transported back to the life I aim to fully return to.

15 September 2017

I call Jeff Rosser this morning. He's in a lively and optimistic mood as he tells me about a new type of immunotherapy being tested that he's hoping to be a candidate for. It's hard not to feel infected by his love of life. He's a determined little rascal and I love him for it.

I worked with Andy Cuttle at Rolls Royce in Derby five years ago and, although we don't see each other much, we have remained friends. Andy is in the area and has arranged to visit me this afternoon. He has a friendly, relaxed manner and conversation is easy. His company is rejuvenating and a welcome distraction from my *Chemo Fog*.

By the time evening descends I feel more exhausted than I've ever felt. I try to eat the meal Andrea has prepared but can't find the energy to finish it. Also ingesting results in heartburn and nausea. Everything I do requires an effort I struggle to find. My fatigue has reached a new climax.

The *Chemo Fog* is in charge and there's little I can do to combat it, I simply have to let it take me and give in to it.

18 September 2017

Has it really been three weeks since the start of my last treatment cycle? It has passed by in a haze of disconnected, forgotten moments. Despite the *Chemo Fog* intensity I am delighted to reach the half way milestone. We arrive at the MacMillan suite at Macclesfield Hospital for day one of cycle five. I feel weak, heavy and slow.

I mentally prepare myself for the torture that awaits and post the following on Winning:

> *So here I am at the half way point of my chemotherapy treatment. About to start round 5 of 8. The oxaliplatin the amazing nurses pump into my veins makes for a painful and rubbish day/week. But I remain positive. It's all downhill from here.*

The usual supportive messages arrive in their masses as we meet with my oncologist before treatment commences. Oncology attempts to be an exact science but there are many variables to consider in determining the correct chemotherapy prescription. Too little and cancerous cells may survive, too much and permanent damage may be the result.

I have often wondered about this during my treatment and I've come to the conclusion that a little permanent damage would be a good outcome. It would indicate that I have taken as much chemotherapy that my body can tolerate, so maximising the damage to cancerous seedlings that may still be in my system. Feeling a little permanent discomfort in my nerve endings would be a constant reminder that the cancer is unlikely to return.

I could live with that.

But my oncologist is concerned. My blood tests indicate that my platelets are low, below normal levels. This is a side effect of chemotherapy. Platelets are colourless blood cells that help to clot blood, so they are vital, life-sustaining and integral to the design of the human body to self-heal.

My platelets are regularly monitored and there is evidence that I have a mild form of thrombocytopenia, a low blood platelet count. This is not unusual but my chemotherapy treatment has to be paused for a couple of weeks to allow my platelets to return to an acceptable count.

We discuss how I'm feeling and my other symptoms. It seems I may also have an ulcer. It is common for stomach ulcers to form during treatment but my gastric symptoms are fairly mild. With the right diet, I can both increase my platelet count and encourage my ulcer to heal. A two-week dose of antibiotics will help.

I follow up on my previous Winning post:

> *Woah!! Stop press. Platelets (sticking plasters that stop you from bleeding) are way down. I may have an ulcer and some other symptoms have concerned my oncologist. He said he was killing me too much.*
>
> *Decision taken to defer the start of session 5 for 2 weeks. Delighted to have a 2 week break from treatment but means the end date is further away! Not sure what to make of it really.*
>
> *Thought I was feeling more crap than usual.*

In response Kayleigh Smith posts a gif of a roaring Incredible Hulk. Whilst green is an appropriate colour to symbolise how I feel, I'm not sure I can quite manage to throw large, heavy objects nor strike an angry Mr Universe pose.

2 October 2017

The lack of treatment over the last two weeks has made little difference to the *Chemo Fog* that burdens me. I have followed the recommended diet and completed my course of antibiotics. The heartburn still lingers a little but is disappearing.

We meet my Oncologist at 10:45am to discuss my condition. My platelets are still low. Too low for a course of IV oxaliplatin. However, it's important that the chemotherapy treatment continues. To compromise I am to start the two week course of capecitabine but to miss the IV oxaliplatin. I will provide blood samples each Friday so that recovery of my platelets can be monitored.

We leave the hospital armed with two weeks' worth of capecitabine tablets. It's wonderful to feel pain free and to have avoided the oxaliplatin torture at the start of my three week cycle. I just have to hope that this doesn't result in the survival of cancer seedlings somewhere in my system.

I post the following on Winning:

> *A visit to Macc hospital with my rock Andrea Barker. I start round 5 of 8 having had a 2 week break from treatment after round 4. It seems my platelets continue to head in the wrong direction. Therefore my oncologist has decided not to give me oxaliplatin (the chemo poison that goes straight into my veins). However I do have to continue with capecitabine (chemo by tablet).*
>
> *I remain positive thanks to the love and support from Andrea, my sons and friends. Forever grateful xx*

Included in the many responses I get a football analogy, an army analogy and something I have to google:

> David Shaw – So the football analogy = 5/8 treatments – You are in the quarter finals. Other teams are winning around you. The Doctor is stopping Zlatan playing but you can keep playing Felani. And you still hope to qualify for Europe. Fans still packing the grounds. All good, usual platitudes, it's a long season…. Take it one game at a time…… you don't win anything with kids …. Etc
>
> David Carson – Mate, if your platelets are going in the wrong direction they seem very much like an army officer with a map – geographically confused! They'll head in the right direction if you have a strong and robust word with them (worked with us army types for years) and I'm sure Andrea could assist in that way only women can. Plus having one less poison coursing through your veins has to be a good thing dude. Keep ya chin up mukka you're over half way.
>
> Pete Munro – Nil illegitimi carborundum!

To save you googling it, Pete Munro's Latin comment translates into:

"Don't let the bastards grind you down."

4 October 2017

Andrea and I meet Chris Smart at The Congleton War Memorial Hospital. He gives me my routine six-month, post-op check-up and is satisfied with my recovery from surgery. He has read my notes regarding the difficulty of my chemotherapy treatment and reminds me that I am in the best possible hands. Good progress is being made with my treatment and I seem to be bearing up as well as can be expected.

He is delighted about our plans to marry, even more so when I tell him we wish to make a donation to his surgery team in some way. I've worked out a target of £2,000. We are expecting about two-hundred guests to donate about £10 per head. Any more than that will go toward MacMillan and any shortfall will be funded by us. He agrees to consider how this can best be achieved and will email me to let me know.

Giving something back feels good.

5 October 2017

Andrea and I are fortunate enough not to have too many financial worries. My pension and some property provides me with a modest income. Furthermore, years of IT contracting has ensured a reserve of funds in my company account that I can, prudently, draw against. This, together with Andreas business, Paws Tours, gives us both a joint income sufficient to comfortably cover our cost of living.

However, due to my cancer diagnosis and lengthy treatment I have been unable to work to earn money since the beginning of this year. With Christmas looming and a wedding to pay for next year, we review our financial affairs.

Windsor House, our home, is a reasonably large, detached house on three levels. The ground floor used to be an open-plan garage and workshop with living areas on the first and second floors. The front door is accessed via steps to the first floor level.

Over the years of living here the ground floor has been converted into three good-sized rooms. These rooms are currently unoccupied. Two are decorated and furnished as bedrooms. The third requires decorating and is used as storage space.

Andrea suggests that we could let the two rooms out to tenants and hence boost our monthly cashflow. This seems like a good idea. We have plenty of room in shared living areas to cope with additional people and part of the house can remain private to us. However much will depend on the calibre and character of the tenant for our venture to succeed.

Andrea posts an online advert for the two rooms.

13 October 2017

Chris Smart phones. The surgery department is in desperate need of a new headlight system which is used during surgery. It's a highly technical and lifesaving piece of equipment. The advice he has received from the hospital administrators is that it would be better for me to purchase the equipment and then donate it to the Hospital. Donating cash has tax complications for the Trust.

He agrees to forward details of the headlight system and where best to purchase it from. It costs about £2,000. This is an ideal recipient of our wedding just-giving cause.

23 October 2017

I have a friend whom I've known for about three years. She is more than just an ordinary member of the MADS family, she is a life member. You have to be long serving and very important to MADS to be bestowed with that honour.

Fran Dykes is the MADS matriarch, blessed with talent forged from years of acting and directing experience. I was honoured to be directed by her in a play called Pub Quiz is Life, written by Richard Bean. Fran's talent is as inspiring as it is frightening. I loved playing Bunny in Pub Quiz is Life for many reasons but mainly because, as a novice actor, I learnt so much from this life force. Above all that, I also admire her for her energy, independence and intellect. She has a beautiful soul that I cherish being in the company of.

Fran was recently diagnosed with breast cancer and is preparing to have a mastectomy later this week. She will have her right breast removed. Follow up treatment is likely to involve chemotherapy and radiotherapy. I cannot imagine what the psychological impact of breast removal for a woman might be. A common phrase I have used during my chemotherapy treatment is:

"I wouldn't put my worst enemy through this."

Therefore, it is very hard to contemplate witnessing Fran suffer in any way that I have. It saddens me deeply. She has supported me in my struggle with kind words and warm hugs, watching all my pain and sorrow. Now her own cancer pilgrimage is about to commence. Without the benefit of the naivety that I had, it must be a frightening prospect.

Quite by accident I discover a Rocky Balboa poster on the internet which pretty much sums up how I feel. Fran is about to get hit hard. However, there are many admirers who will help her to keep moving forward.

How Winning is done

With Fran on my mind we arrive at Macclesfield Hospital for the start of my sixth out of eight treatment cycles. The oncologist is keen to meet us before treatment begins. He has reviewed my case in-line with newly published research data and has evaluated that my system has been sufficiently cleansed with chemotherapy.

The risks of permanent damage are high if the planned treatment continues and it would be for a very marginal gain. He wants to meet me at The Christie Hospital tomorrow to prepare me for the start of radiotherapy treatment.

This assessment comes as a complete surprise. I came to the hospital this morning ready to confront the devil chemotherapy and spit in its eye. I feel ecstatic that I don't have to part with my saliva and that *Chemo Fog* will no longer grip me. Angry that it had to in the first place. Numb, just numb at the enormity of what I've been told. My emotions are in overdrive. I find myself shaking, tearful and laughing. Unsure of myself.

"Andrea, let's go and buy a lottery ticket, this is my lucky day." I cheerfully sob.

I have been hit hard and taken so much pain. It's time to move forward to radiotherapy and leave the chemotherapy in the past. No more IV oxaliplatin, no more capecitabine pills. Sunshine has burst into my life. It will burn away the *Chemo Fog* soon enough and blue skies will return.

We drive home. I had planned for a day of pain, exhaustion, diarrhoea, nausea and couch surfing. Instead I have a new found freedom to enjoy, to live in the moment, be unscripted, to improvise, to do what the feck I want.

Excitedly I post the following on Winning:

> *Off to Macc hospital with my beloved Andrea this morning anticipating the start of chemotherapy session 6 of 8. We got some fantastic news. Due to the impact of the treatment on me so far and new research data we are informed that the 5 sessions of chemotherapy received are now assessed to be enough. So I do not need to complete sessions 6-8. I am ecstatically overjoyed.*

However I now move into the final stage of my treatment, radiotherapy at Christie's. The original treatment plan had this stage scheduled for the new year. We go to Christie's tomorrow morning for a CT scan so my oncologist can determine how much and where the radiotherapy is required for my lower bowel. This is a 5 week treatment and is much less severe than chemotherapy.

It essentially means I can start to return to a normal existence of work, theatre, alcohol..........LIFE!!

My amazing beautiful Andrea has shared every step of the journey with me and together we will cross the finishing line in record time. My brilliant sons, Luke, Max and Cyrus have kept me sane and to everyone else reading this post I thank you for your kind and loving support. I am truly humbled. My final thoughts go to my dear friend Fran who, like me, will beat this horrible disease. She will do it with real style and grace of that I'm sure.

My Winning network predictably responds with warmth and approval. There is also the usual tonic of good humour:

David Clayton – Great news Hans Keith Oldham – amazing resolve! Did you have some of Chadders' rum?
Hans Keith Oldham – OMG! Chadders rum? That's what cured me!
Tony Chadwick – I've applied for a research grant!
Suzanne Copeland – A bloody awesome piece of news right there! Am now sniggering to myself thinking about how appallingly drunk you're going to get! So. One down, one to go. Game on Fran Dykes.
Fran Dykes – Hey…. HK when we get the all clear…. I can see a messy night being had by all!!

Helen Keller, the deaf-blind American author, once wrote that:

"Walking with a friend in the dark is better than walking alone in the light."

6
RADIOTHERAPY
THE CHRISTIE

The Christie Hospital is located in Withington, Manchester. It is one of the largest cancer treatment centres of its type in Europe. The Christie became an NHS Foundation Trust in 2007 and is an international leader in cancer research and development.

Sir Joseph Whitworth, a wealthy Mancunian inventor, left money in his will in 1887 to be spent on good causes in Manchester. His bequest was entrusted to three legatees, one of whom was Richard Copley Christie. He used Whitworths funds to purchase land to allow the movement of the central Manchester hospitals out of the crowded city centre.

A committee chaired by Christie was established in 1890. A Cancer Pavilion and Home for Incurables was founded in 1892. In 1901 it was renamed The Christie Hospital in honour of Richard Christie and his wife, Mary. It was the only hospital outside London for the treatment of cancer alone and active in pathological research.

There has been much investment, research and development since those early days. Today The Christie treats about 44,000 patients every year. It is the lead cancer centre for the Greater Manchester and Cheshire Cancer Network. It covers a population of 3.2 million and runs outreach services at sixteen other locations.

Macclesfield Hospital is one such location and I am one such patient.

24 October 2017

Andrea and I drive to The Christie Hospital to meet my oncologist. The journey takes about an hour through busy, built-up traffic. We drive into a multi-storey car park at the rear of the hospital and inch up to the very top level before we find the last available parking space.

As we walk out of the car park we notice that a number of cars have been abandoned on yellow lines on the main road and down side streets. Although we have plenty of time, we consider ourselves lucky to have found a legal parking bay.

I have to repeat this trip on a daily basis for five weeks for pre-arranged appointments that last only a few minutes. The many risks of running late are noted.

Outside the main entrance is an elderly gentleman attached to a portable IV drip stand smoking a cigarette. It's hard not to be judgmental of him as he coughs and splutters his way through the probable cause of his illness. Nobody deserves cancer no matter what their self-inflicted social habits might be.

I've often heard smokers justify their habit with comments about a relative who smoked all their life and died of natural causes at a ripe old age. Contrary to that, I consider myself to have had a healthy diet all my life and yet I get bowel cancer. There is no logic and I don't have any answers.

I do know that I'm not one for playing Russian Roulette with my life. If I cross the road I'll take the controlled crossing rather than just run carelessly across a busy main road in the hope that I might be the lucky one to make it, unharmed, to the other side.

The bedside manner of my oncologist is equal to that of my surgeon. He is a deeply caring, yet hugely experienced clinician. Today is about preparing me for five weeks of external-beam radiotherapy. It is a cancer treatment that uses high doses of radiation to kill cancer cells and shrink tumours. It is to be delivered from a machine into the area of my bowel where the five tumours were surgically removed with the pinpoint accuracy of fine radiation beams.

Each session is quick and painless, lasting only for a few minutes. I will have daily treatment sessions five times a week, Monday to Friday, over five weeks. It is inevitable that healthy cells in my bowel will also be destroyed. This may cause incontinence. I should also expect some fatigue, particularly after the first couple of weeks, as my body uses extra energy to repair the damage done by the radiation.

Once everything has been explained to us I am given a medical health screening to ensure I am physically ready for the process. Finally I am given three permanent tattoos. These are three tiny dots, one placed on the front of my lower abdomen and one on each side just below my hips.

The beams will be aimed through these tattoos and therefore consistently strike the area of my bowel previously infected. Any possible cancerous cells that might have survived in that area won't stand a chance.

My first session will be on the 7 November and the final one on the 11 December.

27 October 2017

"Happy birthday to you, happy birthday to you, happy birthday dear Andrea… squash tomatoes and stew!"

I'm usually poor at remembering important dates but I've trained hard to remember this one. This amazing lady who has consistently, and without fail, focused on my treatment schedule was born a number of years ago today (it's rude to tell!).

There are lots of presents and a meal out in the evening to celebrate.

28 October 2017

Becky Connolly replied to our 'room to let' advert a week ago. Today she moves in with the help of her father, Martin. Both Andrea and I instantly like them both. Bex is an intelligent, witty, thirty-something, workaholic and styles herself as a professional medic and academic working on her PhD. She has at least three jobs that we can make out and Congleton is a central location for them all.

We consider ourselves to be very fortunate to meet and befriend such an amazing lady, let alone to have her as a tenant.

3 November 2017

Today, we are helping Max buy his first car and drive him around various car show rooms. As we sit waiting to be seen by a car salesman I open Facebook on my iPhone for a quick, casual scroll.

The first post I read is from Jeff Rosser's wife, Di.

It shocks me to my core:

> *I've been putting off posting this message because it's the hardest thing I've ever had to write, but I've had so many lovely messages and cards that I wanted to thank everyone. For any of you who aren't aware, my darling husband Jeff passed away last Wednesday after a short illness. For those of you who knew Jeff and would like to join us, the funeral will take place on Monday 6th of*

November at 11.30 in St Peter's chapel at the Exeter crematorium.

As we want to celebrate Jeff's life, please wear what you want. You are also welcome to join us at the Devon Hotel after the service. Family flowers only. Donations to FORCE and Hospiscare gratefully received.

A very young Jeff and Di Rosser.

Warriors!

Stunned, I cry out "NO!", stand up and run out of the showroom. Andrea, now used to my sudden bouts of anxiety, runs after me. She catches up with me in the car park where I'm weeping for the sudden loss of my warrior friend. I have no words and simply show her the Facebook post on my phone. She hugs me silently while I sob on her shoulder, slowly coming to terms with my grief.

Thanks to cancer, Jeff Rosser leaves behind him a loving wife, Di, a daughter, Sammi and a son, Jed. His parents, brother and many other family members and friends will also suffer from his loss.

"I am going to miss you, Jeff," is all I can say before we return to the car showroom.

Max does eventually buy a car and I feel both pride and excitement watching my son enjoy his life-changing event. But my sorrow returns later with my inadequate response to Di's post:

So very sorry for your loss. The world is a poorer place x

Andrea, supportive as ever, agrees that we should both go to the funeral. There is no way I'll be going alone.

5 November 2017

We drive the four hours to Exeter and book into a hotel, a short distance from Exeter Crematorium. It avoids the risk of being late for Jeff's funeral.

6 November 2017

After a good full English breakfast, we drive to the Crematorium. Outside St Peter's Chapel I greet Jeff's former partner in crime, the benevolent Mr Pete Beaven. I haven't seen or spoken to Pete for many years but it feels like it was just yesterday. I hug an old, familiar friend. I share my Ant and Dec theory with him to honour the loss he must feel. He takes the compliment with a knowing smile but denies ever having met the TV duo.

During the ceremony Di, seated between her children, conducts herself with a calm grace that I greatly admire. It's an extremely well-organised affair. Pete reads a eulogy full of my own memories of Jeff. He's taken a good deal of care to write it in the short time available to him. It is extremely well delivered and equally well received. He has done his mate proud.

Music played a big part in Jeff's life and all his favourite tunes feature in the hour-long service. We witness a celebration of his life. The fact that he is not with us to share it is hard to take.

The reception at the Devon Hotel is overflowing with folk who genuinely loved and admired Jeff. I manage to get some time chatting to Jeff's parents and his brother. It seems Jeff fought his cancer to the bitter end; he was sadly diagnosed as terminal a week before he was due to start his immunotherapy. His final breath came very quickly afterwards and he passed away peacefully in a hospice. It's lovely talking to Jeff's parents. They've always adored him, and he them.

I can't help but think that parents are just not conditioned to attend the funeral of their own child.

As expected, there are many loved ones constantly circling Di, but thankfully we manage to pay our private respects to her before we leave for the long, quiet drive home.

"It's so much darker when a light goes out than it would have been if it had never shone."

– John Steinbeck

7 November 2017

We drive to The Christie in the morning for the start of my final phase of cancer treatment, radiotherapy. Despite a few delays, not least from finding a parking space, we arrive ten minutes early, check in at reception and make our way to the waiting area outside treatment room number eleven.

The radiotherapy machines are in constant use and there is a sign in the waiting area informing patients of how far behind the radiologists are with treatment. Luckily, there are no delays this morning. I've been well prepared for treatment but I'm still not entirely sure what to expect.

After a short while my name is called and I walk through the treatment room door. I am greeted by two very friendly female radiologists. They are aware that it's my first visit and offer re-assurance by asking if I have any concerns. I am asked to remove my coat and shoes and empty my trouser pockets. I leave my possessions on a chair provided.

One of the radiologists guides me towards a treatment bed. I sit down on it, swing my legs up, lie down on my back and look up at the large white machine above me.

The radiologist stands next to me with a large, square tissue in her hands. The other one is busying herself with technology. I am asked to pull my trousers and pants down to my knees and relax. In any other walk of life, I'm not sure I could relax at this request, but in here it all seems very normal. As I start to expose myself the tissue is immediately placed on my groin to protect my modesty.

"Nice touch." I think to myself.

She is well practiced at that manoeuvre. Or is she? The tissue doesn't seem to be very secure, sitting at an odd angle. Maybe she was a little too hasty in trying to save my blushes.

Both the radiologists are now entirely focused on my abdomen as they search for my pin prick tattoos. Satisfied they have located them, I have to lie completely still as they push me into position, lining up my tattoos with meticulous care. Various positional reference numbers are called out followed by another push against my right hip. My body recoils and springs back millimetres from where it previously rested.

Eventually I am in perfect synchrony with the machine. They are happy to start. I lift my hand to scratch my nose and return my arm to the comfortable position it was in, across my chest. The radiologists are dismayed. That movement changed my position by the smallest fraction but enough to have to re-set me. More pushing, recoil and positional number calling follows until, once again, I am ready.

I challenge anyone to relax and remain completely motionless when told to do so. From the very moment the command is given, the body breaks out into the most ridiculous epidemic of itches, pressure sores and joint aches. It's exasperating and almost impossible not to respond with a scratch or a stretch.

I close my eyes tight, but not too tight as that involves unwelcomed movement, and concentrate. I go to a happy place in my mind to block out the various irritations surging through me.

As the radiologists turn away from me to leave they cause a small draft that dislodges the tissue very slightly.

"Now, Mr Oldham, if you could just remain very still, we will administer the treatment from the next room. We will be watching and monitoring you from there so please don't worry."

They leave. I am alone on a hard bed with my trousers and pants down by my knees, a tissue precariously, unsettled on my groin. It takes all my effort to stay in my happy place, fighting the temptation to move. Then it happens. I should have seen it coming; it was inevitable. The tissue finally succumbs to gravity and wafts gently to the floor. I am now fully exposed but still intent on remaining still. It's an absurd paradox. Then a re-assuring voice comes through the loud speaker.

"That's right, Mr Oldham. Keep completely still."

The machine above me springs into action and noisily whirrs around me. High doses of radiation bore into my bowel directed by fine red beams through the tiny dot tattoos. It sounds painful but I feel nothing. In less than five minutes the machine stops.

One of the radiologists appears in the room to let me know the procedure is over and I can move. Maybe it's the exhibitionist in me, but my first instinct is to stretch and scratch before pulling up my pants. Or maybe it's just because I'm used to the anonymity of the medical profession seeing and caring for my every intimate body part. I can't quite decide. The treatment bed is lowered and I'm able to jump off, put on my shoes and collect my belongings. The two radiologists chat to me while I do so, re-setting the treatment room in preparation for the next patient. They don't mention tissue-gate, why would they? The tissue is simply swept up and consigned to a bin with a shrug of the shoulders.

As Andrea and I leave, I collect my appointment card from the reception. Appointments are made each day for the following day. There is no guarantee for the time of the appointment, it's a lottery. So much human traffic passes through The Christie for radiotherapy that it's impossible to provide a regular slot each day. I have to take whatever is on offer each day and, if necessary, try to negotiate a more suitable time. Travelling may prove difficult if I get a rush hour slot. Even worse if I get caught in rush hour traffic with diarrhoea or incontinence!

Arrangements have been made to collect Max's new car after he has finished work. I feel proud watching him drive off the forecourt. I just wish that cancer and its treatment hadn't restricted my alcohol consumption to zero. My son owes me a few late-night taxi runs.

In the evening I post an update on Winning:

> *A visit to Christies with my amazing Andrea to start 5 weeks of radiotherapy treatment. It was an absolute walk in the park. Just as well because I have a couple of job interviews coming up.*
>
> *I had one "tiny" issue however. "Trousers and pants down to your knees Mr Oldham. That's right now lie on your back". A handkerchief sized tissue is strategically placed to protect my modesty. Not for long however as a small draught saw that tissue to the floor during the radiotherapy. "That's right Mr Oldham remain perfectly still" came the tannoy instructions . Man Junk complied. Need to sort this out tomorrow. A sock perhaps??*

The humour of the situation is not lost. Various pictures of posing pouches, cod pieces and childish, infantile remarks, particularly about correct sizes, are returned:

> *Paul Bernardi – I think we still have some of Lyds baby socks if that helps?*
> *Jane Evanson-Horan – A mitten should do the trick Andrea said*
> *Paul Horan – A very small childs mitten*
> *Ally Burrows – So are you radioactive now and do things glow in the dark?*
> *Tony Chadwick – Not like you to be modest. How long did you have to lie*

still for? Just thinking about your notorious capacity issues.
David Shaw – No DELETE key big enough for this imagery. I will resort to drink.

Harrumph!

13 November 2017

The *Chemo Fog* that has placed so many restrictions on my physical and cognitive abilities for the last four months is finally lifting. Whilst I am anticipating some physical fatigue from the radiotherapy treatment it will be insignificant by comparison.

MADS Theatre are planning to produce a play called *Blue Stockings*, written by Jessica Swales, which will run during the week commencing 26 February 2018. Tonight is the reading, an opportunity for anyone interested in auditioning to join in with a group read-through of the play.

Thinking there may be a part for me in it, I decide to attend. It's a fabulous, large-cast period drama. Perfect for my return to the stage at a time I expect to be firing on full cylinders once again. The play was submitted to the MADS play selection committee by my son, Luke, who will assist Kayleigh Smith in directing it.

17 November 2017

I have had seven of the twenty-five scheduled radiotherapy treatments so far and this afternoon's will be my eighth. Andrea wanted to come with me to every appointment, but we soon realised that wasn't going to be feasible; she has a business to run and won't be able to manage a two to three-hour daily interruption. My appointments so far have been sporadically placed during the day but manageable. As yet, I haven't been late or re-scheduled, although I have encountered wait times of up to an hour.

The fatigue is becoming more obvious. I've had enough sessions of gamma rays penetrating and cooking my bowel for my system to start working hard to restore the damage being done to healthy tissue. But I've lived with *Chemo Fog* and this radiotherapy lethargy is mild in comparison.

Despite a mid-afternoon journey I encounter enough roadworks and traffic congestion to risk a missed appointment. Also, I need to go to the toilet. I have worked out where there are various places I can call into en route in the event of an emergency.

I spot a pub that I have pooed in before. The urge is strong and I just about make it to the toilet in time. Phew! But…. no toilet paper! I remain seated and silently listen. There's nobody else about so I flush and, with pants around my knees, hobble awkwardly to the next cubicle. Yes, a full bog roll. I'm not sure how I would have explained myself had I been confronted by somebody entering the toilet as I stumbled, full exposed, between cubicles.

In ten minutes I'm back in the car but now running even later. The traffic is clear, I put my foot down and then FLASH! Damn it - a speed camera. A momentary and stressed lapse of concentration in the wrong place. I'm doing 55mph in a 50mph speed zone. Sod it! Three points and a fine are on their way.

I phone The Christie and explain I'm running about thirty minutes late. No problem, they're running about sixty minutes behind schedule. The thing about my fatigue is that stress is easy to find but hard to deal with. I should have phoned ahead earlier and calmed the feck down.

When I arrive, I'm unable to find a parking space immediately. I'm not going to risk a parking ticket; one fine today is enough. I drive up and down the multi-storey car park until a space becomes available and finally check in for my appointment forty-five minutes late. Even though it's not an issue, just being late whilst trying hard not to be, has drained me. The speeding fine doesn't help either.

Reality soon arrives in the form of a nurse running through the waiting area carrying a baby. The baby is very still and quiet but the young couple running close behind are not. I don't know what's happened but, sadly, the scene speaks for itself. My first world problems are suddenly and cruelly put into perspective.

My name is called as the small fast-moving crowd disappears into a nearby treatment room. I ask the radiologist about the baby and, presumably, its parents as I point in their general direction.

"That's resuscitation," is the only information I'm given.

Ten minutes later I collect my appointment card from reception. I've been given a 4:45pm slot on Monday which means a drive home during rush hour traffic. I explain my dilemma and the difficult journey this morning. The receptionist manages to change it to 3pm.

Today is Friday and I'm therefore required to give bloods after my radiotherapy treatment. It only takes twenty minutes, but means a drive home in rush hour traffic. I eventually return home about five hours after I left this morning.

Having radiotherapy like committing to a full-time job!

21 November 2017

In September 2013, eight-year old Emma was diagnosed with Alveolar Rhabdomyosarcoma, a soft tissue cancer. Part of her treatment involved travelling to Oklahoma for Proton Beam Therapy. Everyone who completed their treatment there got to ring the End of Treatment Bell. It wasn't just a bell but a symbol of hope, of feeling like you are winning the battle against cancer.

Every person who rang that bell felt exactly the same way. The lobby, where the bell was located, was always crowded with people cheering and supporting the latest warrior to ring it.

When they returned to the UK, Emma's parents arranged to make a bell, with its plaque, and donate it to the ward Emma was being treated on at the Royal Manchester Children's Hospital. The Bell was ready for Emma to be its first ringer on the 9 April 2014.

Since then the bell has been rung by many thousands of patients. Each bell costs about £145 to make and distribute. A charity has been set up to send bells out to anywhere in the UK free of charge. This symbol of hope is now distributed across the world for the benefit of cancer patients everywhere. It all started with one young cancer victim.

There is one of these bells in the corridor leading up to the treatment room I visit each day. There are also several others stationed in other parts of The Christie.

The Christie End of Treatment Bell

Today I have a check-up with my Oncologist before my treatment begins. I am waiting in the empty corridor outside his office, seated opposite an End of Treatment Bell. I have stopped and looked at it several times during my visits, reading the words on the plaque on which it is mounted. It inspires me.

Not once have I dared to touch any part of it, rather like a superstitious football player inspecting the silverware before a cup final match. I am completely taken in by the message it conveys. Ringing that bell will be an act of defiance against the horror of cancer. End of treatment, and, through suffering, hope and survival!

As I sit waiting, a young boy of about ten presents himself to me. He tells me his name is Nathan as he holds out his hand, politely inviting me to shake it. I take his hand and introduce myself. He looks thin and jaundiced and has no hair, but that doesn't seem to affect him. He is endearingly respectful and self-assured.

"I've just finished my treatment," he informs me with a wide grin, "I'm with my mum. Please can you film us while I ring the bell?"

"Nathan, it will be my absolute pleasure, an honour, sir. Thank you for asking me."

I gulp as I take the mobile phone he offers me into my shaking hands. I look over his shoulder towards his mum. She is beaming with pride at her son. A huge smile on her face with eyes fixed on him alone.

As I look at her it comes to me that in the English language there are orphans and widows, but there is no word for a parent who has lost a child. If it did exist, I wonder what form would it take. Does it exist in other languages? Should such a word be created in English?

Ask cancer; it will have an answer. It will already have a word with a meaning that is instantly recognisable.

"He wanted to ask you himself. It's been very difficult and we didn't think he would come through it all. He's been brilliant though and he can't wait to ring it." She gushes.

"Well what are we waiting for? Come on, Nathan. Right, I'm ready... and go!"

Nathan holds his mum's hand and gives that bell three loud rings as I film him. Then something quite extraordinary happens. The sound of the bell fills the corridor with people applauding and cheering. I'm not sure where they've all suddenly come from but they're here to support Captain Nathan, a true warrior.

Nathan's hands are raised in victory. Laughing, he takes a bow and waves to the gathering, cheering crowd. They cheer all the more because he's enjoying the victory so much. His tearful mum is mouthing thank you's to everyone.

It is quite a moment and one I defy anyone not to be moved by. While the crowd disperses as quickly as it arrived, I take a few photos of them both in front of the bell.

"Thanks mister. That was sick." Exclaims a very happy Nathan.

"Yes, it was and you deserved every single cheer." I tell him handing back his phone, then turning to his mum.

"You must be very proud."

"Oh, I am. I can't tell you! And thank you."

With that they leave, and I sit alone and cry.

Thankfully, I don't have to wait much longer until I'm called into my oncologist's office. She confirms that my treatment is going well and my bloods are fine. There's nothing significant to report apart from my expected growing fatigue. I'm told to keep going with the radiotherapy treatment.

I'll soon be ringing that End of Treatment Bell.

As I walk past the bell towards my treatment room, a grey-haired, elderly man in his sixties asks me if I will film him whilst he rings the bell with his wife. He introduces himself as Robert; he too has finished his treatment today.

He hands me his iPhone.

"Of course. No problem. I'll take some photos, too. I'm an old hand at this. My pleasure… and go!"

The usual cheering, applauding crowd appears. I don't feel quite the same emotion this time. Not because Robert is any less deserving but because Nathan is a child with a lifetime of happiness now restored to him. His humility born from fighting a condition his mum didn't think he would survive.

Before I return home after my treatment I take great pleasure in posting an update on Winning with a 'feeling inspired' emoji:

> *While I was waiting to see my oncologist at The Christie today I had the privilege of being asked by 10 year old Nathan and then 65 year old Robert to film them while they rang this bell. The corridor erupted into applause and cheers.*
>
> *Quite a moment for them both. I was in the presence of giants.*

My post receives a collective happy tear. The significance of Nathan's and Robert's bell ringing is not lost on anyone. But this comment from Suzi, the wailing banshee, feels strangely menacing:

> *Suzanne Copeland – I've got "you can ring my bell" as an ear worm now. I'll sing it at you later!*

The words "sing" and "at" strike terror deep within me!

I take the feeling of inspiration into the audition for *Blue Stockings*. Suzie is at the audition and briefly carries out her threat. I was right to feel scared. I love being in her company and she's a brilliant actress but her singing sounds like a day out at the zoo.

There are a couple of supporting roles and some minor roles that I could be in the running for. I must do reasonably well at the audition as I'm offered the part of Mr Banks, one of the two support roles I had auditioned for. I am thrilled to accept. Life is starting to feel entertaining once again.

7 December 2017

Tomorrow morning Max graduates from his Master's Degree in Product Design at Nottingham Trent University. His graduation ceremony starts at 10:30am and will finish at midday.

After my radiotherapy session today, The Christie receptionist has given me a 10am radiotherapy appointment for tomorrow morning. I ask for a late afternoon appointment and explain why. There's nothing available after 1pm.

The only option I have is to phone up tomorrow morning and hope for a cancellation. Failing that, I'm told to just turn up and wait for a slot. They will fit me in somehow, but I may have a long wait. It's already going to be a long day so the thought of a long wait at the end of it doesn't thrill me.

This is not an ideal situation but I'm not going to miss my son's graduation. I'll have to get to The Christie whenever I can and wait for however long it takes. The receptionist is sympathetic but insists that missing my treatment is also not an option.

8 December 2017

I call The Christie but they are unable to provide me with an appointment for late on in afternoon.

We set off early to meet Max for breakfast at 9:30am in Nottingham City Centre before the start of his graduation ceremony. He understands that I'll have to leave as soon after the ceremony as possible for my radiotherapy session at The Christie sometime in the afternoon.

The graduation ceremony is a grand affair and the auditorium is buzzing with excitement and celebration. Seeing Max graduate from his Master's Degree in Product Design makes us feel wonderfully proud. Andrea and I meet him for a quick drink and a photograph afterwards. Then we drive home, leaving him to celebrate with his friends.

Max Oldham

graduates in
Product Design MA
Nottingham Trent
University

I arrive at The Christie at about 5pm and have to wait until 7pm for my twenty-second radiotherapy session. The fatigue has worsened during the last week but it is still manageable. It's been a good day and I have one eye on ringing that bell in three days' time.

11 December 2017

I have driven to The Christie twenty-four times in the last five weeks, so the day of my last and twenty-fifth appointment has finally arrived. More than that, it's a milestone, ending a year of suffering and treatment.

I have endured the trinity of a major life threatening operation, chemotherapy and radiotherapy to be as sure as possible that my body is cleansed of cancer. There's only been a short break between each type of treatment.

All three have presented their own unique, hideous symptoms. Hardly recovering from one before moving on to the next. I feel battered and weary. I've lost weight, strength, fitness, intellect and a sense of who I am. Despite all that I feel so happy to have made it this far. I'm going to enjoy ringing the End of Treatment Bell.

The final radiotherapy session goes much the same as all the others. The cumulative impact revealed itself in the last dozen or so sessions with more frequent and urgent incontinence. I am informed that this may take up to 18 months to settle down but by moderating my diet and taking medication I will be able to control it.

I leave the treatment room and fall into Andrea's arms for a celebratory hug and make my way down the corridor to the bell. Andrea stops a few yards from it and films me walking the rest of the way toward it.

I can feel the emotional tension rising in me. The memory of those that didn't have the privilege to do what I am about to do cuts deep.

A long year of undignified, poor health has come down to this moment. I kiss the bell. My lips make my first ever contact with it. I take a deep breath and take hold of the rope with trembling hands. Three very loud and proud chimes follow. As I've now come to anticipate the corridor explodes with people cheering and applauding.

We don't have to ask somebody to take photos of the two of us together. A nurse giving me a slow hand clap steps forward.

"I love this bit. It's so amazing to watch."

Then to Andrea:

"Why don't you give me your phone and I'll take some pictures of you both."

It's a moment I'll never forget. More than the personal satisfaction I get, it pays tribute to all those who have gone before me. An army of giants, of warriors. It also ignites memories for those friends of ours who didn't make it this far.

Three rings on The Christie End of Treatment Bell

Before we leave the Christie for the last time I post an update on Winning:

> *So here it is....the toll of the bell. This signifies the end of my treatment. Three rings. The first two for me and Andrea Barker. We have worked so hard together to reach this milestone. The third needed to be loud enough to be heard by those friends that didn't get the privilege to ring this bell themselves. Jeff Rosser, Al Harrop and Rob Gregory - one day we will hug again.*

To Andrea and my three sons, Luke Oldham, Max Oldham and Cyrus Oldham words cannot express my love and gratitude for helping me to beat this horror. To everyone else reading this you have my love and respect. Your friendship, support and kindness really helped.

My final thought to my lovely friend Fran Dykes. I will be a constant reminder to you that you too will ring that bell. Until then Andrea and I and everyone else that knows and loves you will be with you every step.

The congratulations flood in from those that have stood by me and genuinely cared. My 'Winning' Facebook group started as the easiest method for me to communicate my progress. It has become a place for family and friends to show their love and support. I have to confess that at times it helped to carry me forward. I will be forever grateful.

In the evening Andrea and I celebrate the end of my treatment by dining at Pesto, our favourite Italian restaurant, with Max, Cyrus, his girlfriend Adele and his friend Jay.

7
A RETURN TO LIFE

Although my planned cancer treatment has ended there is still more to deal with. I now face five years of regular check-ups before I am declared 'almost certainly' cancer free. I am still in remission and not yet considered cured.

Furthermore, I face up to eighteen months of slowly recovering from various symptoms as my body continues to heal itself from operational wounds, systematic but controlled poisoning and the destruction of healthy cells by gamma rays.

However, my life will no longer be interrupted nor governed by a treatment plan. I am free to crawl back into life once more. A return to acting, work, holidays, an occasional alcoholic beverage and the odd round of golf are all realistic targets for 2018.

My biggest problem is that the radiotherapy treatment has left me with occasional bouts of incontinence. The damage done to the healthy tissue around my bowel and anus has resulted in weakened muscles. If I need to defecate I get very little warning, I have very little control and it is a painful undertaking. Whilst I tend to enjoy uncertainty and will take calculated risks, the cost of miscalculating my current condition could be highly distressing. Not just for me but for anyone witnessing the potential result.

"Those who dare to fail miserably can achieve greatly."

– John F. Kennedy.

16 December 2017

I have always been willing to push boundaries in life, to find my limits. The hindrances that result from incontinence very quickly define boundaries without the need to seek them out. Incontinence requires caution and not my usual bravado.

This is today's lesson!

I have arranged to meet a former work colleague and friend, Andy Cuttle, at the Mulberry Leaves Pub in Leek for lunch and a catch up. Not only is Andy a mate whose company I enjoy, but he works in a profession I have ambitions to re-join in the new year. Discussing work-related issues will start to re-train my brain and revive my professional intellect, so I'm very much looking forward to it.

However, during the last week, I have been incontinent. Only yesterday I was watching TV in the lounge and suddenly felt the need to go to the toilet. Running up a flight of stairs to the bathroom only encouraged my bowels to open. I didn't make it in time. I had about a ten second warning before the flood gates involuntarily opened.

Under the circumstances, driving to Leek poses a considerable risk. There is nothing but country roads between home and the Mulberry Leaves Pub, about twenty minutes without access to a toilet. In my head, Mr Bravado whispers:

"It'll be fine, you're sitting down, that'll help. You'll be on your own if the worst happens. There's plenty of fields, bushes and trees on the way."

Mr Caution, however, is not happy:

"Don't be ridiculous. You'll shit yourself whilst driving. How will that feel? You could cause an accident as well as have one!"

I tend towards optimism so Mr Bravado comes out on top. Thankfully, I make it to the pub quite comfortably and enjoy chatting with Andy over lunch. I even dare to try a pint of ale, something I wasn't used to because of my year-long diet of drugs. I have suppressed the IT professional in me for a long time and it feels good to let him loose and explore old territories.

Before I leave, I visit the toilet, not because I needed to poo but because I thought it would be useful to try, to de-risk the drive home. I was surprisingly successful. Congratulating myself I return to my car for a pleasant twenty minute drive through the picturesque, sun drenched countryside.

I feel the first rumble after about five minutes, then the second five minutes later, about half way home. A sudden and irritating pressure appears in my sphincter. I clench my anal muscles with all my might and shout:

"NO!"

A temporary reprieve. The turtle head retreats back inside its shell. All this happens whilst I'm still driving but I dare not stop, every second nearer home counts. The second wave hits me a minute later and just as I think I might hold it off, I sneeze. There is nothing I can do. It's a strange and unnatural feeling for a middle-aged man to fill his pants uncontrollably while driving a car. Sod you, Mr Bravado - you encouraged that pint of real ale!

The awkward walk of shame from my car to my front door and up the stairs to the bathroom could have been a scene from Monty Python's Ministry of Silly Walks. Mr Caution whispers in my ear and suggests purchasing incontinence pants and for a second I listen but...

"No not that, definitely not that! Damn you Bravado you know it's the right thing to do."

17 December 2017

Colin and Elle Jacques have responded to our room to let advert. Their son, Tom, will be returning from Berlin in the new year having completed his engineering apprenticeship with Siemens. He will be starting a new role at Siemens in Congleton. Colin and Elle are looking for somewhere for Tom to live and are driving up from Burntwood to view Windsor House and meet us.

Sometimes when you meet people for the first time, you make a connection and just know that you'll get on. Colin and Elle are exactly like that. They talk about Tom with immense pride, much the same way we would discuss any of my progeny.

They stay for about an hour and the conversation is easy and relaxed. We seem to have much in common. In passing, I mention my bowel cancer and the treatment I've undergone. Colin tells me about a close friend of Tom's, Stephen Sutton. He was diagnosed with incurable cancer in 2013 and unfortunately passed away before achieving his dream of going to university and becoming an oncologist.

Stephen was an exceptional student and despite his illness achieved multiple A-stars in his GCSE exams. Before passing away on the 14 May 2014 he completed many of the goals on his bucket list. He endeavoured to be defined by what he could achieve rather than by the time he had left. By doing this, he inspired many others.

Each year Colin organises a local motorbike ride out from Lichfield Rugby Club to raise money for The Teenage Cancer Trust in Stephen's memory. This is underpinned by a website www.ssro.co.uk and this year was the fifth ride out.

I feel inspired by Stephen's story and impressed by the man telling it. Who wouldn't be? Although Tom does not yet realise it, he will have no problem settling in and feeling at home here. He is already starting to feel like one of our own.

18 December 2017

I receive an email from Chris Smart containing a brochure for a Lunar LED cordless surgical headlight system. It has all the contact details required to make a purchase.

25 December 2017

All my sons, including their friend Niall and Andreas mum Pat are with us for Christmas dinner. It's a typically wonderful and festive, family occasion.

The release I feel from cancer victimisation is massive. I even manage to be chef for the day and cook Christmas dinner. It's been quite some time since I have catered for this number but my hard work pays off and I manage to serve a full Christmas banquet.

31 December 2017

It's New Year's Eve and we are dining out at a local Chinese restaurant with the fabulous Rhodes and Bernardi families. We cannot be in better company to see the New Year in.

It is a reminder of how important good friends can be and these folks have proved themselves to be the best with their support of us during 2017. But now it's about 2018 and there is much to look forward to. My new year's resolution is to return to the life I once knew but with more energy and commitment. I've missed being me.

1 January 2018

My social media comment is:

2017…..you sir can bugger right off. 2018….. you sir are most welcome!

3 January 2018

I am keen to start fundraising for our cause in support of Macclesfield Hospital and MacMillan Cancer Support so I post the following link to our justgiving.com page on Facebook:

I hope all my FB friends can support this. Thank you.

JUSTGIVING.COM

Help raise £2000 to purchase a Lunar LED cordless surgical head light system for the surgical team at Macclesfield hospital & donate to MacMillan Cancer Support

We're raising money to purchase a Lunar LED cordless surgical head light system for the surgical team at Macclesfield hospital & donate to MacMillan Cancer Support. Support this JustGiving Crowdfunding Page.

4 January 2018

I still feel the impact of the chemotherapy and radiotherapy treatments but it is manageable. My biggest challenge is managing incontinence. I have to be careful what, when and how much I eat. It will improve over the next twelve to eighteen months as my damaged body continues to repair itself.

Today is all about finding a job. I am as keen as mustard to return to my professional life. Although I'm fifty-seven years of age I'm just not ready to retire from an industry that I have enjoyed working in for many years. I still have ambition and experience to offer. I start searching and identify some possible leads to follow up on.

11 January 2018

I have always enjoyed job interviews. I think if you have the right experience to match the job description you should have nothing to fear and plenty to talk about. Today is my first job interview in over two years and it's for a position in the IT department of the Greater Manchester Police. I've done my research and I'm ready. The interview panel includes the department head for the advertised role, Bob Vaughn-Smith. I feel relaxed, confident, suited and back to my articulate best.

The role isn't the senior position I'm used to commanding but it's perfect to ease me back into working life. Cancer? What's that? Oh yeah, I remember, it's that thing I once had. All gone now.

12 January 2018

My attempts to honour my New Year's resolution and integrate myself back into normal life have started well. I am offered the position I interviewed for yesterday and, despite having applied for other jobs, I readily accept the offer. It will take a few weeks to draw up contracts and process my security clearance, but I'm excited at the prospect of exercising my professional and intellectual muscles once again.

I am delighted with my final Winning post:

> *So this is probably my final post to this group. My recovery from treatment is finally complete. I feel significantly more healthy today than I have felt for over a year. This week I have been signed off by both my surgeon and my oncologist, subject only to planned checkups over the next 5 years. Returning to a normal*

life is gathering momentum. I have been cast in Blue Stockings, opens on the 26 Feb. I am in the running for 4 contract roles and was offered a position for one of those today, following an interview yesterday. I have an interview for my most favoured position next week. I will be holidaying with friends at Centre Parks the week after. Wedding plans are moving forward with invites printed and ready for posting. I have worked so hard and so long to get to this place.

My stubborn refusal to let this horrible disease beat me coupled with the love and support I received from Andrea, my sons, family and friends has got me back in the rat race. It's been a heck of a ride and I am humbled. Thank you so very much xx

The many replying comments are typically congratulatory. I have come to expect nothing less from this mob. I've loved their comments. They've never let me down with their empathy, compassion and humour. That said, I'm really not going to miss posting updates to Winning. Having nothing to say about cancer is a good place to be.

21 January 2018

Colin Jacques sends me a message informing me that Tom has received a contract for his new post at Siemens of Congleton. He flies back from Berlin on 31 January and his first day should be Monday 5 February. In the evening, Colin phones and arrangements are made for Tom to move in on 3 February.

1 February 2018

Andrea and I visit Macclesfield Hospital for the start of my five-year programme of regular check-ups.

Today's visit is for CT and MRI scans, which are all very routine for me now. However, whilst I am there I notice a painting hanging on the wall in the corridor with a plaque on it:

In memory of Pippa Chandler

Although I never knew Pippa Chandler, she was a popular MADS member and ran the wardrobe team before I joined the company. The wardrobe room at MADS is named after her and she was the mother of Cameron Chandler, who directed *Jerusalem*, and the wife of John Chandler, who had often visited me during my difficult chemotherapy days last summer with his current wife Shirley.

Sadly, this much loved lady lost her fight against cancer. The Hospital corridors and the MADS Theatre passageways still seem to resonate with the memory of her. I send a picture of the plaque to Cameron and John with the comment:

"This made me feel better."

As expected, the health check doesn't reveal any nasty surprises. I am still cancer free and planning to remain that way.

3 February 2018

We meet Tom for the first time when Colin and Elle help him move into Windsor House. Not surprisingly, we take to him immediately, in much the same way we took to his parents. He is respectful, courageous and fun. He too talks about Stephen Sutton and how inspired he continues to feel by the friend he once knew.

Cancer is a wretched ogre but it has been integral in creating the drive and ambition I see in this young man.

5 February 2018

Rehearsals for Blue Stockings are going well and the character of Mr Banks is developing nicely. Despite the fact that my body is still working hard to repair damaged tissue I am feeling more energetic with each passing day.

Tonight I go to the reading for a play called *Rumours*, written by Neil Simon. It's a farce so requires high and sustainable levels of acting energy. After the reading, I'm not convinced by the humour in the play, and unsure whether I'm ready to start rehearsing for it so soon after *Blue Stockings*. I probably won't audition for it; instead I'll concentrate on the new job that starts in a few days' time.

8 February 2018

It's been almost a year since my daily life was defined by a respected profession rather than by a serious illness. Today is my first day in my interim post with the Great Manchester Police.

Nothing quite compares to the excitement of starting a new job in normal circumstances. But after battling through cancer treatment and wondering if I'll ever have a return to my usual life, the excitement is trebled. The drive to work takes about an hour, so I'll really have to keep on top of my diet throughout this contract.

13 February 2018

I'm busy rehearsing for *Blue Stockings* and therefore miss the audition for

Rumours. I could have made it, but decide it's not the play for me.

16 February 2018

Tom has gone back to his parents for the weekend. We are impressed enough by him to message Colin with the following:

"Hi Colin. Andrea and I just felt the need to message you about Tom. We completely get why you and Elle are so very proud of him. He's a terrific young man and has connected with us all. He just fits in so well. Tom will definitely go places with his career. He's a pleasure to have around. Please send him back with cake."

The response from Colin tells us they are both very happy to hear how well Tom has settled. There is a promise of cake too.

22 February 2018

Rumours has not been fully cast. Lizzie Bloor is the Assistant Director and the driving force behind the play. It's likely that she will be responsible for directing the actors. She needs somebody to play Len, one of the lead roles. After reading the play again at home yesterday, I have become more convinced that it could be fun to do. Moreover, Lizzie is very talented and I'm seduced by some of her ideas for the production, so I agree to audition for Len and get the part. Well, that's my life mapped out for the next couple of months.

28 February 2018

It's Wednesday of show week for *Blue Stockings*. The run has gone well so far and audiences have been appreciative. But tonight we play in front of only about thirty punters. Snow has fallen heavily, making many roads impassable. I set off early from home and the Range Rover gets me through drifting snow and round abandoned cars. Fortunately, all the cast make it to the Theatre and the show starts on time. One audience member tweets herself marching through the bad weather, determined to make it by curtain-up.

3 March 2018

The last night's performance of *Blue Stockings* receives a standing ovation. The after-show party for large-cast plays typically continues until the small hours of the next morning and tonight is no exception. My thoughts turn to *Rumours*. There's a heck of a lot to do and we open in six weeks. This is exactly the pressure I craved for when I was debilitated for most of last year, feeling lethargic, sluggish, tortured and wondering if I'd ever recuperate back to this privileged lifestyle. Well, I have, and I fully intend to overdose and luxuriate in it.

21 April 2018

After *Jerusalem*, *Rumours* is unexpectedly one of the most enjoyable plays that I've acted in. Tonight is the final night. I've given all I have and don't think I could possibly do another night. In the final scene, I have a long monologue which I deliver as I charge around the set. It's been draining, but the most fun. Lizzie's brilliant direction identified every possible comedic moment and my fellow cast members delivered all that was asked of them.

As is usual with a successful play, new friendships have been forged and existing ones strengthened. The after-show party finishes in the small hours of the morning and saps me of the little stamina that I have left.

25 April 2018

It seems the quality of my professional work has been noted at the same time that an opportunity for a more senior position in the department has arisen. A leadership role has become vacant and Bob offers it to me on an interim basis from the beginning of May. I eagerly accept, as it comes with more responsibility and will help with my rehabilitation back to the type of working life that I am experienced for.

10 May 2018

The memory of my cancer treatment has faded. My focus on work related issues, rehearsals, line learning and ordinary daily challenges has blurred the recollection of the brutality of cancer and its treatment. The restoration of the life I once took for granted has caused me to occasionally forget the symptoms that remain.

Last night, I had a very mild and creamy curry. I am reasonably sure that this is the main cause for the several visits I've made to the toilet at work today. It's been easy enough to manage as I don't have any meetings and the toilet is near to my workstation. However, the healthy tissue in my anus that was damaged by radiotherapy, is still repairing itself. Whilst I get sufficient notice of the need to defecate the weakened muscles are unable to prevent discharge once a certain point is reached. Simply put, I am still at risk of shitting myself uncontrollably.

By 4pm I am convinced that there is nothing else left inside me that will force itself out. To be sure, I take a walk around the site to test my resolve. I feel comfortable and ready to risk the hour-long drive home. I walk to my car, open the door and throw my bag onto the passenger seat. I pause and stretch my abdomen. I assume a crouched position, sit on my haunches and bounce up and down to encourage bowel movement. I consider lying on my back on the grass verge and doing a cycling movement with my legs for additional stimulation but dismiss it as unnecessary. Besides, somebody might see me; it's a step too far. I'm perfectly fine now.

It's within about a minute of driving through the exit security gate of the compound that I involuntarily shit myself. Whatever stools I passed during the course of today were a façade for the diarrhea that now fills my pants. I set off thinking I was safe; I was wrong. The urge is great, prevention impossible. It's a torrential, cascading waterfall of post-masala sadness. There is nothing more I can do but drive home and hope that I'm not involved in an accident (the vehicle type) nor confronted with a need to leave my car. The rest of the journey home is agonising, apprehensive and very tense.

As I approach my driveway I'm on the phone to Andrea explaining what has happened. Whilst she sympathises, I can hear suppressed laughter, and why not? It's our way of dealing with shit that goes down, pun intended!

I ask her to find a large plastic carrier bag and unlock the front door so I can get inside quickly and sort myself out. As I gingerly climb out of the car I feel a warm trickle of movement down my legs so I tuck my trousers into my socks to prevent the unwelcome appearance of faeces beyond my hem line. I carefully walk to the front door like a man with loft insulation in his pants. Andrea greets me, but keeps her distance. With outstretched arms she hands me the plastic bag. I disappear into the bathroom, lock the door and climb into the shower fully clothed.

My shoes are the only items worth salvaging, everything else is consigned to the plastic bag. Once I've thoroughly showered, I get dressed and take the plastic bag to the wheelie bin half-way down the drive. I check the inside of my car. Fortunately there's been no spillage and the leather upholstery is unblemished.

Ultimately, I've come to no real harm. It wasn't a public shitting, but one done in the privacy of my own car. Yes, some clothes are ruined and will never be worn again, but my professional reputation is untarnished. I consider today's episode to be a useful reminder to take even more care with my diet in future.

24 June 2018

The Race for Life is a national event organised by Cancer Research UK. There are a number of planned routes around the country that give people of all ages, backgrounds and abilities the chance to come together and show cancer who the boss is.

There are one-hundred and fifty, five-kilometre races. They're not really races because everyone wins. Thousands of people come together and raise money to beat cancer. Beyond raising money, it's about uniting people against a common enemy. One of the great things, and there aren't that many, about cancer is that wherever you find a victim, you'll also find an army of carers and supporters.

Today I watch such an army run the 5k Tatton Park Race for Life. Ladies from both MADS and Woodhouse Farm run the race in beautiful sunshine, in support of those of us they know that have had or are having cancer treatment.

Collectively, Team #MADSWoodhouse raises about £2,500 for cancer research. I am proud to watch my Andrea represent both teams and complete the course and I feel humbled by those runners that I know. They are making a huge statement and doing a good thing.

14 August 2018

Eighteen months ago, she felt a lump. Today, after lengthy treatment involving a mastectomy, chemotherapy and radiotherapy, Fran Dyes rings the End of Treatment bell at The Christie Hospital.

This beautiful, big-hearted lady has come through her own cancer treatment hell. I could not be happier for her. She has triumphed in style. Her rehabilitation starts today.

28 August 2018

I have been recruited by The Department for Environment, Food and Rural Affairs (DEFRA) to work as an interim IT service design and transition manager on their EU Exit programme.

My role is located at both Crewe and Birmingham, but this week I have to be in Bristol to complete my induction. This role is a step up from the one I had with the GMP and Brexit is starting to get interesting. I am delighted that, once again, I have career choices to make.

1 September 2018

Ten months ago, Becky Connolly moved into one of our spare rooms as a tenant. Today she moves out as a family friend. She has many career opportunities to pursue including the possibility of joining an air ambulance crew in Australia. It's a sad loss but her time has come to move on. With the benefit of social media it's pleasing that we will retain some form of contact.

2 September 2018

Andrea re-posted the online 'room to let' advert a couple of weeks ago when Becky informed us she was moving out. It received an almost immediate response from Chloe Rees, a young lady in her early twenties, fresh out of Hertfordshire University.

She is planning to move to Congleton to start work in the event management industry. Her boyfriend, Rhys Tupper, has also started working in Congleton but his job comes with accommodation. She is in Congleton for the weekend looking at rooms to rent and visits us today. It doesn't take long to be won over by her confident, bubbly personality. The little lady is a class act and we have enough twenty-somethings in the early stages of their careers knocking around Windsor House to know she'll fit in very well.

It's a very easy decision for Andrea and I to make once Chloe has been given the guided tour and left. Andrea phones her within ten minutes and offers her the room. We are delighted that she accepts.

4 September 2018

Andrea and I drive to Macclesfield Hospital for my routine CT and MRI scans. My body has been recovering well and I am confident that it will continue to do so. But today's scans are necessary in order to detect any early signs that the cancer has returned. I have no symptoms and no pain, so I'm sure as I can be that I'm clear of infection.

8 September 2018

Andrea is out riding her horse, Mia, and I'm shopping for a new suit at the Trafford Centre for our wedding in three weeks' time. I get home for 3pm, just in time for Chloe to arrive with her mum Sharon and dad, Barry; they've driven up from the south coast together. 'Baz' and 'Shaz' are delightful and help Chloe move her things into her room. As with Tom, meeting our young tenant's parents is an opportunity to understand how well Chloe has been brought up. Equally, I hope Baz and Shaz can see that Chloe will be settled in a safe and happy environment.

9 September 2018

There's a reading soon for *Gaslight*. It's a well-known play which MADS are going to put on during the week commencing 3 December. I've sourced a copy of the play and read it. The archvillain in the play is Mr Manningham, a fabulous role and one I decide to audition for. Baddies are such fun to act and I can already hear the audience booing and hissing.

8
ANOTHER DIAGNOSIS

Most cancers that are going to come back will do so in the first two years after treatment. After five years, you are even less likely to get a recurrence. Some doctors are unwilling to use the word 'cure,' even if there is no sign that you have any cancer left.

It is generally accepted, however, that your cancer has been in remission for five years from the time your treatment is completed. Only then, your doctor may tell you that he is 95% certain that the cancer is gone for good.

To dwell on the mere probability of a cure and worry that you don't have the absolute certainty of one would be to lose the psychological battle against cancer. You must move on, enjoy life and focus on what you can control, not be imprisoned by what you cannot.

"After one has been in prison, it is the small things that one appreciates; being able to take a walk whenever one wants, going into a shop and buying a newspaper, speaking or choosing to remain silent. The simple act of being able to control one's person."

– Nelson Mandela

11 September 2018

I am contacted by a colorectal nurse at Macclesfield Hospital; Chris Smart wants to discuss my scan results later today. Andrea and I both have a busy schedule today, so I suggest tomorrow when we have more free time. The nurse is insistent, he really would rather see me today. A time of 4pm is proposed. I juggle my diary and agree to the meeting. It all feels like a bit of a nuisance. After all, I'm cancer free, but I have immense respect for Chris and I know him to be a busy man, so if he would rather see me today, then so be it. If only the meeting had been planned and booked a couple of days ago, I could have been more accommodating.

Having cancer has taught me not to self-diagnose but to deal with the facts presented to me by the medical professionals, to rely on their professional analysis. Only then should I be concerned enough to plan my next steps. It is with this in mind, together with a touch of naivety, that Andrea and I arrived at Macclesfield Hospital.

We are first met by my MacMillan nurse. Whilst we wait for Chris Smart she casually asks how we both are and how the wedding plans are going. She informs us that Chris wants to discuss the results of my recent scans with us himself. On that note Chris enters the clinic, greets us with his usual warmth and sits down. He starts by reminding us of the CT and MRI scans I had last week, then concludes:

"I'm sorry to say that the results are not good, Keith. The scans have detected a small lump in your left lung. It appears to be treatable. It is there and needs to be dealt with. Also, I am concerned that the scans you've had may not have identified other seedlings of cancer elsewhere."

"Oh dear!" Is all I can say as I try to absorb what I'm hearing.

But my internal monologue isn't happy. *Oh dear? Oh fucking dear?* Is that the best you've got? I glance at Andrea and, like me, she is sat quiet and motionless, staring at my surgeon, unsure how to react. Needing more information in order to do so.

"I'm going to send you for a PET scan. It'll have to be at another Trust as we don't have one here at Macclesfield. That will show up any infection that might be elsewhere."

"Right!" I respond, still uncertain.

Once again my whole life has been unexpectedly turned upside down. I'm in shock. Andrea grips my hand, tears silently rolling down her cheeks. After all we've been through, this! Mr Chris Smart recognises the need to keep talking, to quickly move us both to an initial acceptance of his diagnosis.

"Look, I know this is disappointing for you both. I feel so angry about it. I was so confident in the treatment you have received. The reason I called you in at 4pm today was partly because I needed most of the day to build myself up to telling you. Out of respect to you both… to find the right words. It's not good news, but let's not be overly alarmed. Whatever the prognosis turns out to be, we have caught it very early and therefore it will be treatable."

"Bugger!" I proclaim, snapping myself out of my malaise. "It's not what I expected to hear but let's just get on with it. We're not beaten yet. If there's more to do, bring it on."

I have become very matter of fact, a stance that Andrea recognises and joins me in.

"You can do this sweetheart. You're strong enough and I'll be with you every step of the way."

Between us we have many questions. The PET scan is an important next step that, despite its name, doesn't actually involve Alfie and Stanley. A Positron Emission Tomography scan is an imaging test that checks for diseases. The scan uses a special dye containing radioactive tracers which are injected into the body. More radioactive material collects in cancer cells than in normal cells. This causes them to appear brighter on the three dimensional image that is created. It is particularly effective in detecting cancerous tissue in the lungs.

With the benefit of a PET scan result, a treatment plan can be discussed. Wythenshawe NHS Trust has the lung surgery expertise, so my case will be referred to the specialist surgeons working there.

We probably take up more of Mr Chris Smart's time than he has available. He is genuinely saddened and frustrated. Patiently, he gives us both all the time we need to accept and understand my condition. It is no wonder that working in the NHS involves long, emotionally draining hours. This incredible man has invested in us both emotionally and professionally. He is committed to ensure a return on that investment.

I tell Chris about my plans to audition for *Gaslight* and ask if my condition or its treatment are likely to interrupt rehearsals or my possible appearance in the play. He knows how much I enjoy amateur dramatics, so it's difficult for him to advise me to let go of this one play. For me it's more than just missing out on a part in a play that I want to perform. It feels like I'm getting sucked back into the life of cancer treatment, a prison I thought I had escaped; a prison where my condition trumps any plans that I am normally free to make.

"No, Keith, not *Gaslight*. But let's get you sorted out so you can appear in many other plays in the future." Is his positive spin.

Andrea and I walk to the car in silence as we independently absorb all the information we have been given. Once in the car, we talk it through. It is said that acceptance is the final stage of the grieving process. The five defined steps are not exactly linear, but we have moved through them rapidly to get to acceptance. More than that, the Rooster fighting spirit has returned. This news is a mere inconvenience. The challenge will be to keep spinning all the plates in my life whilst allowing a short interruption to plate spinning that treatment will involve. Cancer needs to receive a short, sharp shock, not a long, drawn out clobbering. Imprisonment by treatment will only be transient.

It is with this more positive frame of mind that we inform my sons. We phone each of them in turn. Luke and Cyrus are both at home, now living in Macclesfield, but Max is at work. Out of necessity I discuss it with Max on the phone but we visit Luke and Cyrus to let them know in person.

It feels so much harsher putting it into words than thinking about it, particularly following the confidence they had in my assumed recovery. The harshness lies not just in the risk to my life, but in the impact that this will have on them. The key message is that, although it's secondary cancer, the check-up has caught it early and it's treatable. The deep hug I get from Luke, Cyrus and, later in the day, Max, tells me that although they are upset by the news, they have my back.

Having updated my sons I post the following on Winning:

> *So here's the thing. Today Andrea Barker and I were presented with the results of last weeks MRI Scan. It seems we have an opportunity to get back in the ring with cancer and kick its arse. The MRI scan has detected a single small malignant lump in my left lung.*
>
> *It clearly has not heard about battering that 5 of it's mates got when they visited me last year. This time I feel no ill effects but something needs to be done. So I'm going to be booked in for a PET Scan next week. An injection of radioactive dye so that the scan lights up your system like a Xmas tree. That will find any other small lumps and help the diagnosis. A treatment plan will follow......surgery, chemo, radio .... nobody can be sure just yet.*
>
> *All I can be sure of is that life will go on, I will be marrying my gorgeous Andrea on the 29th Sept, my amazing sons and friends will raze up arms with me and the next battle in the war against this horrible disease will be won.*

Kayleigh Smith responds with a gif. It's a clip from Monty Python's '*The Holy Grail*', the scene in which a knight has had his arms and legs cut off but keeps on fighting, shouting: "Come back you coward!" and "It's only a flesh wound!". The gif contains the comment, "I'm invincible."

> *Kayleigh Smith – Keep chopping at that cancer and you'll walk away from it in the end.*
> *Gemma Wilson – Oh Hans Keith Oldham, I don't believe it! I just want to*

run across and give you a big hug again! We will all be with you! I bloody love you guys! Roll on the 29th XxX
Cameron Chandler – Fuck the New Estate and fuck cancer too!
Suzanne Copeland – Oh Keith! Get your drum back out and call up those giants one more time. So glad I cuddled you loads last night. Big love xxxx

The fighting spirit of Rooster is never far away, even in others.

18 September 2018

I attend the *Gaslight* reading. I've already read the play and know it well enough to have identified the dastardly Mr Manningham as a part I'd like to audition for. I have to take my surgeon's advice, however, so I attend the reading partly as a protest to my condition and partly as a way of letting go of my ability to choose.

Cancer may stop me from auditioning, but I refuse to let it dictate the terms of my temporary surrender.

20 September 2018

Andrea and I drive to The Royal Blackburn Hospital, the nearest hospital with a PET scanner. The procedure is not unlike the other types of scans I have already received, with the exception of the injection of radioactive dye. It takes about forty-five minutes to complete. As always, the nursing staff are efficient and reassuring. The results will be analysed and sent to the surgical team at the Wythenshawe Trust Hospital, who will then contact me to discuss my treatment options.

29 September 2018

Today I marry Andrea, the love of my life, my soul mate. All thoughts of cancer treatment are banished; they have no business occupying our minds on this day. Cancer has been an uninvited and unwelcome guest in our lives for too long, but not today.

The Clonter Opera Theatre, surrounded by fields in the middle of the Cheshire countryside, plays host to us and our two-hundred and seventy guests. It's an unusual venue for a wedding, but the owners do a fabulous job to ensure the day runs smoothly and is filled with everything we asked for, and more.

So many unforgettable memories are created this day, aided by many wonderful family members and friends. Every single guest has supported us both, in some small or great way during my cancer treatment. This is a fabulous opportunity not only to celebrate our marriage, but to say thank you.

The donations to our cause have trickled in over the last couple of weeks but today the flood-gates have opened. Our target of £2,000 is smashed by the end of the day and about £4,500 is raised, with still more to come. We are grateful and humbled beyond words. Today our army of giants are no longer hidden behind a few comments on social media but they are here, with us in this one place, and they are very real.

Our ceremony is conducted by the registrar on the stage whilst our guests are in attendance and seated in the auditorium, watching the event unfold. Max and Cyrus are our witnesses and I am seated with them, the registrar and her assistant downstage right.

Suddenly there is music. *'Wonderful World'* by Louis Armstrong, and cue the bride. Luke escorts Andrea onto the stage through a door upstage left. They walk slowly to where I am seated. Luke is led by Alfie and Stanley, who are our ring bearers. It's a beautiful display of family unity. As the bride enters our guests gasp and cheer. It's no wonder, because Andrea looks stunning and I am beyond proud.

The choice of music is poignant for two reasons. It was one of my dad's favourite tunes and has been special to me since it was played at his funeral almost twenty years ago. It is my way of inviting him to today's ceremony. Also, it was played at a particularly dramatic moment in *Jerusalem*, a scene during which Rooster is badly beaten by some local thugs. Despite the music being particularly significant to me it was Andrea's choice for the wedding march. Watching her walk towards me whilst listening to it just makes everything in the world feel perfect.

The rings are retrieved from the collars of Alfie and Stanley and we take our place centre stage and face each other. The registrar is on one side and our guests, the audience, on the other. Unfazed, the registrar expertly conducts the ceremony, ensuring both legal matters and personal details are included.

The moment at the end of the ceremony when the groom is invited to kiss the bride gets a standing ovation. It's magical.

The Registrar asks,

"If anyone should know of any lawful impediment…"

A short break follows for photographs in the Theatre gardens, sipping champagne and chatting to family and friends as a married couple.

The Happy Couple

Unbeknownst to Andrea, Fionnuala and Sara have prepared and brought Andrea's horse, Mia, to take part at this point in the proceedings. It's a lovely surprise and many photos are taken. The close relationship that Andrea has with Mia is obvious to everyone. Both ladies look stunning in white.

The stunning Bride and Bridesmaid

We ask all our guests to return to the auditorium. MADS have prepared a show. Two hours of entertainment hosted by the multi-talented Luke Stevenson. My eldest son, Luke, opens the show with Andy Cantillon. It's a fabulous start. There are so many acts that follow from so many talented MADS members, it's hard to single out any one in particular.

However, there is a moment when Luke Stevenson creates a boy band consisting of me and my three sons. We are encouraged to bust some moves choreographed by Max. Our awkwardness hits a mark with the audience who roar with laughter at the boy band we have become. My 'dad-dancing' is at its very best. I look like bees are attacking me and I'm an easy comedy target. The audience is thoroughly entertained and Luke Stevenson does a brilliant job.

The Bride and Groom with an audience of Giants at their back

Catering consists of buffet food produced by our friend Ursula Evans and a Fish and Chip van, courtesy of the Crewe Fish Bar. Both are a huge success with our guests.

A few words of thanks by me follow. This is my moment to thank all those that have helped make today a special and memorable event. But more than that to dwell briefly on the love and kindness that everyone in attendance has showered on us both during the last terrible eighteen months. The donations to our cause get special praise. It's an impressive sum of money and will certainly be put to good use.

The rest of the evening is not unlike any other wedding party. Luke Stevenson is our singing DJ and gets everyone up and dancing to the set he provides.

Days like this are essential for anyone going through the hell of cancer treatment. I'm not suggesting that if you get cancer you should immediately get married, but spending quality time with family and friends is part of the cure. If it doesn't cure you, then when your time comes you are sure to be remembered with love and affection. Those you leave behind will have an enduring sense of who you are, which can only help them come to terms with their loss. It's also an opportunity to show how you wish to be remembered.

With the new togetherness we have forged, Andrea and I are ready for anything that comes our way.

3 October 2018

We meet one of the junior lung surgeons at Wythenshawe Hospital to discuss the PET scan results. I have three lumps in my left lung. The good news is that the cancer has not spread anywhere else and the three small lumps appear to be localised. The three dimensional PET scan image is displayed to us on a computer screen. The cancerous lumps appear to look very much like the many small lumps of fatty tissue also visible on the screen. It takes a trained eye to identify the difference.

To emphasise the diagnosis, the surgeon draws my condition on a lung diagram. Treatment could just be radiotherapy at The Christie, but surgery is not ruled out. I will need to have heart and lung tests before a treatment plan can be properly recommended.

When we return home I post an update on Winning:

> *Today my wife and I were given the results from the PET scan. I'm happy to say that they represent a good outcome. The cancer has travelled to my left lung. There are 3 lumps, 2 are very small. The fact that they are in the same area helps any planned treatment. The PET scan has not detected cancer anywhere else which is a major relief.*
>
> *Over the next couple of weeks I will have a heart scan and a lung function test. These will provide the additional information required to determine a treatment plan. Based on current known facts the most likely treatment is a period of radiotherapy at The Christie. This should burn away the cancerous cells. The other less likely option is major surgery. This could be a wedge section (dotted lines in diagram) or the removal of my left lung (unlikely but not yet discounted).*
>
> *So it seems the Grim Reaper has tapped me on the shoulder but has been given short shrift. He knows we will win the next battle and he has no business with me. My gorgeous wife Andrea Oldham has been my rock today xx.*

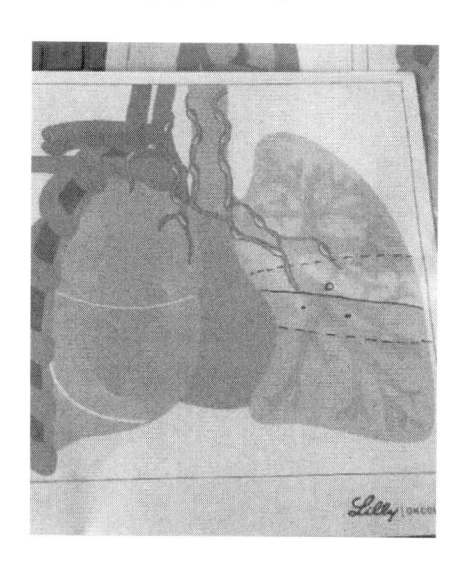

A pad of lung diagrams used to illustrate a lung disease diagnosis

"Go kick its ass!" Is a popular comment in the many responses. David Smith kindly reminds me of the many who have my back:

> *David Smith – It's not taking on the usual suspect, it's taking on an army. Suzanne Copeland – Grim Reaper "Hi Keith I'm ba…". Keith "Yeah, jog on mate!". Grim Reaper "Erm, ok sorry…"*

4 October 2018

Mr Chris Smart is without doubt one of my life heroes. He is right up there with my dad, my wife, my sons, George Best and Sir Alex Ferguson. I suspect that there are many others who feel the same way about this very skillful surgeon. If somebody uses years of training and hard work to save your life it must be quite normal to put them on a pedestal.

I do not want to die and my loved ones do not want to lose me. Not only has Chris prevented my untimely funeral, but he has led the charge in planning my additional treatment. Amongst his words to me when I was first diagnosed was his commitment to provide me with the very best care. He has stood steadfastly by that ever since.

However, his surgical skills are not his most remarkable attributes. He must have saved many lives. The gratitude for that is eternal and comes not only from the patient, but their family and friends. I suspect that surgery is also about taking risks which sometimes do not pay off. Chris, I'm sure, will have sadly lost patients too. This ordinary mortal makes life and death decisions and then has to face the outcome, to manage the consequences. His most impressive quality is the way in which he remains grounded. There is nothing superior about his manner. There is nothing lofty about this man except his physical height. I admire his duty as a human being above his duty as a surgeon.

The donations to our wedding gift fund cause have reached £4,870. Once the Just Giving administration and transactions charges have been deducted, we will still have raised more than enough to purchase the Lunar LED cordless surgical headlight system. With this in mind, I email Chris to update him and to advise him that I will shortly be making the purchase.

8 October 2018

Chris Smart replies to my email.

"This is truly a humbling email, in many ways. I am so happy for you that the day went well. Thanks for keeping me abreast and the link I have read. The best bit of the email…… Mr and Mrs Oldham!!!!

Well done and I will see you soon."

Just an ordinary bloke really, but doing an exceptional job in an astonishing way.

10 October 2018

Andrea and I drive to Macclesfield Hospital for my heart screening and lung function testing. The heart screening takes the form of a heart CT scan. The lung function test involves breathing in and out of a machine to measure the quantity of my air intake, my speed of exhale, ability of my lungs to take up oxygen and strength of my breathing muscles. As it turns out my heart is more than just a swinging brick and my lungs are a fine pair of fully functioning bellows.

17 October 2018

Andrea and I meet with Chris Smart to discuss the test results and consider my treatment options. The lung surgeons at Wythenshawe Hospital want to meet me to discuss surgery. Cutting the cancer out is the more definitive treatment. Radiotherapy may work but is less likely to succeed in the longer term. My heart and lung tests prove that I am fit enough for surgery. The lung surgeons at Wythenshawe Hospital have the expertise to guide me. I am amenable to the thought of giving cancer the harder smack that comes with surgery.

I post an update on Winning:

> *The thing about cancer treatment is the rollercoaster ride it takes you on. My wife and I (I don't think I'll ever tire of saying that) went to Macc hospital today to discuss my treatment following my lung and heart tests. We were informed that the surgeons at Wythenshawe hospital want to meet us to discuss surgery as an option. I could have radiotherapy to burn away the 3 lumps but surgery is the more definitive solution. The thinking is to remove the lower left lung lobe where the cancer is followed by a blast of radiotherapy. The heart and lung tests proved I am fit enough for this option to be considered.*
>
> *So the way I see it is if that's the hardest fight but it results in the best outcome then bring it on. Meeting with Wythenshawe surgeons to discuss battle strategies to be arranged. So cancer NO just NO! As always Andrea Oldham was immense.*

The fighting talk of Rooster, from his army of giants, is the overwhelming riposte:

> *Suzanne Copeland – Yeah. Bring it, cancer, you bitch! Xxxx*
> *Connell Costello – Keep telling cancer to jog on. And if it's being insistent kindly remind it that there's only one person who's allowed to knock you on your arse and that's me and I will be having words.*
> *Neil Burrows – Just looked up fortitude in the dictionary. It had a picture of you looking beautiful*

Only good can come from this lot backing me!

25 October 2018

Andrea and I meet Mr Piotr Krysiac, the thoracic surgeon, and his team at

Wythenshawe Hospital. He is an elderly gentleman who qualified 37 years ago. He has many years' experience and a calm, confident intelligence. So when he strongly recommends surgery to remove the three cancerous lumps, it's advice that is hard to ignore. There is one lump at the very top of my left lung which is easy enough to snip away. The other two lumps are in the lower left lobe and close to a main artery.

Therefore, the option with the best outcome and lowest risk is to remove the entire lower half of my left lung.

Radiotherapy will probably be unnecessary. The cancer is not aggressive and has been identified very early so there is time to decide and plan. I don't need time to decide. I like the thought of having a more definitive option, recommended by a highly-experienced surgeon. It gets my immediate vote.

However, I am encouraged to consider radiotherapy. I agree to do so, but given that my mind is set on surgery, it is booked for the 14 December. This date allows me to take the Christmas period to recover, so that I can then return to work and other commitments in the new year. This time, cancer will be consigned to our memory as a minor inconvenience after it's had a short but firm seeing-to.

We are impressed by the NHS staff we meet today. Recommending the surgical removal of half a lung needs to be done with care. It's not an easy sell. However, they are professional and good-natured. We are calm but determined to fight. The quick-witted banter is a predictable and relaxing outcome. I encourage the snoring, wheezing, farting and pooping jibes that come my way.

When we arrive home I post an update on Winning:

> *So had a chat with the lung surgeon today. It seems that 2 of the lumps are in my lower left lung and the third lump is at the top of my upper left lung. The one on its own is easy enough just to snip away. The other two are dangerously near an artery so the recommendation is a removal of the whole lower left lobe. But that still leaves me with a lung and a half right. Happy days!*

Interestingly the incision will be made in my back just below my left shoulder blade. This delighted Andrea as apparently I snore just a little when I sleep on my back and won't be able to for a while post op. They're not rushing me in for the op either and I've elected to have it done mid Dec. Gutted because I could have auditioned for Gaslight after all......but then again Andrea gets to cook Xmas dinner while I recuperate. The surgeon may choose to take a biopsy with a needle into the infected area. Also radiotherapy hasn't been ruled out, I get to meet the oncologist soon to hear his opinion. My beloved Andrea was immense. We pretty much chuckled with the surgical team throughout the consultation.

Lots of attention is paid to my bodily functions in the returned comments. How unkind! But my kind of humour:

David Smith – Wow, extreme snoring cure, nothing by halves.
Paul Bernardi – Having 2 whole lungs is so last year mate x
Neil Burrows – Never mind the snoring. How Andrea gets any sleep lying next to a hottie like you...!
Rachel Hodges – It's one way of getting out of cooking Christmas dinner! Xx
David Shaw – I can vouch for the fact that you do not snore
Andrea Oldham – I beg to differ Mr Shaw!!
David Shaw – Andrea Oldham He's changed....
Tim Roskell – It wasn't snoring that was a problem when I had to share a house with Hans Keith Oldham some 24 years or so ago....windy fart!!
Suzanne Copeland – Ach lung schmung. It's all sounding like winning.

29 October 2018

I have thought about last week's consultation over the weekend and have conclusively decided on surgery. I don't feel the need to explore radiotherapy as an option. I contact the surgery team at Wythenshawe and let them know. Arrangements are made for me to have a full health screening and surgery preparation a week before the operation.

Now that I have some certainty about surgery on the 14 December, I am duty bound to inform my employer. Jackie Nock is one of the most hard working, supportive and people-centric bosses that it's been my pleasure to work for, very reminiscent of Cheryl Marshall at the Co-Op.

We have a telephone catch-up scheduled each Monday. Once we have discussed business issues, I inform her about my history with cancer, my latest diagnosis and my planned lung surgery. It's not an easy conversation because it risks my future employment and may set my career prospects back again. I have worked hard this year to re-establish my professional self and I really do not want to lose the momentum I have gained.

I explain that I have elected to have my operation at a time that is least disruptive to work. The Christmas period will be quiet despite the current Brexit uncertainty. I estimate returning to work from the start of the second week in January.

I cannot fault Jackie's response. As an experienced leader, I'm sure she has dealt with similar staffing issues before. Her empathy is outstanding and I feel completely at ease with my future employment prospects at DEFRA. It is certainly one less thing to worry about.

5 November 2018

The reading for *Nicholas Nickleby* was last week. Ralph Nickleby is as villainous and manipulative as Mr Manningham in *Gaslight*, so I'm drawn to attending tonight's audition. The play runs from the week commencing 11 March 2019 and rehearsals don't start until early January.

The casting panel is aware of my condition and my planned surgery. They understand that casting me would be a risk but, all being well, I should be recovering when rehearsals begin. I am not hopeful for a part in the play but, refusing to give up, I present myself at the open audition anyway.

Although my audition goes well, I am dumbstruck when I'm offered the part of Nicholas Nickleby. I feel the weight of MADS Theatre standing at my side and backing me, once again refusing to give up on me. Something as minor as a major operation doesn't impact the faith they have in me. It's motivational. Cancer is about to be told that although it might infest my lung, it will not infest my life. I am ready to take a three week break to give it a short but final beating.

11 November 2018

I meet Chloe and Rhys at 06:20am in the hallway to take them to Manchester Airport for their weekend trip to Rome. They've become good friends with Tom, Max and Robyn, and there's not much Andrea and I wouldn't be prepared to do for this extension to our family.

7 December 2018

Wythenshawe Hospital is located in a built-up area and isn't the easiest place to get to. Also, there never seems to be enough parking spaces. What is it about hospitals and parking? Despite these hindrances, Andrea and I arrive on time for my appointment.

We spend the next hour moving around the hospital from one department to the next. I give bloods, have an x-ray and undertake heart tests. Once all this is completed, I am briefed about what will happen on the day I am admitted for my operation. I am also asked if I am willing to consent to my removed lung tissue being used for research. This I am happy to do. Finally, I sign the consent forms and I'm provided with energy drinks and a decontamination body wash for the morning of the 14 December.

I post an update on Winning:

> *An hour spent at Wythenshawe Hospital preparing for surgery next Friday 14 Dec. Today was about bloods, x-ray, cardiac tests (yes I have a heart!), form filling and a chat. I've come away with a goody bag of body wash and pre-op drinks. Happy days. Next Friday is a bit more challenging as they remove the lower half of my left lung. All being well I'll be out in 3-5 days and cancer*

free once again. This time I'm planning on keeping it that way. My amazing wife Andrea Oldham continues to be with me at every step of the way. To my family and friends reading this post you are giants. Thank you for your support xx

Many healing vibes are sent, along with a few other comments:

Tony Chadwick – Good luck mate – we'll have to arrange another catch up in the new year. Now they've found your heart they just need to find your wallet. Hope the pre op drinks go down ok and all goes as well as expected. Pope Francis had a lung removed when he was a youngster and it didn't stop him getting a decent job later.
Becky Connolly – Are you sure it's a heart and not a swinging brick?! Xx
Pete Munro – COME YOU GIANTS!
Jenny Pitcock – As it's my birthday on Friday I'll give you my birthday wish.

Do birthday wishes work on eradicating cancer forever, I wonder? If not, I'll opt for a real heart, my wallet and a decent job!

I phone the company that sells the headlight system and buy one. They can ship it tomorrow. The price has gone up a little. Apparently, they've only ever sold them to hospitals, never to an individual.

13 December 2018

It's my last day at work before my surgery tomorrow. My DEFRA colleagues are generous with their good luck messages.

The headlight system arrived a couple of days ago, so I email Chris Smart to let him know. I have an appointment with him on the 9 January and I suggest that this may be a good time to hand it over to him.

9
LUNG SURGERY
THEIR KNIFE IN MY GLANDS, AGAIN

There are two lobes in the left lung and three in the right lung. A lobectomy is the removal of one lobe. This is the most common type of operation for lung cancer or, as with my case, bowel cancer in the lung. One lung can provide enough oxygen and remove enough carbon dioxide to allow the body to function normally. The only long-term restriction is that removal, or part removal, of a lung will prevent the same strenuous exercise as with two lungs.

Surgery for lung cancer is a major operation and can have serious side effects. Possible complications during and soon after surgery can include reactions to anaesthesia, excessive bleeding, blood clots in the legs or lungs, wound infections and pneumonia. There is also a small risk of death during and immediately following the operation.

The surgeon makes an incision across the back just under the shoulder blade. Some muscle is cut and the ribs are spread apart. The affected lung is then surgically removed. The ribs and muscles are then closed and sutures are applied to the skin. Open lung surgery can take up to six hours. It is normal for the patient to remain in hospital for up to a week after the operation and common to experience fatigue for six to eight weeks after surgery. The chest may be sore and swollen for up to six weeks.

14 December 2018

We arrive at Wythenshawe Hospital thirty minutes early and check in to the pre-op suite situated very near to the operating theatre. The routine here is very similar to the routine at Macclesfield Hospital, but this time without the need to check a stoma mark. The dress code is exactly the same: surgical stockings, netty bag pants and a surgical gown topped off by a pair of my own Crocs.

If ever I get invited to a fancy dress party… hmm maybe not, it's a little indecent!

A nurse asks me my name, date of birth and address in order to properly identify me. I've already signed the consent forms, but hospital protocol dictates that the risks of the operation have to be explained to me again. Once complete, an identity band is placed around my left wrist and a cannula inserted into the back of my left hand. I am now fully prepared for the operation, so the nurse asks me to go through to a surgery waiting room.

This is the moment to say goodbye to Andrea. We've done this once before, but that experience hasn't made it any easier this time. We hold on to each other, not wanting to let go. Whispered "I love you's" are exchanged. We smile and nod at each other and with a final giggle at the fashion icon that I have become, I pick up my overnight bag and leave. No looking back this time. I know Andrea is putting on a brave face for my benefit that will vanish once I am out of sight. The thought of that is crushing enough, I don't need to see it and she wouldn't want me to.

There is nobody else in the surgery waiting room so it doesn't matter that I haven't tied up my gown at the back. I retrieve my phone from my bag and send a re-assuring message to Andrea. She replies immediately, telling me to tie up my gown as I might frighten the nurse. I chuckle and smile at her humour. Happy that she's still holding it together. It's been less than a minute since I was with her and I miss her already.

Andrea has checked us both in on Facebook. I take the opportunity to read some of the incredibly supportive messages being posted by family and friends. They are all very moving. This one, from Tom's parents, is fairly typical, but resonates particularly strongly:

> *Colin Jacques – Be strong together, hold on tight and let your love for each other flow. You can do this and so much more! Col and Elle xx.*

I post an update on Winning:

> *Just said my good bye to my beloved Andrea Oldham and I'm in the surgery waiting room. Feeling very confident of an excellent outcome. I'm blessed to have such beautiful and amazing family and friends. Thank you all for your encouragement and support to us both. It really does count. Is that me they're calling? See you on the other side folks.*

I don't have time to read any of the responses. I switch off my phone and turn my attention to the nurse who has just entered the waiting room and called my name. There is a safe place in a locker for me to leave my overnight bag. The nurse assures me that it will follow me around the hospital to the ward I will wake up on. My belongings are perfectly safe. The locker is just outside the waiting room, around the corner from the theatre.

I enter the small room outside the operating theatre and lie down on a treatment bed. The anaesthetist smiles at me and asks me my name, date of birth and address. This re-assures me that I'm not here for accidental open heart surgery. As I reply he connects an IV line into the cannula in the back of my hand. My internal monologue is busily injecting me with positive thoughts but it is suddenly interrupted by… blackout.

During my operation, Andrea posts the following on Winning:

> *Just a quick update.......The operation was meant to be around 3 hours long so*

I checked at 3.5 hours and they said he was still in theatre and they've just come to me now to say he has just been moved to recovery so fingers crossed he will be out soon........and breathe!!

The death of a spouse or child is on record as being the most stressful life event. So simply waiting while your spouse is going through major surgery with all the risks that it entails is no easy feat. I constantly marvel at the bravery Andrea shows in her determination to stand by me with the optimistic, upbeat and humorous outlook that I need. Trust me, it takes guts!

Over six hours have passed since the blackout, but it feels like I'm immediately hearing and sensing again. My consciousness is alert to noise and inviting me to find the effort to pry open my eyes. At first I refuse, preferring to remain disorientated, half asleep. But noise is working hard to drag me out of my stupor and eventually I submit, slowly squinting my eyes open. I have crossed a line. I'm no longer stranded in my dazed inner self and the world rushes to greet me.

My hand in Andrea's, her big beautiful smile and noise, so much noise.

"Hello, half a lung boy."

I chuckle. This is both funny and informative. Certain I would want to know more, Andrea continues.

"How does it feel to be cancer free again? The operation has gone well. You've done brilliantly. I'm so proud."

"Great... thanks!" Is all that I can happily, but barely, mumble.

My consciousness grows and, as the curtains are open, I can see that I'm in an extremely busy, small four-bed ward. The man in the bed opposite me is the cause of some commotion. He is talking very loudly, not quite shouting but being very objectionable to a man in a white coat.

The man in the bed next to him and diagonally opposite me is snoring chronically. He sounds like a chainsaw through a loudhailer. The ward is an open bay with a nurses' station to my left. The nursing staff are busy rushing around performing various tasks.

Seeing that I am awake a nurse approaches us. She introduces me to all the equipment that I'm connected to. There is an IV drip attached to the cannula in the back of my hand and I'm wearing nasal cannulas for increased airflow. I have access to two devices. The button in my left hand gives me a feed of morphine and the one to my right calls for a nurse if I need one. I am painfully too familiar with all of these.

Happily, I do not have a catheter this time. However, I do have a chest drain. This is a plastic tube coming out of a hole in the left hand side of my chest which is draining fluid off my lung into a bucket on the floor. The tube is about one cm in diameter and the bucket is not unlike something you'd build sandcastles with on the beach but with a lid and a handle.

The nurse takes my observations and scribbles on the record card attached to a clipboard hanging on the footboard of my bed. I feel reasonably comfortable and not in too much pain. This is largely because of the continued effect of the anaesthetic and the pain relief I have been given. When it becomes necessary, and it will, I have morphine available at the touch of a button. I'm surprised I can feel anything at all!

Going through this induction to my condition really does help as it allows me to get a sense of what I'm up against and how I need to deal with it. Andrea is pleased to have me back amongst the living again, even though I'm not entirely lucid. She has already spoken to each of my sons and is ready to post an update on Winning:

> *Keith is now on the ward and is quite naturally feeling very tired. He has numbing drugs (similar to the numbing that you'd receive at the dentist) in order to numb the pain in his back and also morphine for his pain on a pump that he can control. His boys are coming this evening so all is fine.*

There is a collective sigh in the comments that Andrea reads out to me with lots of good wishes for a speedy recovery. Some, aware of the impact of the loss of somebody dear to them, ask after Andrea, recognising what she has also endured.

Watching Andrea read from her phone reminds me that my bag should be somewhere with me. I ask Andrea if she can see it anywhere. Her quick search is fruitless. This is disappointing as I'm now unable to communicate, use my iPad, read a book or have a shave until it is found.

Andrea asks the nurse about my bag and she says that she will ensure it is found and returned to me. I'm not too concerned about it at the moment as I'm in no condition to move too much and I'm exhausted. So much that I find myself nodding off, in and out of sleep.

Andrea is reluctant to leave but there is little point in her staying any longer. Right now I need rest and she will be returning to visit this evening with Max and Cyrus. We kiss, she leaves, I fall asleep.

Despite my exhaustion, my afternoon nap is continually disturbed by the two gentlemen in the beds opposite me. One snores at one-hundred decibels and the other moans incessantly about, well … anything! Mostly about the wound in his chest that he claims is bleeding but that the nurse's claim is healing perfectly well. When the snoring man wakes up he too joins in with the groaning chorus.

The evening dinner trolley arrives and although I am "nil by mouth" I'm hopeful its arrival will calm the ward down a bit.

I'm wrong. Apparently, it only means there's more to moan about.

"What shite are they serving up tonight?"

"Hey… love… pop out and get us a mackies, will ya?"

My bag still hasn't turned up. That, together with the agitation being caused by Dumb and Dumber opposite me, has made me decidedly grumpy. The fact that I am unable to do much about either makes me feel worse. That soon changes when Andrea arrives during visiting hours with Max and Cyrus. It's wonderful seeing their familiar faces and being on the receiving end of their banter.

They all love my dad jokes, they have for years. I've just never understood why they choose not to admit it. I give them one that seems particularly topical:

"Before surgery my anesthetists offered to knock me out with gas or a boat paddle. It was an ether / oar situation."

Not even so much as a smile between them. Quite the reverse in fact. They all scramble for cover in fear of another.

Andrea makes another unsuccessful attempt to find my bag. A nurse who has just started her shift is completely unaware of the loss but promises to find out where it might be.

Before she leaves with Max and Cyrus, Andrea posts another update on Winning:

> *Update: Keiths bag with his mobile, iPad, money, clothes etc has gone missing so he wanted me to let you know that he isn't being rude by not replying.*

This presents an opportunity for a couple of wisecracks:

> *Paul Bernardi – Hey my novel had better not be in there. He swore he was going to read it this week!*
> *Kayleigh Smith – If he didn't want to talk to us he coulda just said….*

In my experience being doped up on anaesthetic, pain relief and the occasional hit of morphine usually means sleep is easy to find. But Dumb and Dumber make sleep impossible.

When they're awake they're too vocal and when they're asleep their snoring wakes the dead.

15 December 2018

I haven't slept a wink. I manage to reach my nurse's bell and press it. A nurse arrives and I explain that I am unable to sleep and ask the time.

"It's 2am. Would you like something to help you?"

"Yes, please. Could you taser those two? I won't tell anyone… honest!"

She hands me a pair of ear plugs. Apparently, she has come prepared. I agree to try them but I don't hold out much hope.

By 3am I am screaming "shut the fuck up!" across the ward.

By 4am I am weeping with frustration, unable to move to escape the infernal rattle shaking the very foundations of the Hospital. It reminds me of the TV programme '*SAS: Who Dares Wins*' when the contestants are captured and psychologically tortured. They are blindfolded and forced to listen to a loud repetitive noise, like a baby crying. Most of them are emotionally broken within a couple of hours. That is a walk in the park compared to this. If I had my phone or iPad and earphones I could at least listen to some music and shut out some of the infuriating noise. Granted I'd still feel the ward shake, rather like a deaf person feeling rhythm by sitting on a boom box, but at least I'd have a chance of sleeping.

By 5am I start to throw anything I can find at Dumb. Dumber is out of reach. But I'm weak and my aim is poor. Within fifteen minutes Dumb's bed is surrounded by litter and I have run out of items to throw. I actually manage to hit him once, on the forehead, with a sweet. He stopped snoring, raised his hand and swotted away something imaginary. Then with a few mouth smacks, he settled back to his rhythmic snore reminiscent of an asthmatic Darth Vader. I regret that it wasn't something bigger and heavier than a mint humbug.

By 6am I have nothing left. I feel empty and broken. Unable to comprehend why they themselves are not woken by the infernal, deafening noise they are making.

At 6:30am they both stop snoring and wake up. They're a tag team, working in tandem. Dumber gets up to go to the toilet. Dumb looks across at me, staring back at him open-mouthed.

"Not easy sleeping in this bloody hovel, is it mate?" He quips.

I continue with my madman death stare but can't find any words. Eventually I just close my eyes, so tired, and hear Dumber coming back from the toilet. I can feel Dumb jabbing his finger in my direction:

"A bit weird... our new friend."

"Is he? You messy sod, look at the state of all this... bits of rubbish everywhere... why is there a Croc on your bed?... and a book, you can't even read!"

I wake again at about 8am to a noisy and busy ward. I've missed breakfast, my first post operation meal. But I'm not hungry, just knackered. The day staff have all arrived for duty and I ask a passing nurse about my bag but she doesn't hear me. She bumps into the bottom of my bed as she rushes by. I could weep. An Asian female nurse takes and records my observations. I must look a forlorn, miserable sight and on the verge of tears. She asks if I'm alright.

"I just want my bag." I reply pitifully, through gritted teeth and with exasperated anger.

She smiles and shakes her head in that Indian way that looks like no but means yes. I have her attention. The small ward is crowded with patients, nursing staff, medicine trolleys, a wheelchair and various items of medical equipment. It's a busy hive of activity. However, this beautiful and efficient nurse is entirely focused on me. Her look galvanises me into action.

Somehow, I find the strength to sit up and swing my legs over the side of the bed and then remove my nasal cannula.

"Please take this out."

I implore her, pointing to the IV line attached to the cannula in the back of my hand. She steps towards me with both hands raised ready to help me back into bed.

"No! I've had enough. I'm sorry but if you don't remove this I will. It's better that you do."

I'm on a roll now, but with no clear plan in my head. In my craziness, the idea has come to me that I'll go and get my bag myself. I can vaguely remember where I put it and I know it's not far.

"Please…"

I hold out my left hand and to my surprise she removes the IV line. Still, nobody has noticed my astonishing and newly acquired strength, except for this one nurse. I slide off the bed and stand. The instant dizziness passes quickly enough. I pick up the drain bucket, now quite full, lean forward and walk.

With my first few steps I ease my way passed a male nurse, Nurse Andrew, and a couple of other nurses. I'm not sure if it's adrenalin or the morphine but nothing hurts too much. By the time I reach the corridor outside the ward I'm in full stride. I can hear Nurse Andrew and another nurse shout after me. I look back and they are chasing me down the corridor. Nurse Andrew pushing a wheelchair.

"Mr Oldham! What are you doing, you'll kill yourself! Come back here at once. No, don't, just stop there, I'll come and get you… Mr Oldham… Keith!"

But, by now, I'm single-minded. Thinking only about finding my bag. I reach the end of the corridor and recognise the door I entered yesterday. I turn left, then right and bingo! The locker is just in there behind those closed shutters. Shutters? Not a problem.

I bend over to grab the shutters to lift them up and I pull. They don't move but everything in my chest cavity seems to. Refusing to give in I tug, yank and heave in various attempts to tear open the shutters. Nothing works; they're locked. On my final and most energetic attempt to hoist them open, Nurse Andrew appears pushing a wheelchair followed by two other very concerned nurses. He sees me stand and wobble.

"Keith… please come back to bed. You've just had a major operation. This… this is silly. You'll damage yourself. Sit in the wheelchair and I'll take you back. Come on now… please."

I've backed away from the immovable shutters. Pain has gripped me, breathing is difficult and I'm sweating profusely. I am unable to stand upright. Finding a sort of bent-over forward, twisted slightly to the left whilst holding on to the wall to be the most comfortable position.

"Nobody is listening," I wheeze, "I've been asking for my bag since yesterday. It's in there, behind those shutters, in a locker. Fetch the key. When I have my bag I'll go back to bed."

"It's Saturday. These shutters are always locked at the weekend. We don't have a key. Why don't you just sit down in the wheelchair?" Nurse Andrew pleads.

"No! I'm fine here." *Well that was a stupid thing to say,* I think to myself, obviously not fine.

"Bring a locksmith to break the lock." I demand.

Is there no end to my foolish idiocy?

It's at this point that Andrea appears. She had gone to the ward only to be told by the delighted Dumb and Dumber that I had 'kicked off' and raced away down the corridor, something about a bag? Andrea followed the commotion, heard my raised voice and rounded the corner to be confronted by her foolish husband in some sort of Mexican stand-off with three members of the nursing staff.

"Keith!" She snaps. "What are you doing?"

"Being a dick!" Is all my breathlessness will allow.

I start to slide down the wall that is holding me up and Nurse Andrew rushes forward and guides me into the wheelchair, picks up my bucket and puts it on my lap.

Andrea crouches down to face me, slumped in the wheelchair.

"Sweetheart, you can't do this to yourself. You shouldn't even be standing up yet, let alone charging around the Hospital. Come on let's get you back to bed."

"Okay babe." I nod weakly, "… bed."

"I don't know how you cope, Andrea. He's so stubborn. He just wouldn't be told." Nurse Andrew chastises but in good humour.

"Don't knock it," she replies, "that stubbornness is what's getting him through all this. Nothing will break him. My husband is a very determined man. Please just get his bag, no more false promises."

"He's a force of nature all right. It's possible that his bag went to another ward. If it's behind those locked shutters… well, we won't have a key until Monday. I'll do my best."

As Nurse Andrew pushes me back to the ward. They continue to talk over the top of me as if I'm not present, something which is becoming increasingly true. I am fading fast. I've had very little sleep and the marathon I've just put myself through has resulted in a searing pain inside and across my chest. Breathing is also difficult.

When we arrive back at the ward, Dumb shouts out:

"Hey… you da man!" Like I'm a re-captured escapee returning to a maximum security prison.

"No, he's not, he's a very naughty boy," fires back Nurse Andrew, leaning down towards my ear in mock *Monty Python* reprimand.

Despite all the grief I have caused, Nurse Andrew retains a certain charm. He's not really annoyed with me; I even sense a friendly admiration. All through my deranged stupidity he had acted in my best interest, doing his best to talk a man off the ledge. He deserves my respect and I have given him none.

Nurse Andrew helps me out of the wheelchair and onto my bed. He checks me over, fortunately no damage has been done. The beautiful Asian nurse is chastising me with smiles and shakes of her head as she reconnects me to the IV line. I immediately call for morphine.

I mouth "thank you" to her and she puts her hand on my arm and squeezes it, smiling and nodding reassuringly.

"Andrew… " I gasp, "sorry… and thanks… respect." These words are punched out between desperate intakes of air and I manage to clumsily grab his hand and grip it momentarily.

"Right, well it's done now. If you wanted your bag you only had to ask. No need for all that performance was there?" … cheeky!

"Ha ha… ah!… hurts when I laugh," I pant.

It takes about an hour of pain relief and remaining still and calm for the pain to become bearable. My shallow breathing is also more controlled. Andrea has spent that time sitting, holding my hand and talking to me. Filling me in on life outside the hospital, doing her best to be a calming, distracting influence. It works.

The dinner trolley arrives and, having missed breakfast, I'm hungry and ready for food. The chest drain is the main cause of my discomfort, followed by the *shark bite* wound across my back. Breathing causes the plastic tube to move inside me and there are many pain receptors in the chest wall that get aggravated. Arm movement causes the wound and damaged muscles to stretch agonisingly.

Andrea offers to feed me but I'm not giving in to that. Using my right arm to lift food to my mouth seems to cause the least tension across my back. I settle for a slow, synchronised, rhythm of movement, eating and breathing.

After dinner has been cleared away, Nurse Andrew appears.

"How much do you love me, Mr Oldham?" He cheerily asks.

I'm not sure why he persists on calling me Mr Oldham. I think it's just his way of being cheeky but respectful.

"It's off the scale, Nurse Andrew, you mean the world to me. Why?"

Nurse Andrew? We seem to have developed pet names for each other by using our real names. Weird!

"This," he replies with a huge grin, suddenly holding up my cherished overnight bag, anticipating eternal gratitude.

"It's not mine."

I sound and look fleetingly disappointed. Nurse Andrew looks at me, then at the bag and then back at me again… uncertain, confused. Gutted!

"… and that's my acting face. Come to daddy, you little beauty. Not you

The Spirit of Rooster

Nurse Andrew, you big lump, my bag!"

Apparently after my operation my bag had followed another patient to the Intensive Care Unit. It's an isolation ward and not the sort of place you burst into looking for a lost bag.

Nurse Andrew had had a coffee break with an ICU nurse this morning and mentioned my lost bag in passing. The connection was made and my bag was brought out of the isolation ward to be restored to its rightful owner.

With Andrea's help I check through the contents. All my possessions are untouched. My iPhone and iPad reconnect me to social media and I post an update on Winning:

> *So the story of the day. My overnight bag (containing lots of important life supporting stuff including my script Cameron Chandler and your book Paul Bernardi) has eventually arrived by my bedside. It went to intensive care. Lucky for me I didn't. The giants sent me to the right place. I am eternally grateful.*

These two concerned responses couldn't be more different:

> *Paul Bernardi – Thank the Lord. Was dead worried about my book there (oh and about you and the rest of your stuff obvs!)*
> *Ann Dean – Glad your bag turned up. What a worry for you. Keep winning, heaps of love xxx.*

If only they knew the truth of the morning's jaunt around the hospital corridors.

After a further rummage through my bag, I come across a survival kit that Stuart Riley had kindly put together for me, containing lots of goodies. I hungrily start munching my way through it and post another Winning update:

> *Now tucking into my survival kit Stuart Riley. There is another part to the story. This morning nobody seemed to be taking my lost bag seriously which I last saw in admissions. I recalled Roosters response. I unhooked myself from all*

the lifesaving gadgets (except the drain obvs) and gingerly marched myself to admissions followed by a small posse of unhappy hospital staff.

I was convinced it was behind some shutters. Said Shutters were locked and no matter how hard I tried I couldn't leaver them opened. At this point the pain & sweating kicked in. Fortunately Andrea Oldham who had just arrived to witness the scene convinced me of my stupidity and nurse Andrew caught me, dropped me into a wheelchair and reconnected me with lots of wires, drips and stuff. Can't see what the fuss was about.

My foolishness is rightly exposed:

Tina Gray – Wow how naughty of you!! Bet you had a royal telling off from the Mrs xx
Fran Dykes – Like Rooster you were probably high on drugs
Suzanne Copeland – Pfft. Where's Ginger when you need him to gopher?
Claire Taylor - ?!! thank goodness for Andrea
Neil Burrows – That's the attitude

By mid-afternoon I am exhausted. The IV morphine has brought my pain back under reasonable control. I spend most of the afternoon falling in and out of sleep. Andrea sits patiently by my bedside having pulled the curtain around me. She wants to be with me in the moments I am awake, to fuss over me and make sure I am comfortable. I eagerly accept this demonstration of love.

Andrea is kindly offered something from the evening dinner trolley. Later, Tom also visits. Chatting with him is always easy and relaxing. It's great that he's made the effort. When visiting hours end and Tom has gone I encourage Andrea to go home. I'm comfortable and she's thought of nothing but me all day. Time to go home, be with Alfie and Stanley and open a bottle of wine.

The nurse's shift has just changed and the incoming ward charge nurse records my observations. She advises me that it's time to remove the IV morphine and prescribe me with oral analgesics instead. I can't but help feel that this is a little too soon but I'm keen to recover and get released so have no objection. The IV line is removed from the cannula in the back of my hand and oral pain relief is discussed and a prescription is written up.

During the course of the evening the pain in my chest worsens. I consider myself to have a high pain threshold. It is something that I have always had and cancer has, occasionally, found the limit of my threshold. But, this pain is becoming quite disturbing. The smallest breath I take causes instant pain in my chest around the area my drain is located.

It's a well-known fact that breathing is a life-preserving bodily function and pain is a stimulus that humans seek to avoid. Movement causes more intake of oxygen, which results in pain, which stops me breathing and increases my need for oxygen, for which my chest heaves and moves. It's a vicious circle. So I sit very still, close my eyes and concentrate on minimal breathing and pain management.

I'm in this state for about an hour when the snoring begins. Calling for a nurse will require the supreme effort of movement. I open my eyes hoping to see help nearby. My curtains are drawn, damn it! My emergency button is too much of a stretch away. I have had vocal training and know that it doesn't take much breath to project my voice. I steel myself, and, trying not to break the rhythm of the shallow breathing I have established, I call:

"HELP!"

Unfortunately, Dumb and Dumber have established a rhythm of their own and emit a loud snore at the exact same time as my SOS call. Also, calling out hurt, a lot. I curse the snoring chuckle brothers and go back to concentrating on shallow breathing and pain management. In doing so I come to realise that I might not actually make it through the night.

I have faced the prospect of my own death before and have witnessed others deal with their own certainty of it. So it is no stranger to me. I remember the Doctor advising Rob Gregory to think about how he wished to be remembered. If I am to die tonight I want my wife, daughter and three sons to know how much I love them and that they were in my final thoughts.

I start to think about other messages I want to leave behind. I'm in a dark, lonely place but everything is crystal clear. There are things I must write down in case I don't make it. I am calmly processing emotions, decisions and actions that are now vital to me, given the little time think I have left.

"Remembering that I'll be dead soon is the most important tool I've ever encountered to help me make the big choices in life. Because almost everything – all external expectations, all pride, all fear of embarrassment or failure – these things just fall away in the face of death, leaving only what is truly important."

– Steve Jobs

Suddenly, a nurse pulls back my curtain to do my observations.

"Just checking in on you, Keith. How are you feeling?"

"Need… pen… and… paper," taking a shallow and painful breath between each quietly spoken word then:

"think… I'm… dying… can't breathe… pain!"

"What? Well, not on my watch," she affirms as she picks up the clip-board from the footboard and reads the record card attached to it.

She quickly disappears and returns in less than a minute with my prescription of analgesia and a glass of water.

"Take this now." She hands me a small paper pot with three pills in it and the glass of water.

I do my best to synchronise movement and swallowing with the low rhythmic breathing I have established. I have to compromise briefly on the breathing but my pain management is good and I swallow the three small and very bitter pills.

The nurse, recognising my distress, stays with me for a while and offers reassurance. Within thirty minutes the pain has abated and my breathing has eased considerably. No need for a pen and paper just yet, I think to myself, but it felt close!

The nurse returns later to see how I am. The pain relief she gave me was very strong and it is vital to keep on top of my pain medication. I ask if anything can be done about the rumble of thunder coming from the beds opposite as I really would like to get some sleep tonight.

"Hmm…" came the reply, "… rest assured Mr Oldham that regular observations will be undertaken throughout the night."

I take that as code for: 'if the little buggers aren't quiet they'll get woken up!' I put my ear-phones in, turn on some music and close my eyes. Looking, perhaps, for the sanctuary of '*Rob World.*'

I still don't get much sleep, partly because of the pain I still feel but mainly because of the loud, unrestrained farmyard noises coming from the two beds opposite me.

However, I had correctly decoded the nurse's message. The noisy twosome are occasionally but '*accidentally*' disturbed during the night by a nurse having to take regular observations, perhaps even more regular than normal.

16 December 2018

At about 6am I give up trying to sleep; after all I've had at least three or four hours. That constituted a good night's sleep for the likes of Margaret Thatcher and Sir Winston Churchill, so why not me.

Whilst I listen to the sound of revving motorbikes I Google 'snoring,' looking for a miracle cure. I discover that snoring occurs as a result of narrowing of the airway during sleep. When we sleep the muscles of the airway in the mouth, nose and throat relax and the passages become smaller. This causes the soft tissues of the airway to vibrate. That vibration creates the sound of snoring.

I visualise narrowing the airways in the throats of Dumb and Dumber just a little bit more… until silence… only then releasing my grip!

My pain is manageable now that my medication is under control. However, I have noticed that my heart rate seems to increase without warning but only for short periods. It causes me to sweat and my breathing becomes harder. It first happened when I woke at 6am but it was hardly noticeable so I dismissed it. I have another episode while breakfast is being served and, whilst it is not severe, the palpations are more pronounced.

Shortly after breakfast a doctor appears to review all the cases on the ward. Dumb is first. Yesterday he was complaining about pain in the surgical wound in his chest that he insisted was bleeding. This morning the doctor is explaining that the wound is dry and healing quite well. He should be ready to go home today.

"Brilliant!" I think but hope he doesn't live within a two mile radius of the hospital; the distance I calculate the sound of his snoring will travel. However, Dumb has other ideas and is resisting going home despite the fact that he is the most mobile and vocal patient on the ward.

"It might start bleeding again, doctor, do you think I should stay in until tomorrow just in case? I think it might be infected!"

"It's not infected but let's take another look at it later on today."

Dumber is next and he can't wait to go home. Unfortunately, he has had minor heart failure and they want to keep monitoring his heart condition. Sadly, he's going to be in hospital for a while.

By contrast, I've hardly noticed the gentleman in the bed to my right. He has slept pretty much the entire time I've been here. How? Surely he must be deaf! He is sleeping now so the doctor looks at his record card, decides not to disturb him and moves toward me.

He explains that he wasn't involved in my operation, but he has discussed it with the senior surgeon who performed my lobectomy. The surgery went as planned and the three cancerous lumps were successfully removed.

I ask about the chest drain. I'm surprised, but delighted, to learn that once the drain is removed I may be allowed to go home. The drain is not ready to come out yet as my chest is still discharging fluid. The good news is that the absence of bubbles in the fluid indicates that there are no air leaks in the remaining half of my left lung. The fluid discharge will continue to be monitored and is currently showing signs that the drain may be removed as early as tomorrow.

Whilst he is explaining my condition to me I feel more heart palpitations and my forehead starts to sweat. I am slightly more breathless but able to tell him what's happening to me. He takes my pulse but is not overly concerned.

Apparently, it is a common reaction to the trauma my body has experienced and will leave me feeling tired. I am prescribed with IV magnesium sulphate, otherwise known as Epsom Salts. My surgeon will be visiting the ward tomorrow to assess me and answer any more detailed questions that I may have.

The doctor calls a nurse and explains what he has prescribed and that my condition should be closely monitored. The nurse disappears and returns with a bag of fluid which she hangs from my IV stand and then attaches the IV line to the cannula in my hand. The slow drip of magnesium sulphate begins to trickle into my system.

I had hoped to get up and start moving around the ward today, but being attached to both a drip and a bucket makes movement a bit more restrictive. For now, I force myself out of bed and just stand still for a while. Dumb takes this as an invitation to engage in conversation. Not content with talking to me from the comfort of his own bed he walks towards me and stands at the foot of my bed.

"They don't know owt these doctors. It's fucking ridiculous. This chest wound is infected. I should be in intensive care me ya know… have you tasted the slop they serve up?... and sleep is impossible in here… noisy nurses over there… "

But all I can hear is "blah, blah, blah, blah, blah!!"

I am too exhausted to cope with him, the partial cause of my exhaustion. I'm beginning to wonder how I'm going to rid myself of this tenacious, complaining mancunian when Andrea arrives.

Thank goodness, I'm saved, but no!

Dumb persistently continues talking at me, over the warm greeting from my wife. I want to tell her about my pain medication, the doctor's visit, the drain, the IV line and well, everything.

"Mate!" Holding up one hand to stop his chatter. "Do me a favour and just pull the curtains around my bed will you?"

I hope my request, delivered as politely as I could muster, will finally dismiss him. My hand has the same effect as the raised hand of King Cnut trying to stop the tide. Dumb continues his innate drivel whilst pulling the curtain around my bed and, unbelievably, the three of us!

Andrea and I look at each other and I start to laugh. I find his blatant obstinance and rhino hide sensitivity beyond irritating; it's actually absurdly funny.

"Just stop talking… please… can you just leave us alone… thank you. My wife is here to visit me… please go away!"

I wave the back of my hand toward him and spit each word out with a firmly directed venom, whilst trying to control my paradoxical need to chuckle.

"Oh, yeah sure… erm… soz!" Dumb turns and leaves.

As I open my mouth to speak to Andrea, his head suddenly appears through the curtain.

"Cuppa tea anyone?"

I give him my silent death stare.

"Er… that's a no then?" he responds apprehensively.

I smile and nod. He returns to his bed.

"Miserable bugger!"

He whispers loudly at Dumber, pointing in my direction.

Once Andrea and I have caught up with each other behind the privacy of the magic curtains I post an update on Winning:

> *The good news is the that pain is now under control. The drain is likely to be removed tomorrow. The bad news is that getting the pain under control has triggered a fast and irregular heartbeat. I'm exhausted but now face a drip of magnesium sulphate that will take 5 hours to administer. Deep joy!!*

A titter is never far away:

> *John Chandler - I take it you won't be at the mulled wine evening then?*
> *Kayleigh Smith – Course he will …. He just needs to bring his drip and we'll sort it*
> *John Chandler – Kayleigh Smith true, wine intravenous and hopefully appropriate clothing!*
> *David Shaw – Isn't that Epsom Salts? They should prescribe a trip to Old Trafford that will get your heart rate down and send you soundly to sleep*

The afternoon passes slowly as the IV Epsom Salts slowly saturates my system and revitalises me. My heart rate has continued to behave itself. The senior ward nurse removes the IV line and records my observations. She is pleased that I am stable but is unable to dodge the intervention from Dumb as she returns to the nurses' station. Once again he is drawing attention to his chest wound and doing his best to convince her it is infected.

"The doctor said I should stay in overnight and he will look at it tomorrow," he grumbles deceivingly.

Despite his obvious dishonesty, and to his delight, she confirms that he will be staying in hospital at least until tomorrow. I actually start to feel pity for this man and wonder what his home life must be like for him to be so keen to prefer being cooped up in this cramped and soulless hospital ward.

Watching him devour his evening meal I start to understand him a little more. Regardless of his constant complaining, in here he gets food, a warm bed and a roof over his head. He is also around people he can chat to and others that will take care of him.

I realise that he hasn't had any visitors in the time I've been here. Neither does he have a cannula in his hand. In fact, I can't recall him ever receiving medication. Although my sympathy for him grows, I still struggle to tolerate his whirlwind presence and the noisy disruption that comes with it, particularly in my fragile condition.

Once again Andrea serves her time and spends the day and most of the evening with me. Some of it entails simply holding my hand and watching over me as I fall in and out of sleep. It is hugely comforting and I wonder how the rejected but needy, like Dumb, cope without the unconditional affection I am showered with. With my new-found empathy I really should stop referring to him so disparagingly and ask him his real name. But then, some habits are too hard to break.

Once the IV line has been removed I get out of bed and walk the ward with Andrea. Carrying the bucket is a bind and I have to be careful not to catch the plastic drainage tube on anything. The unrestrained abandon I feel by moving around is intensified by not having a small team of nurses chasing after me.

17 December 2018

I'm awake at 5am for the third morning running. I feel like I've been denied sleep, forced to stay awake by the purring growl of the overweight Bengal tigers opposite me. I resisted the urge to smother them with my pillow during the night. Instead, I choose to listen to music, relax as best I can and try to sleep. I manage to get a modest Margaret and Winston nanna-nap before surrendering to the wide-awake club.

After breakfast, the doctors' round arrives and my surgeon, the talented Mr Piotr Krysiac, appears at my bedside and pulls the curtains around me. He confirms that surgery went exceptionally well and he's confident that all the cancerous tumours were removed. The heart palpitations I experienced yesterday are not a great concern. The drain is no longer discharging fluid and can be removed this morning. There is no evidence of air leaking out of my lung. My pain medication is under control.

He tells me that once the drain has been removed I can go home to convalesce. My case will be referred back to Chris Smart and no further treatment will be necessary.

Andrea arrives shortly after the doctors' round and she is delighted to be bringing me home today. Despite my exhaustion and the pain I feel I am ecstatic. I have gone through three days of pain, fear, sleep deprivation and psychological noise torture. I am ready for the comforts of home.

I post an update on Winning:

> *I've just met my surgeon. Heart is fine and the drain will come out this morning. Home this afternoon. I think they're going to miss such an awesome patient.*

There are many congratulatory comments from #teamsupporthanskeith who welcome the fabulous news.

Whilst we are waiting for a nurse to remove the drain I notice that Dumb is energetically talking to a doctor. He's telling him that the doctor he saw yesterday said he would have to stay in hospital until Wednesday (today is Monday) to ensure that his wound is clear of infection. The doctor, clearly confused by this falsehood, sounds adamant that Dumb is well enough to go home. Two nurses arrive with a medical trolley to remove my drain so I'm not sure how this discourse is eventually settled.

The curtains are pulled around my bed and one of the nurses asks me to stand and remove my hospital gown. She inspects and removes the dressing around the hole in the side of my chest. I am instructed to exhale as much air as possible, to empty my lungs. The nurse then pulls purposefully at the tube. The rapid movement of the flexible, soft silicone tube through the inside of my chest wall is the strangest feeling. It isn't particularly painful. I am surprised by the length of tubing and the fast pace with which it falls away. It feels so unnatural; it's not part of me but is moving inside me. The moment I am free from it, the other nurse seals the exit wound with stitches and I inhale.

It's wonderfully liberating to be able to suck in air without feeling pain, to take a deep breath. The solid mass that was once inside me, that prevented me from filling my one and a half lungs, is no longer constricting me. A home visit from a District Nurse will be arranged to remove the stitches in five days' time.

Once my medication has been prepared, I can go home. I pack my overnight bag and get dressed in the freshly laundered clothes that Andrea has brought for me. They smell of home, a contrast to the fusty, man-sweat, yet hygienic, odor of the ward. We don't have to wait long for the nurse to arrive and talk me through my medication.

I am also given a device that tests and exercises my breathing. It's called a Voldyne 5000. I am encouraged to first exhale all the air from my lungs and then breath in deeply and rapidly through the mouthpiece. The strength of my inhale is measured by a rising piston. Normal lungs should easily register the highest unit of 5,000. However, I am barely able to register 500 units. I dread to think what I would have registered whilst I was restricted with the chest drain.

Before we leave I notice that Dumb is tucking into his dinner and looking quite pleased with himself. I suspect he has caused enough confusion to stay a little longer. Dumber is sleeping silently. Damn him, he never did that for me!

As we walk past the nurses' station one of the nurses calls us over and shows me my post-surgery x-ray. I'm impressed enough to take a photo of the image on the screen as a keepsake. My lungs are a black shadow on the x-ray image. The shadow on the left is smaller than the one on the right. She asks me about any recent bowel movement. I realise that I haven't actually had a poo since before my operation. She points at the light grey shadows underneath my left lung.

"Yes, it looks like you're quite impacted… here, here and here… just in the space left by the half lung you used to have."

I don't feel the need for a poo right now but once I'm home and relaxed I suspect it'll take a painful couple of hours to shift that lot!

I was right, it does!

10
RECUPERATION AGAIN

The human respiratory system is a series of organs responsible for the intake of oxygen and expelling carbon dioxide. The primary organs of the respiratory system are the lungs which carry out this exchange of gases as we breath. The average adult takes over twenty thousand breaths each day. The removal of the lower left lobe does not stop this important bodily function, but, due to the reduced air intake capacity, it can take time to adjust.

While you may be able to return to work within six to eight weeks, your doctor will advise you to avoid heavy lifting for the first several months. This is to prevent strain on the chest muscles and the incision. It can take up to a year to feel almost no effect of the operation. That said, the recovery period after a lobectomy is different for everyone.

Healing can be aided with breathing exercises and the avoidance of environmental toxins such as smoke and chemical fumes. Once recuperation is complete, living with a reduced lung capacity doesn't impact everyday tasks or life expectancy. However, a person with one lung won't be able to exercise as strenuously as someone with both lungs. Dwelling on this thought, I wonder what that means for me.

Life should not be measured by the number of breaths we take, but by the moments that take our breath away.

18 December 2018

After my short, but exhausting, stay in Wythenshawe Hospital I had thought that sleep would come easy for me. Although, I fell asleep quickly enough last night, I woke several times during the night, and not just to take pain medication.

I have three comfortable sleeping positions that I tend to rotate into during a full night's sleep. Unfortunately, none of them are conducive to a lobectomy. I find myself waking up several times and gasping for air as if my half-lung has been crushed by my sleeping position. My breathing is long, deep and slow as I try to regain a normal pattern.

A couple of times I put my head out of the window to suck in some fresh night air. On one occasion, I woke with a sudden urge to poo and ran to the toilet, gasping for breath. My new normal!

After breakfast I feel energetic enough to post an update on Winning:

> *Came home yesterday afternoon. This mornings jog around the park was a most welcome diversion. Now for the underwater charity swim across the lake. Might give the cycle ride a miss.*

The humour is not lost on some:

> *Fran Dykes – Funny man!*
> *Paul Bernardi – You tried to change a tyre last time if I recall!!*
> *Susanne Copeland – The only thing that surprises me about this is that you passed on the cycling!*

I then thought that actually seeing my half a lung might be quite interesting… and my impacted faeces of course!

I post my photo of it on Winning:

There it is ....gone!!

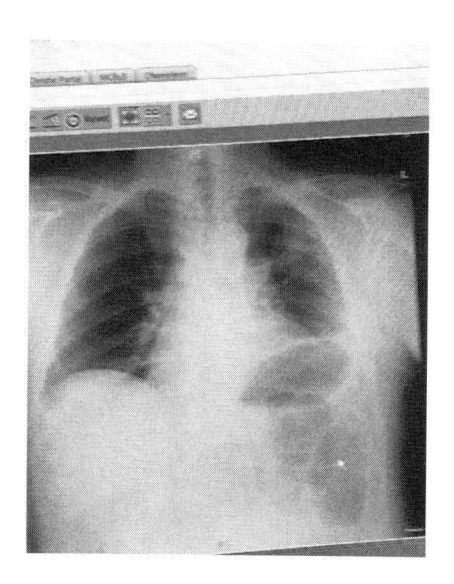

Let the banter commence:

> *Paul Bernardi – Nice lungs*
> *Julie Bernardi – You know you shouldn't put topless photos on social media don't you!!*
> *Neil Burrows – we can rebuild him*
> *Stephen Donnelly – Exposing yourself like that you'll catch a chill*
> *Andrea Oldham -*

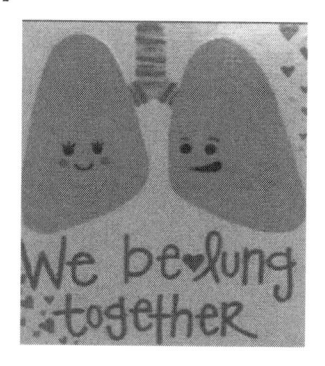

19 December 2018

I get a phone call from Chris Smart. He is aware that I've come through my surgery successfully and I'm convalescing at home. He thanks me again for purchasing the headlight system and thinks that handing it over to him on the 9 January represents the ideal opportunity. This man always breathes confidence into me. He follows up with an email.

"Hi Keith

Further to our phone conversation today I have been speaking to our Comms Manager, Chris Gorman who is copied in here.

He will ensure everything is done by the book and be there in clinic. It would be great for the trust to have some photos taken on the day as well so we can publicly thank you for you kindness and generosity. Jackie please can you confirm the clinic time with Chris.

Finally Keith well done for getting through your surgery and have a HAPPY CHRISTMAS.

Chris"

I am thrilled to be giving something back.

20 December 2018

It's a last minute decision, but I'm feeling just about well enough to attend the annual MADS mulled wine evening at the Theatre with Andrea. My appearance comes as somewhat of a surprise to my fellow thespians. I am somewhat surprised myself, it was less than a week ago that I had half a lung surgically removed.

They are mostly a huggy, kissy, crowd and the more affectionate among them delightfully forget my condition with the warmth and strength of their embrace. We don't stay long, but long enough to feel convinced that I'm on the mend.

22 December 2018

The District Nurse visits me today to remove the drain hole sutures. One of the stitches is very tight and has grown increasingly uncomfortable, so I'm rather pleased to have them removed. She inspects my wounds and comments that they appear to be healing nicely.

I have been using the Voldyne 5000 daily. My exhale is now registering almost 1,500 units. It's a useful guide to my recovery. However, the sudden bouts of breathlessness that have woken me during the night have occasionally befallen me during the day. I have noticed that they seem to start with a faster and erratic heart rate. The experience is intermittent, doesn't seem to be triggered by anything in particular and stops after a few minutes.

In the evening, I am lying on the sofa, resting and watching TV. I become aware that my heart is beating faster than normal. I can feel my chest pounding. My breathing becomes laborious. I can't explain it, as I've been lying very still on the sofa. At first I ignore it, thinking that it will cease after a few minutes. It doesn't. After fifteen minutes, I stand and pace the room, breathing deeply and slowly. It's not painful, but it is confusing and tiring. Both Andrea and Max have become increasingly concerned. Talking is difficult but there's been little sign of it stopping for thirty minutes when I manage to say:

"Ambulance!"

Andrea is on the phone immediately, describing my condition and symptoms to the ambulance service. They keep her on the phone until an ambulance pulls up at the bottom of our drive about fifteen minutes later. The two ambulance paramedics charge into the lounge where I am sitting on the sofa trying to remain calm, breathing heavily and sweating. They attach me to what I think is a mobile ECG machine with a number of leads taking readings from different points on my body. It measures the rate, rhythm and electrical activity of my heart. The ends of all the leads have to be placed at certain points on my body to ensure a correct reading. A normal heart beat is about seventy beats per minute. Mine is racing erratically along at between one-hundred and fifty and one-hundred and eighty beats per minute. There is no obvious explanation for this, but it is highly likely to be the result of my recent surgery.

My condition is monitored for a few minutes and the lead paramedic suggests they should take me into hospital. Hearing this, my fast-beating heart sinks. There was I thinking I'd be home for Christmas. Rather than driving the ambulance up our narrow driveway, I am pushed to it in a wheelchair. Once in the ambulance I am strapped down on a trolley and taken to Macclesfield Hospital with Andrea. On the way, my condition continues to be monitored and my heart beat peaks at two hundred beats per minute.

On arrival at the Hospital I am checked into the resuscitation department at A&E, attached to an ECG machine and a cannula is put into the back of my right hand. Andrea posts a comment on Winning:

> *Currently in the resus dept of a&e after a trip in the ambulance with Keith who has an irregular and fast beating heart beat. Normal heart beat is about 70, marathon runner is 160 and Keiths heart beat is ranging between 158-182 however it peaked to 200 in the ambulance. I wouldn't mind but he was only lay on the sofa!! Apparently this is nothing to worry about as everything else is normal??!! Currently he is praying it won't result in an overnight stay. Apart from this Keiths recuperation is going ok*

There are a lot of "hope he's okay", "big hugs" and "warrior" type comments, but then there's always that one friend in the crowd:

> *Suzanne Copeland – I'm sorry. I should never have text him that boob pic! Hope he's back to normal soon.*

My heart rate returns to normal without medical intervention within an hour of admittance. By midnight, I'm advised that I'll be staying in hospital overnight for continued observations and so that the cardiac consultant can take a look at me tomorrow. I phone Max to update him and he drives to the hospital to take Andrea home.

Once again, I have been hopelessly reliant on Andrea and I am so grateful that she's in my corner. She's tired and tearful when she leaves but I know Max will take good care of her.

23 December 2018

I'm admitted to the male cardiac ward at about 1am. My heart rate has continued to remain stable. Sleep doesn't befriend me. I have struggled to sleep in my own bed at home so there's little chance of it in here. Despite all six beds being occupied, it's a quiet ward and I wonder if that's got anything to do with the fact that all the occupants have heart conditions.

I chat to some of the other inmates over breakfast. They've all been residents here for weeks. Evidently, monitoring and treating a heart condition takes time. It can take many weeks to gather reliable diagnostic information and a long time to recover from heart surgery.

The elderly gentleman in the bed opposite me tells me that he is terminally ill. The frankness with which he discusses it doesn't surprise me. He has clearly accepted his fate. I've learnt to respect such openness by showing an interest, listening and asking some direct questions; to validate him. With acceptance of this kind comes immense courage. He is more worried about the wife he will leave behind than his own loss of life. I am deeply humbled by this distinguished gent, a legend in my modest opinion. In his presence, I feel like a fraud for worrying about the possibility of being in hospital over Christmas.

At 11am, the cardiac consultant visits me to discuss my condition and the ECG results. There is nothing actually wrong with my heart, it is likely to simply be responding to the stress my body feels post-op and during recovery. My heart rate was unusually high and I did the right thing coming into hospital. But I am considered to be at a low risk of having cardiac problems, so he is happy to send me home. He suggests a prescription of beta blockers to slow down my heart beat if it becomes necessary. He also recommends that I return for an Echocardiogram as a precaution. This is a scan which provides a detailed view of the structures of the heart. I am euphoric at the thought of going home, despite my weariness.

The elderly gentleman gives me a thumbs up and congratulates me on being the quickest escapee this ward has seen for some time. His remaining quality of life will come mainly from the interaction he has with those around him that care enough to give him time and make him smile. I suggest he should form an escape committee and I'll be his secret liaison to the outside world. I'll meet him at the hospital boundary at midnight with a change of clothes, a map, a food parcel and a new passport. He enjoys the banter and I'm happy to have cheered him up a little and in my own small way.

I phone Andrea with the news of my escape. She loves Christmas and so is doubly delighted that I'm able to come home today. Also, we have been invited by Paul and Julie Bernardi to their home for Christmas dinner, something we have both been looking forward to.

Whilst I am waiting for Andrea to pick me up I tuck into a rather tasty turkey dinner served up from the dinner trolley.

I post an update on Winning:

> *Home for Xmas. Marvelous. After being monitored overnight I'm considered to be a low risk. I'm being discharged with beta blockers for use in the event of a repeat prolonged and uncomfortable episode. I also have an echocardiogram planned in to check out the old ticker.*
>
> *There was talk of a lengthy stay to continue monitoring but I prefer the pragmatism of feck off and come back if necessary. My beloved Andrea Oldham is on her way to collect me. Happy days.*

The Christmas cheer is aplenty in the many responses that my post receives. I'm just thrilled that I will be sharing in it from home, rather than via social media from a hospital bed:

> *Paul Bernardi – Good news – still on for Xmas dinner?*
> *Hans Keith Oldham – Absolutely. But I have to say I had a turkey dinner in hospital. The standard has been set…… expectations have been raised. Just saying!*
> *Paul Bernardi – I'll let the Mem Sahib know she's up against the might of the NHS*

It won't be the first time that Julie Bernardi has fed me so I know she won't have much competition! I have found hospital food to be quite good, but not that good.

When Andrea picks me up we find laughter in the fact that I have stayed in hospital for bowel, lung and now heart conditions. I seem to be moving through vital organs at a rapid pace and I agree with her that enough is enough now. It's my time to enjoy a healthy life, starting with our Christmas and New Year's Eve plans.

25 December 2018

Andrea and I spend Christmas morning with Luke, Max, Cyrus and Niall exchanging Christmas presents. It's so much fun and I'm thankful to be involved. At midday, the boys leave in order to spend the afternoon with their mum. Then, it's Christmas dinner at the Bernardis for Andrea and I. Julie Bernardis culinary expertise knocks the might of the NHS right out of the park. A few party games follow and it feels good to be celebrating amongst close friends.

27 December 2018

I'm still struggling to sleep through the night. Frequently waking and gasping for breath. I visit my GP who prescribes some very strong sleeping pills. I am advised to take one twenty minutes before bedtime, or two but only when necessary. Tonight I take one and it works. I get the first complete night's sleep that I've had for a couple of weeks.

31 December 2018

A time to reflect on the past year.

I am proud to call Kayleigh Smith my friend. Kayleigh, like many of my MADS friends, is hugely talented and has been supportive of both Andrea and I, particularly during my cancer treatment.

I read her year-end 'Obligatory 2018 round-up' on Facebook which opens with:

> *I don't immediately think much has happened this year, but when I look back I find quite a bit to be proud of.*

She's right, there is, and she goes on to share her 2018 achievements that she is most pleased about. She concludes her post by listing:

> *Some of the awesomeness that inspires me and keeps me going.*

Her mum, dad and brother are wonderful folk and rightly get called out. In amongst her friends she lists:

> *Fran Dykes for travelling difficult roads with bravery and style.*

> *Hans Keith Oldham for being the bionic man and never letting his own burdens stop him being there for his friends.*

I am genuinely choked, this time emotionally rather than physically. She is so right about Fran. As for me, I have been on the receiving end of so much care and attention during 2018 that I never saw myself as somebody who had the energy to give it to others. Thank you Kayleigh.

Our New Year's Eve is spent at the home of Mike and Sarah Rhodes and in the company of many other friends. Like the Bernardis, the Rhodes are fabulous hosts and the group that gather to see in the new year are intent on celebrating. We could not be in better company.

I've heard it said that true friendship multiplies the good in life and divides its evils. That can certainly be said of tonight's mob.

1 January 2019

Before embarking on the very early morning, five-minute drive home from Chez Rhodes, I take two sleeping pills. Yes, two! I'm intent on starting the new year with the best possible night's sleep.

When we get home, we bump into Rhys. I chat with him briefly on the stairs, go to bed and immediately fall into a state of unconsciousness.

At least, that's what I thought I had done. When I wake from my deep, ten-hour slumber, Andrea tells me what I had actually done. Apparently, after arriving home, I had sat in the lounge having a natter with Andrea and Rhys in what seemed to be the drug-induced state of a complete half-wit. I babbled incomprehensibly for ten minutes, stood up and declared I was off to bed. As I left the room I bumped into furniture, the door and the wall. I moved like a pin-ball bouncing off objects before finally disappearing through the lounge door and up the stairs.

All that without having drunk a drop of alcohol. Now that's what I call a good night!

2 January 2019

Inspired by Kayleigh Smith I post the following 2018 round up on Facebook:

The Spirit of Rooster

Don't normally do year end round ups but thought I'd give 2018 a shout out.

Started the year feeling I'd beaten cancer having rung the bell at The Christie. Got back into work with the Greater Manchester Police. Had an absolute riot playing Len in Rumours with a fabulous and talented cast. Changed jobs to work for DEFRA on their EU Exit strategy.

Married the love of my life Andrea Oldham . This was the absolute highlight of the year, she's my world and we're very happy together. Clonter Opera proved to be an excellent location and so many friends supported us in so many amazing ways. Who will ever forget the MADS show and the talented Luke Stevenson?

We gave up wedding presents and raised about £5k for surgical equipment at Macc Hospital and to donate the balance to Macmillan. I've been privileged to be cast as Ralph Nickleby in MADS next play, Nicholas Nickleby. I round the year off by knocking six bells out of cancer for the second time. I'm now cancer free again and recovering from the removal of my lower left lung.

On balance I rate 2018 as a fantastic year not just because of the incredible loving Mrs Oldham and the bursting pride I have for my 3 sons but we have seen humanity at its very best. Family members, friends, MADS, work colleagues, NHS employees have all been a constant reminder that the single dominant human emotion is love. Please cherish it throughout 2019.

Inspiration is contagious.

If you respond to feeling inspired then any action you take as a consequence, inspires others. So it seems from the many comments that my post attracts. I wonder how far inspiration will be passed forward and what good will come from it.

3 January 2019

Leading up to my surgery and during my recovery from it I've been busy learning my lines and developing my character for Ralph Nickleby. Tonight is my first rehearsal. I'm not yet at my best but my current state of health is improving daily. I am pleased to be registering almost 2,500 units on the Voldyne 5000, a steady enough progress.

7 January 2019

Three weeks after my lobectomy and I'm back at work. I'm working from home today and catching up on the many emails I've received during my absence. Although I'm not yet fully recovered, I feel strong enough for what I consider to be light duties. Today's measure on the Voldyne 5000 is just over 3,000 units. I consider that to be an accurate reflection of my continued recovery.

9 January 2019

I have an appointment with Chris Smart at Congleton War Memorial Hospital. My recovery is going well and my health is improving. My five year programme of cancer check-ups will now start again under his control. A colonoscopy, CT scan and MRI scan will be arranged in a couple of months' time.

Chris Gorman, The Trust Media and Communications Manager is invited to join us in the clinic. Andrea and I are delighted to hand over the headlight system purchased with the donations from our wedding guests. Chris Gorman takes some photos of the event and interviews both Andrea and I for the story behind the donation. It's a story that will appear in the Trust's online magazine.

When I describe the tortuous daily journey to The Christie for radiotherapy treatment, Chris is encouraged to confide in us.

There are plans to extend the services offered by The Christie's outreach unit at Macclesfield Hospital to include radiotherapy treatment. This will require a new building at a considerable cost. More details are yet to be announced but it is very likely that funding for this will require charitable donations.

Andrea and I decide that this would be a more personal and fitting cause for the extra funds we have raised. Chris agrees to pass on our details to the Community Fundraising Team at The Christie who will contact me at an appropriate time after the plans have been announced.

10 January 2019

There is an important work-related meeting scheduled in Birmingham that, after some thought, I have decided to attend. As long as I move slowly and don't exert myself, I don't get too breathless. I'll be fine. What's the worst that could happen?

The journey involves a twenty-minute drive to Crewe Train station, from there an hour-long train ride into Birmingham New St station, a fifteen-minute walk to the office building and finally a lift to carry me the ten floors to the office.

I arrive with enough time to get a cup of coffee and respond to a few emails before the meeting begins. Then it happens! A fire bell test is always taken seriously, but is often seen as an unwelcome disruption. This is doubly true in my case, because the exit to the building is via the ten flights of stairs and not the lifts.

So it's with a considerably reduced lung capacity, with one lung still in a state of disrepair, that I have to tackle the ten flights of stairs. I simply take my time to descend and find myself to be the last to evacuate the building, along with a man hobbling on crutches.

After the fire test is complete, many return to the office via the stairway. However, along with the man on crutches, I'm content to wait the twenty minutes it takes to return by a lift.

Disabilities come in various forms, some not as visible as others.

14 January 2019

I have four children, all of them busy adulting. I have taken each of them to Las Vegas for a week with a friend as a twenty-first birthday treat, all expenses paid to include various trips and shows.

My youngest son, Cyrus, is twenty-three on the 7 August. My cancer has so far prevented us taking him and his lovely girlfriend, Adele, on their long awaited Las Vegas trip. This year Andrea and I are determined to put this right.

Having agreed on dates for the holiday and after researching best deals, I book the trip for the four of us. We will be staying at the MGM Grand, located on the Las Vegas Strip, for a week in September. A number of tours have yet to be planned which will include various shows, quad-biking in the desert and a helicopter flight to the bottom of the Grand Canyon for a champagne picnic. It finally sets the record straight.

Also, Andrea and I haven't had a holiday for over three years. The Vegas trip feels as much a celebration of beating cancer as it does a belated twenty-first birthday celebration.

16 January 2019

Andrea and I drive to Wythenshawe Hospital for an appointment with Mr Krysiac, my lung surgeon. My shark bite scar has healed well. I tell him about my erratic breathing. He responds by simply reminding me that I have had half a lung removed. It may take up to a year to feel completely normal again.

Interestingly, as we move around the Hospital we keep bumping into William Roache who plays Ken Barlow in Coronation Street. We are not exactly star struck but can't help but notice that he is quite spritely for somebody who, at the age of 87, holds the Guinness World Record for the longest serving actor in a televised soap opera.

17 January 2019

Posting what I consider to be a final update on Winning, seems to be becoming, habit forming. This time it's just got to be *final*:

> *Recovery from the lung operation continues to go well. Every day is a noticeable improvement on the previous day. My "shark bite" scar has almost healed and my reconstructed left lung is filling with air. I'm not quite pain free but I'm getting there. We met with my bowel surgeon last week who is now back in control with regular health checks over the next 5 years. We met with my lung surgeon yesterday who seemed somewhat surprised and delighted at the pace of my recovery. I am cancer free and do not require any more treatment.*
>
> *As for life ... I returned to work last week, I'm cast in MADS next production as Ralph Nickleby in Dickens Nicholas Nickleby and we've booked a holiday to Las Vegas in Sept.*
>
> *When visiting Chris Smart (Bowel Surgeon) we presented him with the surgical equipment we purchased with the funds raised at our wedding (more news and photos of that to come). To give something back to the team that saved my life was a beautiful thing. We are eternally grateful to those who donated. It really mattered.*
>
> *My amazing wife Andrea Oldham continues to be unrelenting in her love and support for me. You, my family and friends, have all helped carry me along with your warmth, humour and love. Life is good xx*

It feels so good to post this comment as it draws a line under two years of brutal cancer treatment. It's a statement that says I've come through the worst of it and I'm well enough to get back into the life I had planned.

"You can be a victim of cancer, or a survivor of cancer. It's a mindset."
– Dave Pelzer

I couldn't be happier and the responses recognise it:
> *Paul Bernardi – So that you don't take too much on I think it's great that your*

next MADS role is a curmudgeonly old git – not too much of a stretch for you there! All the best buddy, always here for you (mainly to take the piss admittedly)

Suzanne Copeland – Only wish I could love this post twice. I echo Paul Bernardis musing on your next role. Big love xx

Pete Munro – 'Ave it!

Tim Roskell – Great stuff me ol mucka. I don't know what the hell you're made of but you should bottle it, label it and sell it! (but also acknowledging it's the Andrea Oldham back up care that might be difficult to bottle)

Paul Horan – that's all fantastic wonderful news, just to say now you have done all that can you sort this Brexit mess. Love you brother x

20 January 2019

The East Cheshire NHS Trust published the following online article two days ago. I rather enjoy the thought of giving something back to those responsible for saving my life. I'm proud enough to share the link to it on Facebook.

Congleton man Keith Oldham (right) with his wife Andrea and Macclesfield Hospital consultant colorectal and general surgeon Chris Smart.

Local cancer survivor's £2,000 gesture of thanks for life-saving care.

The Spirit of Rooster

A local cancer survivor has thanked a surgeon who operated on him by raising funds for a £2,000 cutting-edge piece of equipment. Congleton resident Keith Oldham raised the amount to purchase a top-of-the-range surgical headlight for Macclesfield Hospital, following successful treatment to remove a bowel tumour in May 2017.

Keith, aged 58, was so grateful to consultant colorectal and general surgeon Chris Smart that when he and his wife Andrea got married in September, they asked for donations to cover the cost of the equipment rather than gifts. Thanks to the generosity of the couple's family and friends, this raised much more than the £2,000 required for the headlight. Keith is now planning to donate the remainder of the funds raised to a local cancer-related cause.

Keith said: "Chris is an amazing guy and has a fantastic bedside manner. He's now one of my heroes and I'll never forget what he did for me, along with the staff at the MacMillan Centre and on Ward 1 at Macclesfield Hospital. "Throughout my experience with the NHS, the staff at every level have been wonderful, from the housekeeper who brought me a cup of tea in the morning after my surgery to the consultants who oversaw my care. I've experienced such wonderful humanity and I wanted to give a little back by fundraising for this additional piece of equipment which will benefit Chris and, in turn, his patients."

Mr Smart added: "I am extremely grateful to Keith for what he has done for us. Despite everything he has been through he has remained amazingly positive and continued to think about helping other people. "This very high quality piece of kit will help me and my colleagues to work even more effectively when performing surgery in areas like the pelvis, which can be very hard to see into."

Keith, who works as a freelance IT contractor, has been through several rounds of chemotherapy and radiotherapy and has also had additional tumours removed from his lungs in recent months. However, he has been determined to maintain a positive attitude to the situation throughout in order to help comfort his family and friends, including his three sons. He is also keen for his story to be shared as a positive example to other cancer patients.

If you would like to raise funds for East Cheshire NHS Trust's official charity ECHO, please go to www.echonhscharity.org for details of how you can get involved.

When Chris Gorman interviewed us for the article he mentioned charitable funding that will be required for the 'soon to be announced' development of a radiotherapy unit at Macclesfield Hospital. The unit will be an extension to the services currently offered by The Christie. Andrea and I agreed that this should be the recipient of the additional funds raised by our wedding justgiving.com cause. To be able to offer radiotherapy treatment to local patients without the tortuous drive to The Christie and back gets our resounding vote.

2 February 2019

Chloe is moving out today, as she and Rhys are moving in together. They are renting a house about a mile away. We have also found a new tenant who is moving in tonight; let's call him Bob. When we first met Bob he seemed decent enough and was looking for somewhere short term to stay until he could find somewhere near to his workplace to live.

I haven't invented Bob. He really did move in. I've just changed his name.

3 February 2019

I call in to the new home of Chloe and Rhys on my way to the Theatre to help move some of their things in. The original point of renting out our two spare rooms was to ease our cashflow whilst I was out of work.

However, the pleasure that our tenants Becky, Tom, Chloe and Rhys (not officially a tenant, but as good as one!) have brought into our lives has been a gift. To witness these youngsters starting to forge a life for themselves, with so much future promise and potential, reminds me how precious and short life is.

In the afternoon I help with the set build for *Nicholas Nickleby* at the Theatre. This involves a lot of heavy lifting, sawing, hammering and climbing. By the time I get home I can feel that my half-lung has had a thorough workout.

7 March 2019

Bob has found somewhere closer to his workplace and so has given notice that he will be moving out on the 9 March.

We have all grown irritated by Bob, so none of us are too displeased to see the back of him. It's likely that we would have asked him to leave had he not served his notice. Our irritation with him is born from his general lack of respect. He tends to mope around the house in misery and seems unable to engage in any sort of pleasantry. There's been no falling out with Bob, we are just glad to be seeing the back of him.

Andrea and I wake this morning and discuss him before we get up. Late last night after we had gone to bed we heard him bumping up and down the stairs staggering to and from the toilet. He'd obviously had too much beer to drink, despite his early departure to work this morning.

Andrea is the first one up. From the top of the stairs she can see a lump of mud on the step that leads into the lower ground floor bedroom area. Cursing, she walks down to pick it up. Curious with what she now holds in her hand she takes a closer look. A solid human turd, no less!

I emerge from the bedroom wondering what the screaming, cursing, running and flushing toilet were all about to be confronted by Andrea gagging as she furiously scrubbed her hands in the bathroom sink.

I am no stranger to human poo management and Andrea has cleaned up her fair share of dog poo. Words cannot describe the revulsion we both feel. Bob, you absolute disgrace! Also, you must have actually stepped over it on your way out this morning.

I can sympathise with incontinence, but clean it up for fuck's sake! My instinct is to empty his possessions in his room into bin bags, leave them at the bottom of the drive and change all the locks before he returns from work.

Once rational thinking has taken control of our emotions and murderous designs, we remind ourselves that he's leaving in two days and we still have his deposit.

9 March 2019

Bob moves out but his deposit does not. Thank goodness.

16 March 2019

It is the final night for *Nicholas Nickleby*. The play has received some positive audience feedback. My opening night's performance on Monday was poor by my own standards but, thankfully, significantly improved for the rest of the run.

I had breathing problems on occasion but adapted quite well. In summary, I am satisfied with my efforts particularly given that rehearsals ran in parallel with my recovery.

28 March 2019

A colonoscopy is a procedure I don't think I'll ever get used to but it's one I will have regularly over the next five years. I'm booked in to have one early tomorrow morning.

I manage to drink all the moviprep and suffer the consequences of emptying my bowel. The whole process takes over two hours and by the end of it I feel empty. There cannot possibly be anything left inside me. I go to bed feeling exhausted by the two-hour exertion.

I'm instructed to take another dose of moviprep before tomorrow morning's colonoscopy. To do so would mean getting up at 5am. I cannot believe it's a worthwhile exercise. I'm surely already empty and clean inside. Foolishly, I decide not to bother.

29 March 2019

I don't have very fond memories of the last colonoscopy I had but this morning's procedure seems so much worse. I realise, to my shame, that it's my own fault.

The additional discomfort is entirely due to the fact that I have not emptied my bowel properly. Some brown moviprep gravy is painfully discharged during the colonoscopy, forcing itself round the colonoscope inserted into my anus. This has also made Chris Smart's job of spotting any anomalies in my bowel more difficult. He does his best to navigate through the obstructions which should not be there and which cloud the picture being presented on the monitor.

I can only apologise. I had one thing to do, ONE thing!

On his way out of my colon, he does spot a polyp. This is a projecting growth of tissue from my bowel wall. It is quite normal to have a polyp or two, any more than half a dozen would be a concern. Some polyps can become cancerous.

Chris Smart is not concerned as the polyp is isolated but decides to take a biopsy for analysis to be on the safe side. He takes care to repeat that he is not concerned by the appearance of a single polyp and it's not something I should worry about.

After the procedure is complete, I return to the changing area where I am able to thoroughly clean myself and get dressed. I notice that my record sheet states 'inadequate' under the heading *bowel preparation*. This is disrespectful and inexcusable. I have failed to play my part in a routine procedure. I must do better in future.

9 April 2019

This morning's medical treat is a CT Scan with contrast. The contrast is injected into me via the cannula put into the back of my hand. After the procedure, I am reminded to drink plenty of water to help flush the contrast out of my system.

I have a busy afternoon and I am on front of house duty at MADS Theatre in the evening. It is here that I realise that I have failed to adequately hydrate. An irritating rash appears on my legs and on part of my stomach. I assume that it is a reaction to the contrast still in my system. I drink four pints of water, one immediately after the other. When I get home I take an antihistamine tablet.

What happened to the commitment: 'I must do better in future?'

24 April 2019

The Brexit can has been kicked further down the road by the dysfunctional UK politicians mandated to deliver it.

A new EU Exit date has been agreed; anytime up to the end of October this year. As a consequence, the new Defra EU Exit services under development, with my support, are to be moth-balled. My role is, therefore, no longer required. Sadly, my contract is immediately terminated.

Jackie Nock is genuinely sorry to let me go. I hope the opportunity to return to Defra one day will arise as I've enjoyed working for this large, essential, supportive and ethical Government Department.

14 May 2019

Chris Gorman calls me and asks if I would be willing to attend the Trust AGM and talk about my cancer treatment experiences. Chris Smart will be presenting one of his initiatives, Colorectal Pathways. A patient testimony would work well with his material. This represents another opportunity to give something back, so I readily agree. The AGM is on the 4 July.

17 May 2019

I am beginning to wonder about my planned MRI Scan when I receive a call from Macclesfield Hospital requesting I attend for one at 1pm next Monday. It will complete all the procedures required for my cancer check-up.

19 May 2019

It is exactly two years to the day that I had my bowel surgery. But more importantly today is the Simplyhealth Great Manchester 10k run. Three of my Theatre friends Rob, Stuart and Rachel are taking part. A small group of us from MADS have planned to travel with them by train into Manchester to watch them.

Each of the three runners are raising money to donate to their chosen charity. Rob Copeland is raising money for Cancer Research and is running with the names of *Maureen* (his gorgeous mother-in-law), *Fran* (Theatre friend and his occasional pretend wife) and *Keith* (me) on his back. Rob has prepared well and although his thoughts are on the race he will also be mindful of those of us who have fought and survived cancer.

I will be watching them run, happily cheering from the side-lines. Non-attendance is not an option for me. Rob was the first person to befriend me at MADS. He helped me through my early years as an amateur actor and we have remained good friends since. Stuart and Rachel have been supportive of me throughout my treatment and are amongst the best friends I have at MADS. Rachel, a hugely talented actress, played the part of Dawn, the mother of Roster's son, in *Jerusalem*. Stuart is quick-witted, genial, intelligent and exceptionally articulate. Sharing an early manuscript of this book with him for his feedback was a shrewd and gratifying move.

As we have arranged to catch a train into Manchester I have to manage the risk of incontinence. I have a light and early breakfast which settles well. Eating or drinking any more may disturb the limitations of my bowel and cause the urgent and painful need to poo. I find thirst and hunger so much easier to cope with than incontinence, especially in crowded areas, with infrequent toilets.

The event is extremely well-organised and attended. Tens of thousands of runners take part, the majority doing it for charity. Cancer is the dominant charity cause. The Christie, Cancer Research and the Dianne Oxberry Cancer Trust are all well-supported. Manchester is making the statement that cancer has many enemies.

Rob, Stuart and Rachel all charge round the course to the best of their ability and there is a collective sense of pride amongst us for their individual performances. These three giants could have jumped Stonehenge in a single bound today.

Rob, Rachel and Stuart – each one a Giant!
Simplyhealth Great Manchester 10k run

20 May 2019

I arrive at Macclesfield Hospital for my 1pm MRI scan with contrast. One of the technicians asks me lots of questions and fills out a form. The final question on the form is:

'Have you ever had a reaction to the contrast?'

I tell him about the rash I got after my CT scan last month. This is unusual so I get questioned about this several times by different members of staff. There's even a referral to a consultant.

The conclusion is that I'm having a different contrast today and, as long as I drink plenty of water after the procedure, I should be fine. I'm confident that I will be.

On my way out I bump into Chris Smart quite by accident. He's dressed in his scrubs so I sense it's a busy day for him. Nonetheless, he walks towards me with a smile and shakes my hand. He confesses that the CT scan had identified small dots of something in my liver. Upon seeing this, another consultant had arranged the MRI scan which should provide additional detail about what these dots are.

It's nothing to worry about at this stage and once he has the MRI scan results he'll call me in for a chat. I trust Chris with his professional skill, his honesty and his humanity. If he tells me it's nothing to worry about then I'm very willing to take that at face value. Although a seed of doubt has been planted, it's within my control not to let it germinate and grow.

Today's appointment is one of the few that Andrea has not been able to attend with me. She made me promise to phone her on the way home. Telling her about the chat with Chris Smart is not easy, but I try to convey it in the same way that Chris told me. Had she been with me she would certainly have asked Chris more questions than I did. I felt that it was best to save the questions for when all the results have been analysed.

When I arrive home, I drink several pints of water over the course of the afternoon to help flush the contrast out of my system.

I'm not making that mistake again.

24 May 2019

I receive a phone call from Angela Jeff, one of the colorectal nurses working with Chris Smart. She has the results of the MRI scan. I feel nervous because I know something of concern is in my liver that needs to be explained. Angela is well aware that I must be worried so she doesn't move immediately to explaining what has been identified. Instead choosing to tell me that Chris Smart has asked her to let me know the results and that there is nothing wrong with me. That re-assurance has come first. I am now ready to hear what the fuss was about.

When a collection of blood vessels form a lump, it's called a haemangioma. It's quite common for benign haemangioma to occur in the liver. They are quite harmless and do not need treatment. They are certainly not cancerous. I have two small haemangioma in my liver, it's nothing to worry about.

Being diagnosed with cancer and then being treated for it has many ups and downs, a rollercoaster of emotions. One week the results can be positive, the next week life threatening. I have learnt that it's important to remain emotionally stable, to respond equally stoically to both good and bad news.

"To meet with triumph and disaster and treat those two imposters just the same."

– If
Rudyard Kipling

25 May 2019

I post an update on Winning:

> Last Monday my surgeon informed me that the CT scan I'd had a couple of weeks ago identified two small lumps in my liver. Yesterday I was informed that the lumps were no more than haemangioma – blood vessels forming into lumps and nothing to worry about. Andrea and I met with triumph and disaster and treated those two imposters just the same. I remain cancer free. Next check-up

in 6 months time.

The teasing drama of my update is not lost on some:

> *Fran Dykes – Hells teeth I held my breath whilst reading this ... Hurrah for no stupid cancer cells*
> *Hans Keith Oldham – Fran Dykes I held my breath for 4 days. Not easy with half a lung!*
> *Simon Waring – You know how to put us through an emotional rollercoaster ride in just a few sentences my friend. Oh and "that" poem is very special to me and is a great example to live by.*
> *Suzanne Copeland – Your liver has evidently coagulated due to lack of alcohol! Status started as ☹ and ended as ☺ xx*
> *David Wilkinson – Mr Wilko heard to shout "Oh fuck" quickly followed by "thank fuck"! Come on you giants xx*

A magnificent 'Spirit of Rooster' shout from Mr Wilko, the professor, award winning actor and fine narrator!

12 June 2019

Facebook reminds me that today is Jeff Rosser's birthday. I'm unable to ignore it and post a message wishing him happiness wherever his soul happens to be.

11
CAREGIVING

Breast cancer is the most common type of cancer in the UK. About one in eight women are diagnosed with breast cancer in their lifetime. If it's detected and treated in the early stages there is an excellent chance of a full recovery. Therefore, it's vital that women regularly check their breasts for any changes. Anything unusual should be immediately examined by a GP and, if necessary, referred to the NHS experts.

The first noticeable symptom is usually a lump. Most lumps aren't cancerous but should be examined to be certain. Male breast cancer is very rare. Less than 1% of all breast cancer cases develop in men.

"Caregiving often calls us to lean into love we didn't know possible"
– *The Inspired Caregiver*
Tia Walker

29 June 2019

Today Andrea tearfully informs me of a small, painless lump she has found in her left breast whilst in the shower. The exposure she has had to cancer, and its shameful destruction, through her care for me, is a double-edged sword.

Most importantly, it has motivated her to check herself regularly and act immediately if anything suspicious is found. But she has witnessed my suffering, and the slow painful death of others, at close quarters. Therefore, the uncertainty of a small lump results in a self-diagnosis derived from the suffering of others, rather than the simple facts of her own condition. It's frightening.

Whilst it's natural for us to fear the worst, because we have seen and felt the worst, Andrea resolves to contact her GP on Monday for an appointment. We settle on the thought that it's probably nothing to be alarmed about, fatty tissue or a cyst, but needs to be examined by professionals, just in case.

1 July 2019

Andrea phones her GP surgery and attends an appointment this afternoon. The GP acknowledges the lump, but is unable to offer a clear diagnosis. To be safe Andrea will be referred to the breast screening clinic at Macclesfield hospital. She will be contacted by phone later this week to arrange an appointment.

3 July 2019

The breast screening clinic finally calls Andrea with an appointment for the 19 July. It feels like a tortuously long time to wait, but sadly there are many referrals, causing a two-week wait for screening.

Maintaining a positive outlook during the next two weeks is within our control. It's not going to be easy though, as Andrea finds the uncertainty and doubt very unsettling. Cancer has already attempted to make an impact by inflicting an emotional, if not a physical, blow.

4 July 2019

Andrea and I attend the East Cheshire Trust AGM at Macclesfield Hospital. We are met by Chris Gorman outside New Alderley House. He takes us to the Board Room where the AGM is being held. On the ground floor of this building is the breast screening clinic. It's an uncomfortable reminder of Andrea's forthcoming appointment.

Whilst we stand outside the board room waiting for it to be vacated, we meet Mel, the senior ward sister for surgical ward 1. This is the ward I was admitted to following my bowel surgery. Chris informs me that Mel was recently recognised by the Trust for her compassion, one of the six NHS cultural C's. It's easy to see why. Mel is relaxed, happy and friendly. She is also here to co-present with Chris Smart, so she knows all about colorectal pathways.

Whilst chatting to Mel I decide that, in sharing my cancer treatment experience, I will talk about the importance of compassion during and after treatment. It's clearly an important aspect of the care that the NHS provides, as it has become something they celebrate. I am also delighted to learn that Michael, who cared for me so well during my stay on ward 1, is still enjoying his newfound career.

The PowerPoint material used during the introduction to the AGM contains the dashboard image of our justgiving.com page. It's a picture of the End of Treatment Bell coupled with a headline of the cause. There's also a reference to the surgical equipment that has already been donated and the online article published by Chris Gorman.

I start my presentation by flattering Chris Smart for his surgical skill and bedside manner, remarking that his commitment as a human being always comes before his commitment as a surgeon.

I then tackle my cancer treatment experience in chronological order from initial diagnosis to current day, pausing to highlight specific observations. I conclude with an anecdote about the rather stern but efficient senior nurse who had whispered so lovingly in Rob Gregory's ear the day before his illness was confirmed as terminal. I have to confess that I stumble emotionally at the memory of it, but this only serves to provide more dignity and pathos in the telling. If there is a better example of compassion in the NHS, I'd like to hear it.

My audience chuckle and silently sob into handkerchiefs in all the right places. I like to think that I make them feel proud to be part of the extraordinary organisation that is the NHS. Andrea and I chat briefly with the two Chris' as we leave and they both express the importance, to the Trust, of listening and reacting to patient feedback.

19 July 2019

Over the last two weeks, Andrea and I have constantly reminded ourselves that whatever the lump in her breast is, it feels small and she found it very early. However, she has a deep-rooted fear of needles which has caused her to become very anxious about today's appointment at the breast screening clinic.

In 1997, the mental health community officially recognised needle phobia in the *Diagnostic and Statistical Manual of Mental Disorders*. Now mental health experts estimate that needle phobia, sometimes called belonephobia, may affect up to 10% of the population. For most, like Andrea, it results from a bad experience in their formative years. Therefore, the best way to avoid belonephobia is for parents to correctly deal with the fear the first time they notice it in their children.

Like most irrational fears, the longer you have it the harder it is to overcome it. All humans are born knowing how to be afraid. It's a necessary survival mechanism. However, irrational fears are those that may not have any real basis in reality but still scare you anyway. Working out how to deal with such phobias has been challenging neuroscientists for decades.

We arrive at New Alderley House ten minutes before the appointment.

Andrea in fear of the treatment and me feeling like a hopeless bystander. I'm not used to being the patient's carer in our relationship. I really don't like seeing Andrea struggle, frightened of the treatment and worried about the outcome.

After a short wait in the general waiting area we are taken to the clinic waiting room. First Andrea has an ultrasound scan and a mammogram (a breast x-ray).

Once analysed, the results of these tests can be categorised in any one of five ways:-

1. Normal breast tissue
2. Benign lump (not cancer)
3. Abnormal or uncertain but probably benign
4. Suspicious and possibly cancer
5. Cancer

We are led into the doctors' surgery hoping to be told the lump is nothing to worry about, maybe a category two. After weeks of uncertainty, of trying to remain positive, the first fork in the road is ahead. The doctor will either direct us home with nothing to worry about, or *cancer*. It's a tense moment as we sit holding hands.

The various categories are explained to us. Andrea's condition is assessed as a category four. My head spins, thoughts racing on, searching for an answer, trying to evaluate what that means for Andrea. She remains silent and motionless. Tears trickle down her cheeks.

Andrea and I embrace, holding on to each other tightly. It's our worst fear. Cancer has blighted our lives again, but this time there's a seismic shift in roles, Andrea is now the victim and I am the carer. My instinct is to wish I could take the bullet instead. Andrea's instinct is to feel terror; she knows cancer too well.

The doctor falls silent whilst we come to terms with the inconclusive diagnosis. She continues only when we have regained enough emotional strength to start asking questions.

The lump measures 5mm x 7mm. Anything smaller than 15mm is considered small and, therefore, this is tiny. However, the tests have revealed enough to suspect it to be cancerous but the only way to be certain is to take a biopsy of the lump. This procedure can be performed immediately but the results will take another week to obtain before they can be discussed.

A breast biopsy is a surgical test that removes tissue or sometimes fluid from the suspicious area. Cells are removed by way of a large needle, following a local anesthetic. They are then examined under a microscope and further tested to check for the presence of cancerous tissue. A biopsy is the only diagnostic procedure that can conclusively determine if the suspicious area is cancerous.

The diagnostic investigation has now moved in a direction that plays to Andrea's belonephobia. It is a fear that she is forced to confront immediately. We are taken to the treatment room where Andrea is asked to remove her upper clothing and lie down on a treatment bed. She has always said that if her life depended on having an injection, she would not allow fear to be an impediment, that somehow she would face her fear for the greater good. This theory is about to be severely tested.

The doctor explains that the procedure will first require the injection of a local anesthetic to numb the pain in her left breast. After a short wait, the biopsy needle will be inserted into the lump and a sample removed. This will be repeated four times. The doctor will use an ultrasound image to guide the biopsy needle into the lump.

I can see the horror and fear etched into Andrea's face as she contemplates the pin cushion that her left breast is about to become. In my role as carer, I have to quickly work out what Andrea needs from me in support. It doesn't take long. She grits her teeth, grips my hand, closes her eyes and turns her head away from the doctor, towards me. All thoughts of the procedure are banished from her mind as she talks rapidly about anything that comes to mind; holiday to Las Vegas, dog walking, Mia.

My job is to keep that conversation going, provide the distraction she craves and hold tightly onto her hand.

I once witnessed Andrea attempting to give a blood sample, a simple painless procedure that lasts a few seconds. She screamed, hyperventilated, questioned every movement and eventually refused to give any blood. Had she persisted she may well have fainted.

Not so today.

I watch the doctor swab her breast, inject it with a local anesthetic and take four biopsy samples, one after the other. The biopsy needle is as large as a small knitting needle. With an ultrasound probe in one hand the doctor uses the image on the monitor to guide the needle into the lump, to then remove a sample.

Once four samples have been taken, a small titanium marker is inserted. The lump has been reduced to almost nothing in size such that the site has to be tagged.

The response from Andrea throughout the procedure is nothing short of miraculous. She remains calm, chatty, humorous and distracted. She completely misses the doctor declaring that he has finished and continues chuckling at a funny story she is telling. Eventually I manage to cut in:-

"It's all over sweetheart, finished."

"What?" Opening her eyes. "Finished? Really? But I didn't feel anything."

"Exactly." Declares the doctor knowingly. "Well done, I could see you were frightened. You've been very brave, nice and relaxed."

Before we leave the clinic an appointment is made for the following Friday so that the results of the biopsy can be discussed with us. Waiting for, potentially, life-changing results understandably creates uncertainty and doubt. Fear often follows.

Today I helplessly watched my wife face her worst fear with courage and dignity. Okay, not quite Amelia Earhart, Anne Frank or Rosa Parks but, knowing the extent of her fear, I was so very impressed by what I saw. I am hugely proud of her. Whatever cancer throws at her, this little lady has got the courage and spirit to handle it.

I have come to the conclusion that watching your loved one suffer from cancer and its treatment is far more punishing than I had imagined. You stay close, but feel inadequate. At a loss, constantly trying to find ways to ease the burden of the victim. It's the simple things that count; the hand holding, the smile, the hugs. It takes understanding, patience and a selfless courage to provide the right re-assurance precisely when it's needed.

It is something that Andrea has been doing consistently well for me over the last couple of years. I am determined to ensure she receives the very same quality of caregiving from me.

"I learned that courage was not the absence of fear but the triumph over it. The brave man is not he who does not feel afraid, but he who conquers that fear."

– Nelson Mandela

22 July 2019

Tonight there is a MADS audition for a production of *Nell Gwynn* which runs from 2 December to 7 December. The audition is unusually early for a MADS play. However, this production contains a good deal of singing and dancing, both ensemble and individual pieces. This is a slight departure for MADS, so casting the play earlier than normal will allow a longer rehearsal period to work on the difficult musical numbers.

I audition for two roles, those of King Charles II and Thomas Killigrew. The audition is rightly challenging and I feel fortunate to be cast in the role of Killigrew, a historical figure born in 1612 and a playhouse manager believed to have introduced Miss Gwynn to his stage. At least that is what is told in Jessica Swale's play.

It's a large-cast play which includes my son, Luke, and many other talented MADS friends. The experienced and very talented Fran Dykes is directing it. I am delighted.

26 July 2019

A week has passed since Andrea's biopsy and her category 4 diagnosis. During that time, we have resigned ourselves to the thought of cancer and a lumpectomy. Nonetheless, it is still a shock to hear the surgeon confirm that the lump is indeed cancerous.

There is, however, a slight twist. The unexpected often arises when being treated for cancer. Andrea has a lymph node just inside her left breast near the site of the lump. If the cancer has traveled the lymph node will be infected. There is no evidence to suggest it is but the doctor wants to discount that possibility. This means another biopsy, this time on the lymph node.

Fear grips Andrea once again.

Despite feeling quite positive on arrival at the breast screening clinic, the confirmation of cancer combined with the prospect of suffering another biopsy needle is just too much. I watch my wife stiffen, eyes widen and quietly sob as she faces the doctor, listening to his prognosis. Then she turns to me. I smile back at her and hold her hands ready to offer strong words of encouragement.

"No!"

She is abrupt, firm and assertive.

"It's not going to do this to me. I'll be ready, doctor."

Her hands are raised as if to regain control. She has bounced back with impressive speed and I could not be more proud.

"I came here expecting the lump to be cancerous. I'm still scared of needles, but I coped with the biopsy I had last week. I can do this."

Arrangements are made to return to the breast screening clinic next Friday to biopsy the lymph node. Once the results are known a treatment plan can be discussed.

30 July 2018

Claire Ferguson calls from The Christie Charitable Fund office situated in The Christie Hospital. She is a senior communities fund raising manager and we discuss the funds Andrea and I have raised and the donation we wish to make to The Christie at Macclesfield Project.

Arrangements are made for us to visit The Christie this coming Friday for a photographed cheque presentation. Claire will be on hand to meet us and discuss any questions we may have.

2 August 2019

We haven't visited The Christie since I rang the End of Treatment Bell. Not only is the drive there a stark reminder of that time, but it is also a nod to the radiotherapy treatment that Andrea may require.

We meet Claire Ferguson at the charity centre on the ground floor just inside the main entrance. She greets us both with warmth and a welcoming smile. After I complete a bank transfer for £2,760 the display cheque is written and photographs are taken.

Claire has done her research and knows my cancer story well. She is genuinely saddened to hear Andrea's diagnosis and acknowledges that the Christie at Macclesfield Project will not deliver in time for Andrea's possible radiotherapy. Nonetheless, we leave feeling proud at having raised money that many others will benefit from.

Donation to The Christie at Macclesfield Project.
With Claire Ferguson

A *catharsis* is an emotional discharge through which one can achieve a state of moral renewal or achieve a state of liberation from anxiety. This is what donating money to such a great cancer cause feels like to us both. The kindness of so many good people stands behind this donation. It's a huge defiant statement against cancer and a springboard into a life less troubled.

To celebrate our new found catharsis, we book a family holiday to the Greek Island of Skiathos (*Mamma Mia* was filmed there) in July 2020. It'll be my sixtieth birthday and a wonderful time to share with my wife, sons, their girlfriends and any of our friends who wish to join us. To escape the damp British summer and enjoy the warm sun in beautiful, idyllic surroundings will be just perfect.

6 August 2019

At the first rehearsal for *Nell Gwynn,* it dawns on me that it's going to take a lot of singing and dancing hard work to reach the standards expected by MADS. Particularly as I don't quite have the voice of an angel. We are encouraged to use whatever meagre musical talent we have, with gusto.

9 August 2019

Andrea is steeling herself against her fear of needles as we make our way to Macclesfield Hospital for her lymph node biopsy. The uncertainty of her prognosis is an additional burden. Recognising that laughter is an antidote to stress we chat, giggle and chuckle for the twenty minute drive.

In the surgery we are met by a different doctor. He is very aware of Andrea's fear of needles and discusses it with her, taking time to carefully explain the procedure. He is extraordinarily empathetic and considerate.

Andrea lies on her back and turns to look away from the two local anesthetic injections she is given. Her coping mechanism is distraction. Her hand firmly grips mine as she talks about dogs, horses, holidays and anything that comes to mind.

Two biopsy samples are taken. Andrea grimaces a couple of times as the doctor watches the monitor to guide the end of the needle into the lymph node. The sudden but brief, sharp pain Andrea feels is contrary to her previous biopsy experience. It is a painful reminder of her fear. Her grip tightens and her conversation becomes more urgent and energetic. She is afraid but in control. This lady is determined to win.

The lymph node is in a less fleshy part of Andrea's left breast, toward her armpit. This probably accounts for the discomfort during the procedure and the bruising that it causes.

"I'm so sorry I'm such a hopeless wimp. You must just want to knock some sense into me, to keep me still and relaxed," repents Andrea, as she gets dressed.

"Not at all," replies the doctor. "You were very brave. Also, the hospital discourages slapping patients these days. It's considered bad form."

The antidote of humour in the face of adversity is a beautiful thing.

10 August 2019

Andrea's painful bruise contains most of the colours of a rainbow. That doesn't stop Stanley from using it as a launch pad to jump for his favourite ball.

Ouch!

16 August 2019

It's a wet and miserable day as we make our way to the hospital for Andrea's lymph node biopsy result. The weather dampens our mood a little but not our determination to face what lies ahead.

We are met by Andrea's surgeon, Mr Jalal Kokan. It doesn't surprise me that he understands her anxiety as he carefully explains his findings. The lymph node wasn't a lymph node after all but fatty breast tissue. There is no evidence of cancerous tissue in the biopsy. Mr Kokan goes on to explain that he has reviewed all the scans taken so far and has discovered a shadowy area in need of further investigation.

Andrea is tearful; Mr Kokan pauses. Now more concerned about how she is feeling rather than delivering diagnostic information. This man knows how to manage human frailty. His empathy is as impressive as we have come to expect from the NHS.

He falls silent, allowing Andrea to question and express her fear. Only when she is ready does he proceed, generous in giving her the time she needs to assimilate his analysis. It's important to him that not only does she understand what he is telling her, but that she also comes to terms with it.

He clarifies that his investigation is making good progress but that he wants to take a closer look at the shadowy area in order to discount it; to be more certain about the prognosis. To do this he is proposing a digital breast tomosynthesis (DBT).

This type of scan will provide the higher resolution result in 3D that is required and can be undertaken immediately. Compression is used to improve the image quality so there is some discomfort.

Andrea has regained her composure and is led into the treatment room. I return to the waiting room where Andrea joins me in a short while after her DBT. We wait here for two hours.

It's the waiting that feeds uncertainty and heightens anxiety.

Eventually we are called into Mr Kokan's surgery. Moments later he walks purposefully into the room and, before sitting down, faces Andrea and immediately says:

"It's good news. We now know you only have one problem, the small lump in your left breast. There is nothing else to worry about."

The relief from the agonising tension that his words bring is palpable. He is very aware of the need to confirm this outcome definitively and before anything else. Andrea's relief causes her to immediately burst into tears and tremble. It's what we both wanted to hear when we first walked into the clinic with such determination this morning.

But cancer enjoys the drama and torture of uncertainty, the unforeseen, the unexpected. Particularly anything with new and grisly complexities. It takes courage, fortitude, bounce and the spirit of Rooster to face cancer's twisted pleasures and come out on top, to win.

Andrea and I hug.

It's in moments like this that any caregiver should provide essential emotional support. Simple acts of calm re-assurance, to be the giant that Andrea needs.

With a more certain diagnosis Mr Kokan discusses the lumpectomy for which the date of the 16 September is agreed. Andrea has a number of horse riding holidays and our planned trip to Las Vegas, all of which have to be considered. She will be admitted as a day case for the operation, two days after our return from Las Vegas.

Surgery will involve a left ultrasound, wire-guided, local excision and sentinel biopsy under general anaesthesia. All the associated risks are discussed and although they generate some nervousness we leave the hospital with the feeling of having had a positive outcome today.

21 August 2019

Wedding gift for fund from kind duo.

This is the headline that appears in the Macclesfield Express today under other news about The Christie appeal. Our story, including the display cheque photograph, was provided by The Christie Charity Centre.

A couple of minor facts are inaccurate, but it's mostly well written. It's a good story, one amongst many, for the tenacious project team and it's fund raising ambitions.

22 August 2019

The *Nell Gwynn* cast meet at the Theatre for a read-through. The singing and dancing is taking shape, but rehearsals now begin for the rest of the play.

24 August 2019

Andrea leaves for a long weekend of horse riding in Wales with her like-minded friends. Nothing will slow this lady down. She's going to do the thing in life that she most loves doing; riding Mia.

26 August 2019

It's a warm, sunny day. Tom has served notice that after eighteen months living with us, he is moving out next weekend. Colin and Elle have arrived to help him move his belongings to his new home. It's about a mile away and his new accommodation gives him more personal living space and is also cheaper.

Before he drives off in his car he joins me in my office for a brief chat and a man-hug. He's become like an extended family member to us. We'll miss him.

It is during a little clear out of my own that I come across my old and trusted golf clubs. They've been stored under the stairs for the last five years, sad, lonely and untouched.

I've often thought about returning to the sport that I thoroughly enjoyed playing for so many years. Not only would it help improve my fitness but I simply miss playing it. I'm just not sure if I'm physically ready to start swinging a golf club again. My scar may restrict upper body movement, my muscle memory has faded, breathing can be difficult and I sound like I'm making excuses.

Impulsively, I throw on a golf shirt, put my clubs in the car and drive to a local nine hole golf club at Cranage. It has a driving range, perfect for practicing my swing.

I last wore the golf shirt five years ago and it feels looser on my slimmer frame than I remember. On arriving at the club house I buy one-hundred range balls. I'm nervously anticipating my scar to be tight, my muscle memory to be a shadow of what it used to be and my half lung to cause occasional breathing difficulties.

It has been said that golf is a good walk spoiled. Not so for me today. I don't play to the standard of Rory McIlroy, but then I didn't expect to. Only in my wildest dreams would I play that well. However, I do manage to swing as well as I used to and strike the ball cleanly into the area of the range I am aiming at.

I'm comfortable with all my clubs, even the fairway iron that I always found difficult. It feels like I never stopped playing and I leave the driving range wondering who will be up for a leisurely nine holes with me now that I have rediscovered my golf mojo.

My left shoulder blade feels a little sore and my breathing did get heavy enough for me to sweat more than normal, causing me to pause occasionally for a rest. However, I can improve on this lack of fitness. It's a challenge I am more than happy to meet.

During a particularly frustrating round of golf many years ago my buddy once pointed at me and said:

"Keith you know what your problem is don't you?"

"No, what?" Expecting advice on grip or swing.

"Your problem is that you've got a lump of shite on the end of your club."

Curious, I held up the driver I was holding and closely inspected the club face for any attached, unwelcome and interfering detritus.

"No, the other end," cackled my buddy, clearly playing mind-games, and hoping to unsettle me, immediately before I was due to play off the tee.

27 August 2019

On the 6 September, Andrea and I plan to travel to Las Vegas with Cyrus and his girlfriend, Adele. It's our twenty-first birthday present to the, now twenty-three year old, Cyrus. It's also the first holiday abroad that we've have had in over three years. The trip, booked in January, has been postponed until now thanks to cancer.

I've attempted to arrange travel insurance a number of times. However, when I have answered the questions about health and discussed our cancer treatments I was told that coverage is either not available or comes at the cost of thousands of pounds. The cheapest quote I've obtained thus far has been £1,250.

I have come to the conclusion that the best option is for Andrea and I to travel uninsured. I decide on one last attempt and phone insurewith.com, a cancer specialist insurance company recommended by a long suffering cancer victim friend.

The insurance agent guides me through an impressive series of health questions to make sure that they fully understand the cancer conditions of us both. Some of these questions are scripted, but others are not, especially when seeking to explore, in greater detail, the answers I have already given. This recognises the fact that cancer has many variables that cannot all be understood by a standard set of questions.

Having carefully recorded all my responses the agent puts me on hold whilst he refers my request for a travel insurance quote to a medical specialist.

After a five minute wait I am offered a more manageable quote of £231.45, which fully covers all four travelers without any health restrictions. I estimate this to be twice the cost for any traveler without a cancer treatment history. I accept the quote and purchase the insurance cover, happy in the knowledge that I'm unlikely to find cheaper cover elsewhere.

Cancer can hit victims hard, financially. Not only can treatment restrict one's earning potential but lifestyle costs, like travel insurance, can increase.

Thankfully, there are market specialists, like insurewith.com, who understand the true nature of cancer and can customize products, and their costs, to individual cancer victims.

28 August 2019

An unexpected letter arrives from The Christie Community Fundraising team thanking us for our donation of £2,760, in lieu of wedding gifts. A certificate of special thanks is enclosed.

The letter confirms that our donation will be directed to the much-needed Christie at Macclesfield Fund.

Furthermore, the new centre will transform cancer care in East Cheshire, bringing essential cancer services together into one purpose-built unit. It will deliver local specialist access to radiotherapy, chemotherapy, holistic support, information services, outpatient care and palliative care to local cancer victims.

Andrea and I are both really quite pleased with ourselves.

The certificate is an unexpected and respectful touch. We are both still so overwhelmed by the generosity of those who put their hands in their pockets for the cause we are supporting.

> **Certificate of special thanks to**
> **Keith and Andrea Oldham**
> for raising a wonderful
> **£2,760.00**
> in support of The Christie
>
> Signed: ....
> Date: 22nd August 2019

Special thanks from The Christie

This morning I have one of my scheduled check-ups with Chris Smart at Congleton War Memorial Hospital.

Chris isn't available, so we are met by one of his registrars. He reviews my notes and we agree on key treatment dates. As expected scans, blood tests and a colonoscopy will all be arranged in the coming weeks.

I am in the best possible health and have every reason to be optimistic about the future. Nonetheless, my extraordinary NHS team is regularly monitoring my progress very closely.

They will continue to do this for the next five years. I could not be in better hands. It's a firm foundation from which to continue my recovery with confidence.

29 August 2019

A serious fault has occurred with the emission system on Andrea's car. Without her car, she is unable to run her business or tow her horse box. We take her car to the mainline dealer in Macclesfield and discuss the problem with the senior engineer. He's a pleasant young man and agrees to investigate the problem and provide a quote to correct it. It may take a few days to put right, so Andrea will use my car in the meantime.

The engineer phones Andrea later in the day to explain his findings and, in a very matter-of-fact manner, quotes a total of £2,500 for the job. This is far more than either of us expected and too much for Andrea to deal with. It's a shock and she immediately bursts into tears and fires back a garbled response.

"Oh no! I need my car for my business. How much? That's our holiday fund. We haven't had a holiday for three years. I've just been diagnosed with breast cancer. It's so unfair. I just can't cope."

To his credit the engineer asks if she is alright. The job for the car has suddenly become less important to him. The tears of this lady, pouring out her heart about her cancer diagnosis, has moved him.

Without hesitation he reduces the quote to £2,000, offering a further reduction if he can source discounted parts. It's the maximum he can knock off the quote and it's a significant sum. It's the only act of kindness he can offer on the phone.

I wonder if he too has been touched in some way by this terrible disease. His immediate and unexpected kindness is the reverse shock that triggers calmness and gratitude in Andrea.

30 August 2019

Neil Jeff, you sir, are a nursing genius.

As we walk into the surgery for Andrea's pre-operation appointment we are met by senior nurse Neil Jeff. We both recognize him instantly as the same nurse that completed the pre-operation for my bowel cancer operation on 19 May 2017. This gives us an instant morale boost, as our memory of this man's care is nothing but positive.

He methodically works through the medical history questionnaire, recording every relevant detail. Andrea's notes clearly state her needle phobia. Neil questions her about this with an empathy and understanding that makes me wonder if he too is afflicted with the same irrational fear. He is not, but his rapport gets Andrea's attention. Today we have met another NHS giant.

There is a moment in which he suddenly remembers us both from two years ago. He has also read our recent fund raising press release, which helps to jog his memory of us. This encourages a more relaxed and personal conversation, which helps to explore Andrea's needle phobia further.

Although she is scared, she is no fool. She is using courage and laughter to fight the urge to turn and run away. Neil recognises this and shields her with his professional honesty and a wit to match hers.

Once Andrea's heart and lungs have been examined, it's time to take bloods. Andrea has prepared her left arm with Emla numbing cream. She grips my hand and looks away from Neil as he places a tourniquet on her upper left arm, tightens it and gently taps the vein he is about to enter.

He is in that single-minded clinical zone. Concentrating, to ensure the successful completion of a correct and effective medical procedure whilst, at the same time, offering care and compassion to the patient. His attention is focused on both the procedure and the patient. Keeping the conversation going, he swabs the point of entry and injects the needle with the words:

"You'll feel a little scratch… now."

Andrea flinches, tenses, then relaxes. She is quietly counting as I watch her blood drain into a small blood culture bottle. Her foot is tapping to the rhythm of her count. The whole procedure takes a count of twenty to complete. The needle is then removed and a cotton wool ball is pressed onto the puncture wound and firmly taped down. A small amount of blood has oozed out onto the cotton wool, but Neil has managed to carefully conceal it from Andrea.

I know this lady. From the moment she woke this morning she has been petrified by the thought of giving blood today. Only those with an irrational fear can possibly understand what she is feeling.

I have been told that I am fearless, not courageous; there is a difference. Andrea has faced her worst fear again and come away relaxed, smiling and laughing.

"I'm just amazed at how easy and painless it was, Neil. I'm sorry for being such a difficult patient and thank you so much." Andrea turns to face Neil once more.

"Nonsense. You were so relaxed, just brilliant. Probably more relaxed than me. I think I need to lie down for a while too. Talk about pressure!" Neil replies with a mock gasp.

"I was worried that if the pre-op is a bad experience, I'm not sure how I would have coped with the operation itself. But I think you might have just cured me of my needle phobia."

"That's great, but I'm sure you would have coped. If not, we've still got the straps to tie you down with!"

We roar with laughter at Neil's joke, in a way that only a release from tension makes possible. Andrea and I both now have the confidence we need that the operation will go well. She feels able to just about deal with anything that comes her way.

I also need to give blood today so we make our way to the Phlebotomy department. On our way Andrea gushes:

"He probably doesn't realise what he's done for me. Everything has changed. Needle phobia was my biggest barrier. I just didn't realise how easy an injection really is. I'm cured."

Spoken like a woman whose sight has suddenly been restored.

We leave the hospital, each with a cotton ball taped to our left arm and drive to a local pub, in a happy mood, for a celebratory lunch.

My wife and I have so much in common, even diseases!

4 September 2019

Andrea collects her car from the dealership in Macclesfield. All the emission problems have been fixed. The total charge is £1,641, about £900 less than the original estimate.

The engineer we met on the 29 August has proved to be a man of his word and has reduced the cost as much as he has been able to. Not only by reducing the cost of labour but also by passing on the discount the dealership normally gets on engine parts.

This act of kindness from him causes me to wonder if he is motivated by his own cancer story. He didn't share one with us, but there was a notable uplift in customer service when he had heard of Andrea's struggle. He seems inspired to pay something forward, maybe he's just a decent human being. I suggest to Andrea that we take the £900 saving and place it all on a roulette table in a Las Vegas casino.

I'm not sure she is convinced that it would be a wise investment.

6 September 2019

We fly to Las Vegas from Manchester Airport with Cyrus and Adele.

To say we are excited is to understate our feelings. Being denied a holiday like this for the last couple of years, due to serious ill health, has made the anticipation of it even more enjoyable than usual.

Las Vegas has a lot to offer and we have much planned, including a helicopter ride into the Grand Canyon, quad biking in the desert, various shows, fabulous restaurants, visiting the many casinos and lazing by the pool. Aside from all that, spending time with Andrea, Cyrus and Adele presents an opportunity to build lasting happy memories.

12 September 2019

We are due to fly back to the UK tomorrow. Andrea's lumpectomy is scheduled two days later.

In order to face your fear you must first come to understand it. To do that, it has to be examined and questioned. Andrea and I have always agreed to talk freely and honestly about her cancer and the operation to remove it, in order to normalise it. Doing this has not spoiled our holiday, but rather removed a shadow that might otherwise have existed.

Setting a goal and feeling rewarded for facing your irrational fear is a positive way of overcoming self-sabotaging and negative thoughts. Repeating *if I do this then I will achieve that* becomes a positive affirmation and a self-fulfilling prophecy. With this in mind, I suggest a gift from us both to her to signify beating cancer. A cancer ribbon tattoo perhaps, or a piece of jewelry. Given her fear of needles and love of jewelry, her choice is obvious.

Explaining the reason for the purchase to the jewelry store assistant creates an immediate and excited response. He produces an affirmation ring and suggests the removal of three diamonds, replacing them with pink sapphires, to give the effect of a cancer ribbon.

He could do this today and the ring would be ready for collection tomorrow morning before we check out of the hotel.

"Perfect." Was our joint response.

14 September 2019

We return tired and jet-lagged from Las Vegas. It was a holiday that lived up to our over-inflated expectations.

In the evening we eat out with friends and then go to MADS Little Theatre to watch a play called *Dinner* performed by my company. The cast includes my son Luke and his girlfriend Amy. It's a thoroughly enjoyable way to get back into normal, post-holiday, UK life. By the time we get to bed, however, we have been awake for over thirty hours and feel exhausted but happy.

16 September 2019

We arrive at the surgical day ward at Macclesfield Hospital at 7:30am and check in for Andrea's scheduled lumpectomy. The nursing staff are on top form and their friendly chatter with Andrea immediately relaxes her.

Then the physiotherapist stumbles into the room.

"Ah, Mrs Oldham, Andrea… yes, Andrea. I'm the physio, glad to see you've got your trainers on. We are going to start with a light jog around the hospital. Follow me."

Andrea half stands, smiling and slightly confused, almost prepared to run out of the hospital with this comedian. I look on, wondering if this man should be taken seriously.

"Only joking," he chuckles. "I mean, do I look like I could jog to the end of the corridor, let alone around the hospital?"

"No!" I'm thinking. "You do not. But I do like your sense of humour. It's just what the doctor ordered."

He continues with his witty banter to his appreciative and captive audience as he explains and demonstrates the various arm and chest exercises Andrea is asked to do after surgery. Satisfied that his routine has both informed and amused the patient, he moves on to his next victim in the opposite bay.

I didn't know physiotherapy could be so entertaining.

The admissions nurse reminds Andrea that before surgery she will require two procedures in preparation for surgery.

The first is the insertion of a wire into her left breast. This will clearly signpost the lump that the surgeon will remove. It will be inserted under a local anaesthetic.

The second is an injection of radioactive liquid called a tracer. During the operation, the surgeon will also inject blue dye into Andrea's breast. The dye and the tracer drain away from the breast tissue into nearby lymph nodes, colouring them blue for easy identification. Up to four lymph nodes will be removed.

A pathologist at The Christie will then analyse them for evidence of cancerous tissue. If any is found, it means that the cancer has travelled and may appear elsewhere in her body. This is something the next planned treatment will have to consider. It is unlikely that Andrea's cancer has travelled. Although no evidence has yet been found to indicate this, it is nonetheless important, and surgically simple enough, to be certain.

We are sent to the breast screening clinic at New Alderley House with another patient requiring the same procedure. Andrea chats with her during the five-minute walk. I sense that she is developing a siege mentality by bonding with the welcoming nursing staff and this patient. Through this, most things become possible as confidence develops. This will then feed her courage.

On arrival at the clinic, we are informed of a two-hour delay in the delivery of the radioactive tracer from The Christie and, therefore, the insertion of the wire will be done first. This is performed by the same doctor who completed Andrea's second biopsy. He remembers her.

As a reminder, both doctor and patient briefly discuss the biopsy and Andrea's needle phobia. Awareness created, both are ready to manage the irrational fear of needles. The doctor, full of empathy and compassion, carefully explains the procedure and the patient courageously steels herself for her impending nightmare.

"Talk to me about horses."

Is the request from Andrea as she lies on her back, eyes closed, facing away from the treatment table and tightly gripping my hand. Now prepared for a local anaesthetic injection.

The nice doctor obliges. I had forgotten that during Andrea's second biopsy he had spoken about the horse his wife owns and which he helps to look after. This is a fact that would have positively defined the doctor for Andrea. The conversation is exactly the distraction Andrea needs as the injection is prepared and administered.

After a short wait for the anaesthetic to take effect, a wire of about eight inches in length is inserted into Andrea's left breast by about one inch. The doctor uses the ultrasound scan to guide the end of the wire into the cancerous lump.

The wire protrudes out of the breast, but is taped down to ensure it remains stable. Despite the horse chatter, a large tear eases out of Andrea's right eye and trickles down her cheek. This is an expression of fear, not pain, but it's the only obvious sign of it. Above the surface, the swan glides majestically in the sunshine, but beneath the water line legs are paddling like crazy in weeds. Once again, this lady's courage steps forward and crushes her fear.

"You never know how strong you are until being strong is the only choice you have."

— Cayla Mills

Wire insertion complete, we return to the waiting room where we settle down on a comfortable armchair and sofa for a power nap. About an hour later the dye arrives and Andrea is led away. She returns ten minutes later. It was an extremely slow and painful injection and one she would not want to repeat. However, despite the trauma, she remains calm and in control.

We walk back to the surgical day ward where Andrea changes into surgical stockings and a hospital gown. She is both physically and emotionally ready. As she pops over to the nurses' station to ask when she is likely to be taken to the operating theatre, it dawns on me that I don't feel quite ready to let her go yet. I step out into the corridor to look for her and see her coming towards me, laying down on a theatre trolley.

Gulp, that is unexpected!

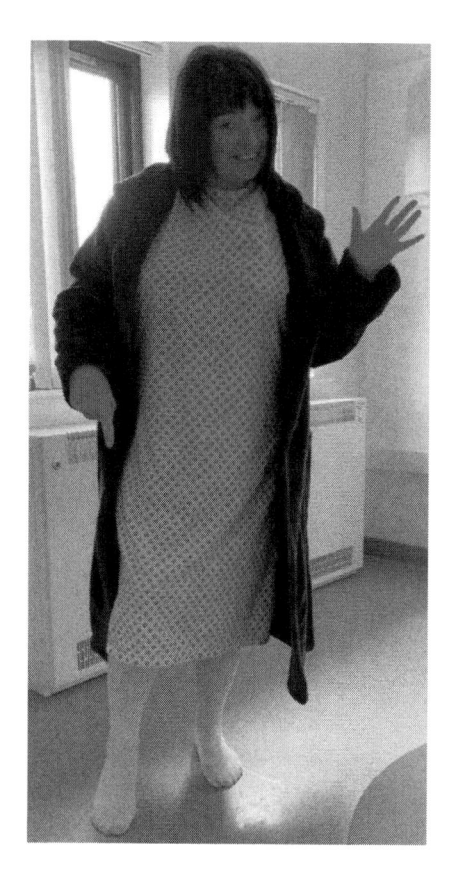

Andrea Oldham
Hospital fashionista

Parting from a loved one as they turn towards an operating theatre to face the risks of a major operation is something I have yet to experience.

Despite all the preparation for Andrea's lumpectomy, it takes all my emotional energy to adjust to the unexpected suddenness of seeing her on a theatre trolley being pushed down hospital corridors. This is a time to show strength, unity and re-assurance.

Caregiving can be lonely and emotionally draining.

"The operating theatre is just down here. This is as far as you can go, Mr Oldham. Phone us about 4pm. Andrea should be back on the ward by then and we can update you."

Andrea and I face each other and smile, radiating love. Each trying to re-assure the other. I know she's in good hands and the operation is not too complicated. She knows what parting from me on my way to surgery feels like.

We kiss and smile. I turn and walk away. After a couple of steps I pause to listen, a lump rising in my throat. My heart leaps as I hear Andrea's very distinct laughter a few meters down the corridor behind me. She's relaxed and I just know she is going to be okay.

With that thought, and refusing to turn around, I continue walking and go home.

Rather than phone the ward, I decide to simply return at 4pm. As I pull into the hospital car park my mobile phone rings. It's Andrea, she has just come round and is back in her bed on the ward. She sounds groggy but the operation has gone well.

I run to her ward and five minutes later I'm sitting by her bed, happily watching her munch on toast and sipping sweet tea. I pass Andrea's jewelry to her, including the new ring we purchased in Las Vegas. The time has come to enjoy the fruits of positive reinforcement and the customised cane ribbon ring is her reward.

Positive Reinforcement Ring.
I had cancer, cancer never had me.

Whilst Andrea excitedly puts on her new ring, I notice that she has black pen marks on her shoulder and chest area like bad tattoos. I also discover that most of her upper body is patchily stained brown by surgical cleaning fluid rather like a poorly applied false tan. The strangest thing, however, is that the whole of her left nipple is aqua blue.

"What the dickens…?" I begin to ask.

"The surgeon injects the blue dye through the nipple."

Declares the nurse, anticipating the end of my question, as she appears through the curtain.

"It's quite normal and may take a couple of weeks to clear up. The longest I've ever known is eighteen months."

Adds the doctor, reassuringly, as she follows the nurse to Andrea's bedside.

"Although, that is very unusual. It's usually only a couple of weeks."

The doctor was part of the team that operated on Andrea. She describes how well the operation went and that Andrea played her part very well. The cancerous lump was successfully removed and has been sent to The Christie pathology department for analysis. This and the lymph node histology will be available in about ten to fourteen days and will be discussed with us both when we return for a check-up in two weeks' time. For now, it's all about recovery.

Andrea remains in her bed and convalesces for a couple of hours until the nurse appears with analgesic drugs to discharge her with. These are discussed and handed over. Once an appointment is made for a check-up in a fortnight, we leave. It's been a long and exhausting day but with a very satisfying conclusion. Despite her discomfort and restrictive upper body movement Andrea is relieved she has no more needles or surgery to deal with.

When we arrive home we receive the usual energetic greeting from Alfie and Stanley, neither of whom seem to quite grasp the tender condition Andrea is in. I put on the kettle whilst Andrea disappears upstairs. Before the water in the kettle has boiled I hear a loud scream. Imagining another Stanley mauling I charge upstairs to find Andrea in our en-suite bathroom staring into the toilet, exclaiming:-

"I'm turning into Papa Smurf. Look!"

I peer into the bowl and see aqua blue water. The blue dye injected into Andrea's nipple has worked its way through her system and now finds itself in our toilet, being flushed away.

19 September 2019

I receive an email from Chris Gorman. As expected, he starts by asking about Andrea, hoping she is well.

He tells me that I made a powerful impression on the Macclesfield Hospital Board last month at their AGM. Therefore, the Board has asked if I would be willing to talk again, but this time on camera. They wish to make a video for training and induction purposes.

I am more than happy to do this and arrangements are made for us to meet at the Congleton War Memorial Hospital next Thursday to film the video.

Andrea is recovering well from her operation despite some bruising and swelling. Her left nipple is still blue but she is no longer leaking like Papa Smurf.

24 September 2019

Andrea has an appointment to check her wounds and dressing. Her scars are evidence that she is stronger than the cancer that tried to hurt her. She has some swelling under her left arm. Fluid retention is expected as a result of the removal of the four lymph nodes. This has given her some discomfort, but it has been manageable.

The appointment is at Macclesfield Hospital's MacMillan Suite. We haven't been in there since my chemotherapy was administered such a long time ago. We reminisce on arrival. It's strange to think that this time we are here for Andrea's benefit.

Mr Kokan enters the clinic with a nurse and a medical student. He sits facing us both and immediately informs us that the lymph node pathology results have arrived from The Christie earlier than expected. It's good news; there is no evidence of cancer. It hasn't, therefore, travelled from the small primary tumour that was successfully removed. As far as he knows Andrea is now cancer free.

The news is unexpectedly early and stuns us both. We expected the histology next week and had no warning we would get it today. It takes a few seconds for us to grasp it. Feeling dazed and unsure comes before the welcome relief of acceptance. It helps that Mr Kokan's smiling face confirms his words. Andrea bursts into tears and I am left shaking with relief. Comprehending news like this feels life changing. More so than a huge lottery win. Being the richest person in the cemetery is pointless.

Mr Kokan removes Andrea's dressing and inspects his work. He suggests that the fluid causing the swelling should be drained. Andrea hardly flinches as he draws excess fluid from under her arm with a long thin needle. Emla cream is not required. The endorphins, otherwise known as the happiness hormone, surging through Andrea's body are more than sufficient to suppress any lingering concern about needles. The dressing is not replaced as the wounds are healing well.

Andrea's cancer is described as a grade two invasive ductal cancer, 15mm in size and located in one area. The tumour was tested for Ki67 protein. High levels of this protein found in cells indicate that the cells are dividing and growing faster than normal. The test reveals a low to medium rate of 12.9%. There are, therefore, no signs of lympho-vascular invasion.

All this analysis determines Andrea's ongoing treatment. She will have fifteen sessions of radiotherapy at The Christie. This will be planned over a three-week period during November. There is nothing that suggests it is essential, but radiotherapy will reduce the risk of cancer recurrence in the future.

She will also be prescribed Tamoxifen, a small pill to be taken daily for the next five years. This will reduce the Ki67 level in her system. Annual mammograms for the next five years will continue to monitor her health and provide an early indication of any disease returning, something we both now feel confident will not happen.

Anybody who tells us today that the NHS is failing should be prepared to enter into a robust debate. We have experienced the very best surgical skill, outstanding and trusted pathology analysis, pharmaceutical excellence, a comprehensive treatment plan, the high confidence that the involvement of The Christie invokes and a scheduled five-year pathway to freedom.

But more importantly, all of this was delivered with the compassion of a saint and at a pace to suit both the patient and her carer.

Without doubt, one of the most beautiful things about Britain is the NHS and the people who work there.

On our way home, Andrea posts an update on her Facebook page. The many responses are as supportive, happy and congratulatory as we have come to expect.

Today humanity wins; cancer loses.

26 September 2019

I wake up early this morning ready to meet Chris Gorman and film a training video based on my cancer experience. Unfortunately, Andrea is in some discomfort. The area under her left arm is swollen due to more fluid retention, something we were told to expect. I call Chris to postpone this morning's filming so I can take Andrea to the drop-in clinic at Macclesfield Hosptial.

We don't have to wait too long for Andrea to be seen by a senior nurse. The procedure is reasonably straight forward. Although Andrea closes her eyes and faces away when the long needle is inserted and fluid is drawn out, she doesn't flinch. I hold her hand and she chats to me in the same relaxed manner as when we were by the swimming pool in Las Vegas. She has come a long way since that first biopsy needle.

"When you've got your eyes closed, you don't feel anything!"

Exclaims a smiling Andrea as we leave.

29 September 2019

One year on and we are still married and very much in love. Today is our first wedding anniversary. We blinked our eyes and in an instant, we've been married for a whole year. Time is one of life's greatest diminishing assets.

The more good use you make of it the quicker it seems to slip through your fingers. Despite the torment of cancer, our lives have been busy, happy and fulfilled. Time has flown but we have been both pilot and navigator. Deeply offending cancer by being masters of our own destiny.

We exchange simple gifts and acknowledge the many congratulations received. Facebook reminds us both of our wonderful wedding at The Clonter Opera one year ago today. The photos that are posted by our *giants* are bright, colourful and happy; a weaponised contrast to the misery that cancer would have had us suffer. In the evening, we dine out with Max and his lovely girlfriend, Robyn.

It is the best of times.

1 October 2019

Andrea has been getting intermittent shooting pains in her left breast. These have become more regular during the course of the day. She takes two codeine phosphate pain killing tablets. They make her feel drowsy so she sleeps for most of the afternoon. I'm concerned enough to call the breast care support number and speak to Nichola, one of the nurses. The stabbing pains are quite normal. When asked, Andrea confirms that there is no redness around her scars.

Mr Kokan has referred Andrea to Dr Lisa Barraclough at the cancer resource centre at Macclesfield Hospital for advice on further management of Andrea's condition. The appointment is tomorrow at 10am so Nichola will check her then.

2 October 2019

Andrea wakes this morning in considerable pain. The wound under her arm is red and swollen. The analgesic she has taken makes her feel light-headed and dizzy.

On arrival at the cancer resource centre, Nichola shows us both into the clinic. On inspection she confirms that Andrea's wound is infected and prescribes a course of antibiotics. Andrea also has some fluid retention. No fuss is made when the long needle is inserted into Andrea to drain off the fluid. Needles have become her new normal.

Nichola then proceeds to inform Andrea of all the risks associated with radiotherapy and Tamoxifen. An appointment for the radiotherapy planning session will be made, probably for the last week of this month. At this session she will have two, small, pin-prick tattoos. This will provide a target for the radiotherapy beams to ensure the right area of her breast is consistently treated. The fifteen radiotherapy sessions are likely to commence the following week.

Finally, a further appointment is made with Dr Kokan for next week in order to inspect Andrea's wounds once the antibiotics have had time to start working.

Before leaving the hospital, we collect Andrea's antibiotics and Tamoxifen from the pharmacy.

Once home, we realise that there was no discussion about the Esmya tablets that Andrea was asked to temporarily cease taking. These were prescribed to reduce the size of a 12cm fibroid. This is the least of our worries.

Cancer enjoys making an apparently straightforward recovery more complex. To twist the knife, make the path a little less certain and thereby to toy with your emotions, to tease you to the very core.

It is here, in one's soul, that the battle against cancer can be won and win it we will.

12

RENEWAL

The sun sets to rise again the next morning and the phoenix must burn in order to emerge from the ashes. So it is with recovery from cancer treatment for both patient and carer. Andrea's recovery from the operation is almost complete and a new day is upon us. We are ready to emerge blinking into the daylight and to fully engage with life once again.

To witness severe suffering as a result of cancer shifts the mindset and introduces a fresh and positive perspective. Our renewal has commenced.

4 October 2019

I receive an email from Louise Dobson, who is part of the fund raising campaign team for The Christie at Macclesfield project. The team is currently producing a 'case for support' document which will be given to fundraisers to explain why their help is needed.

Louise has read the recent press release about the donation Andrea and I made to The Christie and the reason for it. She has used it to write a quote from me that she would like to use in the document and asks if I will permit the following to be printed:

"Both myself and my wife have had radiotherapy at The Christie for our cancers. We know exactly how grueling it can be to not only go through radiotherapy every day for five weeks, but also to have the added stress of long journeys to and from Manchester. It is almost unbearable. Being able to have treatment closer to home will make a huge difference to patients in the future."

Whilst the quote isn't entirely accurate, as Andrea has not yet started her radiotherapy treatment, it does make a good case in favour of The Christie at Macclesfield project.

I phone Louise to discuss it and agree that the slight inaccuracy doesn't really matter. Having experienced the car journey to The Christie with me already, it's a point that Andrea already agrees with. The quote serves its purpose as it stands and I agree that it can be used.

8 October 2019

We drive to Macclesfield Hospital for Andrea's check-up. The antibiotics have cleared up the infection but the wound is still weeping a little clear fluid. This, we are told, will soon stop. The wound is healing well.

Damn it! I receive a notice of intended prosecution from Cheshire Constabulary for driving 45mph in a 40mph zone on the way back from Macclesfield Hospital on the 2 October. I was caught in busy traffic by a manned camera. I remember seeing the man holding the camera, but I didn't think he was pointing it at me, nor that I was speeding.

What is it about me and driving to or from hospitals? According to the Government driving license website, the three points I received whilst driving to The Christie for radiotherapy treatment will, fortunately, expire in November next year. When I was first diagnosed with cancer I would not have imagined that my experience would almost span the lifetime of a traffic offence penalty.

9 October 2019

A letter arrives today from The Christie Hospital confirming Andrea's radiotherapy planning appointment for 21 October. She sheds a little tear and I comfort her the best I can. Apart from the wound that is still weeping fluid she is recovering well enough physically, but is prone to occasional melancholy.

In her sorrow, she often asks the question "why me?". On the surface, this question appears to encourage self-pity. However, I believe it's just her way of saying that cancer and its treatment is hard and uncertain. Asking the question "why me?" is an inherent way of asking for help. Help I am more than willing to provide.

The appointment is a reminder that more treatment lies ahead. The normal routine she desperately desires is still weeks away. Recovering from cancer can fool you into thinking you've regained all your strength and that you've restored your life earlier than you actually have. It's a long, tiring and, often, miserable process.

15 October 2019

I drive slowly and carefully to Macclesfield Hospital for my second health screening since my lung operation. I am scheduled for a CT Thorax abdomen pelvis scan with contrast.

I had drunk four pints of water before the appointment and so, as we arrive at the X-ray department, I dash to the toilet for much needed relief. Andrea has found somebody to chat to whilst I check in and I then take a seat in the waiting area. It's about fifteen minutes before my appointment is due. However, almost immediately a male radiographer enters and calls:

The Spirit of Rooster

"Mrs Oldham? Mrs Oldham, please."

I look up, about to speak. I hesitate as I'm trying to work out what has surprised me more. The fact that I have been called fifteen minutes early or that I am now a Mrs and not a Mr. Andrea joins me, as if on cue, laughing and pointing at me:

"Well I am Mrs Oldham, but I think you'll find that you want Mr Oldham."

The confused, grinning, bespectacled radiographer looks back at his notes, then at me:

"Well, I stand corrected. *Mr* Oldham if you'll come with me please. I think I'm going to rather enjoy sticking a needle in you!"

"I'm not going to feel a little prick am I?"

"No, no, no, not at all… yes, yes, you are. Particularly when wearing one of those hospital gowns."

With the jovial banter complete I strip, put on a hospital gown and then join the cheerful radiographer in the small surgery. I read and sign the risk assessment form as the radiographer prepares a cannula. The cannula is necessary so that the contrast can be easily injected into my system during the CT scan.

"All joking aside, Mr Oldham I am actually quite good at this."

He remarks as he tightens the tourniquet around my upper arm, tapping a vein in my antecubital fossa (the medical term for the inside of the elbow).

"As good as the nurses at The Christie? They have got to be the best in their profession."

"Nobody is that good; except me, of course. Now just clench and unclench your fist. That's it, pump up your vein and let's bring it to the surface."

I am relaxed and inspired enough to actually watch my antecubital fossa being swabbed and the cannula being inserted into a vein. The happiness that this radiographer is determined to share does not distract him from completing a perfect, clinical execution.

"I didn't feel a thing."

"Good. Chemotherapy can often degrade the vein so when we get a particularly difficult patient we often send them to the MacMillan suite downstairs to have the cannula inserted. They're masters with a needle and could probably find an active vein in a corpse."

The CT scan that follows has become a normal and well-practiced process for me. The contrast makes me feel slightly more nauseous than usual. But that soon passes and we then drive slowly and carefully home. No careless driving offences today.

17 October 2019

I meet Chris Gorman at the Congleton War Memorial Hospital. He regrets not filming my presentation to the Trust AGM but is determined to capture my experience on film today. He leads me to a quiet, private room with a view of the garden through the window, behind the seat he asks me to sit in.

Once again I talk through the timeline of my treatment. I emphasis the importance of compassion from the medical staff toward patients, providing anecdotes of when I have encountered it. I suspect that much of the film will end up on the cutting room floor. Chris is confident that he can create something meaningful for the hospital's induction training, from the edit.

21 October 2019

Today, Andrea and I drive to The Christie for her radiotherapy planning meeting. She will leave with all the information she needs for her treatment,

The Spirit of Rooster

an appointment for her first session, a couple of tattoos and a good deal of confidence in the medical staff involved.

Andrea is feeling despondent and vulnerable. The prospect of more cancer treatment and the biopsy wound that still hasn't completely healed is making her feel somewhat sorrowful and weak. The thought of a tattoo needle is also causing her some additional distress.

The radiologist who meets us is both charming and witty. She is determined to put Andrea more at ease. Unfortunately, as Andrea's wound has not quite healed, she must have it inspected by a doctor before committing to radiotherapy treatment.

This is an unexpected blow. Once you've prepared yourself for any sort of cancer treatment, to face the prospect of delaying it is frustrating and dispiriting. The doctor is busy at the moment, but will see us as soon as she can.

Whilst we are seated in the waiting area, a lady collapses into a chair a couple of seats away. She lands rather ungracefully with a loud thud, followed by an exhausted:

"Oh fuck...argh!"

We both look at her, to our left, as she struggles into a more upright position.

"Pardon my French," she giggles, hand raised to her mouth.

"I'm in quite a bit of pain and sometimes my potty mouth gets the better of me."

Little did Andrea and I realise it, but we were about to begin a brief conversation with one of the most inspiring women we have ever met.

We sit with her for no more than ten minutes. Listening intently, questioning occasionally. Our mouths wide open, eyes watering, hearts pounding and minds racing, trying to come to terms with her situation. Her relaxed and genial manner belies her tragedy. As she tells it, she smiles, laughs and shrugs her shoulders.

She has clearly come to terms with the rare form of spinal cancer that is starting to cripple her. It is terminal. Before death greets her she will suffer terrible pain, a cocktail of drugs, a wheelchair, paralysis, muscle weakness, retention, incontinence and spinal deformities. She is receiving radiotherapy treatment to keep her alive and mobile long enough to sort out her affairs. Today is session eight of thirty that she has planned.

The medical staff at The Christie have been, and are being, amazing. Each day, she travels from home to The Christie using adapted patient transport provided for her. It takes two hours each way.

"I'm only forty-eight years old. If I could just have one more Christmas I'll die happy." She chuckles.

We sit, completely absorbed. This is her new *normal*, no longer her tragedy. She is refusing to let it be that. Out of respect for her *normal*, I ask:

"Who will you spend Christmas with?"

"My daughters. They're in their early twenties and understand this ... this ... awful situation. But my son, he's only twelve. He shouldn't have to understand it, he's too young and doesn't really get it. That's hard ... he ... it's just so hard."

Her voice quivers for the first time and her trembling hand wipes away a tear.

"But..."

Bracing herself, she continues:

"... they're my only priority right now. The sad thing is that my son's dad has never been in his life but suddenly wants to be. He really is so unfit to be a father. He's an alcoholic, doesn't want to work and lives in a run-down area in another city. I just can't leave Jason with him. He would have to move away from his family and friends, it would be a complete disaster. So, on top of all this, I'm fighting a legal custody battle to ensure my boy can have a good life with good people who care about him."

I have so many questions to ask. "What's your name?" is an obvious one that seems to have bypassed us both.

But, a nurse suddenly appears in front of our new, inspiring friend and helps her to her feet before I can ask. The familiar way in which the nurse manhandles the patient and the shared laughter it invokes suggests a warm friendship. Before she is taken from us I just get the chance to say:

"Wow. You are one amazing lady. Thank you for sharing that with us and bloody good luck."

It's a pathetically underwhelming and irrelevant response, but what else is there to say?

The nurse and the patient link arms, chuckle and slowly make their way toward a treatment room at the other end of the corridor. There is no tension or sadness, only warmth and laughter. Anyone watching them could be mistaken to think they were closely related.

"If you have been brutally broken but still have the courage to be gentle to other living beings, then you're a badass with a heart of an angel."
— Keanu Reeves

"Well, that puts things into perspective. How inspiring is she? After listening to her story, why, oh why am I feeling so sorry for myself? Tattoo? Radiotherapy? Bring it on. If she can smile her way through all that, then I can respect her enough to do this."

Determination has returned to Andrea. When we arrived at The Christie the cancer monster whispered in her ear:

"You are not strong enough to withstand the storm."

Andrea has just whispered back:

"I am the storm."

Minutes later we are in a doctor's clinic. Andrea with renewed grit. Her wound is healing but, as a precaution, the radiotherapy treatment will start one week later than planned. However, all the preparation, including the three freckle-sized tattoos, can be completed today.

"Excellent. Let's do this!"

Strong, resolved and ready. Andrea is led away while I return to the waiting area. I can see one of the end of treatment bells at the other end of the corridor. I quietly reminisce of my time with it and hope that it's robust enough to withstand the three rings that the mighty Andrea will give it once her treatment is complete.

Caregiving can often encounter courage, fortitude, grit and inspiration.

30 October 2019

Paul Bernardi has recently acquired the benefit of an annual health check from his employers, an addition to his reward package. Being a man of a certain age, he recently decided to book himself in for a full health screening at a nearby private hospital.

I receive a message from him informing me that his doctor had phoned to discuss an anomaly in his prostate. He is being referred for further tests and is concerned.

Paul has steadfastly supported us throughout our cancer treatments and knows more about the impact of this plague than the most. I call him to discuss it, to offer strength, but privately wonder how this will play out.

5 November 2019

Paul has seen his consultant today. The prostate felt normal to the expert finger, but it is larger than it should be. There is a greater than fifty percent chance that it's okay.

An aging man has hormonal changes that can naturally enlarge the prostate. He feels re-assured that even if it is cancerous, it will have been caught early and is treatable. He has been booked in for an MRI scan followed by a prostate biopsy.

8 November 2019

This morning, I receive a phone call from Nick Molyneux, the communications officer for The Christie NHS Foundation Trust. He is helping to organize a Christmas concert in Macclesfield town centre on the 17 December to raise money for The Christie at Macclesfield project. He asks if Andrea and I are able to attend and wants to meet us to discuss how we could support the event.

As luck would have it, we are due at The Christie today for Andrea's first radiotherapy treatment at 4pm. Our plan is to then meet friends from the MADS Little Theatre for a meal and then afterwards go to an Eddie Izzard show at The Manchester Apollo.

At 3:30pm, Andrea and I meet Nick and his colleague, Nichola, at the coffee shop near The Christie charity centre. They would like us to address the Christmas concert audience together and share our stories, perhaps even tell each other's story. Mark Radcliffe, the Radio Two DJ, is hosting the event.

Neither of us take much convincing to participate. We have always been keen to give something back when the opportunity arises. It seems we share this desire with Mark Radcliffe, now in remission from a cancerous tumour at the back of his tongue. He also lives in Cheshire and is therefore considered local to Macclesfield Hospital.

Just before 4pm we make out way to clinic number six for Andrea's first radiotherapy treatment. They're running on time today, so we don't have to wait long once Andrea has booked herself in.

A few minutes after walking into the radiotherapy suite Andrea reappears, smiling and completely unfazed by the treatment she's just had. It really is a quick, painless and easy undertaking. The major downside is that the drive, of up to an hour to and from The Christie, makes it a much more mammoth task than it should be. The Christie at Macclesfield project cannot deliver soon enough.

Today, however, our journey is made easier by our post-treatment plans. Cameron, Stuart, Rob and Suzie have kindly booked a nearby restaurant to meet up in, before a drive across Manchester for Eddie Izzard. If Andrea has any initial treatment worries, it is in this most excellent and jolly company that they very soon evaporate.

25 November 2019

Run-up week for *Nell Gwynn* begins today, so the cast has to attend rehearsals every evening from 7:30pm to very late. The *Team Nell* effort thus far has been tremendous.

But this week is also Andrea's last week of radiotherapy and that must be the priority. If Andrea has an evening appointment, I will be with her and, therefore, miss, or be late for, the rehearsal.

28 November 2019

At last, after three weeks of daily treatment, Andrea has her final radiotherapy session. It passes just as routinely the previous fourteen sessions have passed. Only this time, there is an extra special task to perform once the treatment is complete. That moment of defiance against evil, of hope for the future and of remembrance for those less fortunate.

It is a moment that we have both been looking forward to and Andrea has come to The Christie prepared. She is wearing a t-shirt designed by a lady called Ellie Shipton. Sadly, Ellie lost her fight against breast cancer. She did not get to ring the bell, the bell tolled for her. Before passing, she designed a white T-shirt with the word STRONG emblazoned in sparkly red across the front. It can be purchased at www.personalitee.co.uk and each sale earns a £10 donation to The Christie charity. We didn't know Ellie ourselves, but heard about her from Dave and Petrona Clayton. Her story instantly struck a chord with Andrea. Ellie Shipton's inspiration helps to carry us today.

The corridor seems unusually quiet as Andrea approaches the bell. She pauses to read the words inscribed next to the rainbow as I prepare to record the ceremony. She takes hold of the rope and turns to face me; head held high and with a huge grin.

I had done my best to help this lady through all her treatment, to care for her in a way she needed me to. Much as she had done for me. To watch her now induces a tearful pride.

Yes Andrea! You ring that Bell.

The chime of the bell triggers the Christie response we have become accustomed to; cheering, whooping and applause. The bell rings out another successful treatment. Members of staff and patients alike fill the corridor to celebrate with us. The memory of it will remain with us forever.

7 December 2019

The curtain finally falls on *Nell Gwynn* tonight. It's proven to be a very popular play, it even sold out on a couple of nights. Ticket sales have been exceptionally high and the audience reaction excellent. Great cast, great fun.

9 December 2019

I call on Paul Bernardi as he has a prostate biopsy scheduled for tomorrow. This involves a large needle injected into the perineum which is situated below the pelvic diaphragm and between the legs. Simply put, the needle will be inserted into that area between a man's scrotum and his anus. It's going to be painful so will be administered under a general anesthetic. I stay with him briefly and leave a gift of a child's rubber ring.

10 December 2019

I receive a message from Paul, who is in the post operation recovery room, moaning about a sore backside. Sitting down is apparently difficult and painful. How he chuckled at the stupidity of the swan inflatable. Well he's not laughing now!

14 December 2019

For the last week or so Andrea has had a chest infection causing her to cough and splutter. She has not slept well and has been on a course of antibiotics for a couple of days. Tired and aching, her mood is low. This morning she gets out of bed at about 6am, unable to recover from a coughing fit. A short while later she charges back into the bedroom in tears.

Her left leg is red, swollen and cramping. As I come round from my slumber she is on the phone to a friend, and former pharmacist, Fionnuala Keen describing her symptoms.

I stand and move to sit with her on the edge of the bed. Before I get there she suddenly falls forward and collapses onto the floor, hitting her head on the bedside table on the way. She has fainted. I quickly dismiss Fionnuala and immediately dial 999. Andrea starts to come round after about five seconds but remains groggy as I describe her condition to the emergency services.

Fifteen minutes later, the ambulance crew arrive. By this time, Andrea is sitting up in bed still wondering exactly what had happened. The medic suspects a deep vein thrombosis (DVT). It is not considered life threatening and rather than take her to a very busy A&E department, an emergency appointment is made with a doctor at The Congleton War Memorial Hospital for about an hour's time.

The doctor also suspects a DVT which, he explains, can result from either an operation, a long haul flight, radiotherapy, weight loss or a serious health issue like cancer. Sadly Andrea has ticked not just one but every box, including a brain hemorrhage a number of years ago. What do you give to the girl who has everything? I know - a DVT.

The doctor is confident enough in his diagnosis to start the treatment of blood thinning medication immediately. However a scan of Andreas left leg will be arranged for Monday, at Macclesfield Hospital to confirm the diagnosis.

If it is a DVT, the medication can continue, probably for the next three months. In the unlikely event that it is not a DVT the scan will determine what has caused the leg to swell and redden. To have this thrust upon Andrea, on top of everything she's been through, seems callous and unfair. She is able to walk and the swelling has subsided but it's yet another condition to recover from. However, she is strong and considers this to be no more than an inconvenience. One she will deal with and rise from.

"The greatest glory in living lies not in never falling, but in rising every time we fall."

– Nelson Mandela

15 December 2019

Oliver, the son of Luke Stevenson and Kerry Quinn, crashes into the world. Luke, professional wedding singer, window cleaner and human being genius will marry the lovely Kerry next spring. Renewal of this nature is the best cure for sorrow and self-pity.

Hi Everyone, Can I ask you all to budge up a little bit to make some room for Oliver Quinn Stevenson, born 15/12/2019 weighing 7lb 5 1/2 Oz

No words! Well maybe one. CUTE.

We are all born winners and this little warrior is no exception. Oliver Quinn Stevenson, always remember your greatness.

"Before you were born, and were still too tiny for the human eye to see, you won the race for life from among 250 million competitors. And yet, how fast you have forgotten your strength, when your very existence is proof of your greatness. You were born a winner, a warrior, one who defied the odds by surviving the most gruesome battle of them all. And now that you are a giant, why do you even doubt victory against smaller numbers and wider margins? The only walls that exist, are those you have placed in your mind. And whatever obstacles you conceive, exist only because you have forgotten what you have already achieved."

— *Rise Up and Salute the Sun*
Suzy Kassem

16 December 2019

A scan of Andrea's left leg at Macclesfield Hospital this morning confirms the DVT. It traces the length of her leg up to her hip. A scan of her upper body is arranged to identify how far the DVT has travelled.

If a blood clot breaks free and moves through your bloodstream, it can get stuck in a blood vessel of the lung. This is called a pulmonary embolism and can be fatal. For Andrea, this is a minor possibility that must be discounted. The blood thinning medication is to continue for the next three months.

17 December 2019

We arrive at St Michaels and All Angels Church, next door to the Macclesfield Town Hall, about thirty minutes before The Christie Christmas Concert is due to start. This gives us enough time to meet the fund raising team. We chat with Roger Spencer, The Christie CEO, for much of this time. His knowledge and passion are impressive. He is grateful to us for agreeing to present our story at this evening's celebration and welcomes us into The Christie family.

The Reverend Martin Stephens commences proceedings by welcoming the four-hundred plus sell out audience. The Church boasts wonderful architecture and is beautifully decorated. It's a dramatic and splendid venue, a perfect backdrop for this evenings celebration.

Mark Radcliffe is the evening's host and introduces each act with clarity and professional good humour. He is a Bolton born Radio Two broadcaster, musician and writer who now lives in Knutsford. He was recently treated at The Christie after being diagnosed with a cancerous tumour at the back of his tongue in September 2018 which had spread to some of the lymph nodes in his neck. In Spring 2019, he was told his cancer was in remission.

The Christie family
and the thoroughly entertaining Mark Radcliffe

He speaks of his cancer treatment at various times during the evening. His career relies on talking, yet cancer chose to exploit this by landing at the back of his tongue and then infecting his neck. Mark confesses to have said some terrible things over the years, but this affliction must surely be unfair retribution. Like us, he recognises that humour, with some self-deprecation, is an excellent and spirited way of fighting back and retaining one's sanity.

"They took a walnut size tumour from here and an apple sized tumour from here. My wife said any more of that and we'll have enough for a Walldorf salad!"

Music is provided by the Macclesfield Youth Brass Band, the Fallibroome Academy choir with standout individual performances from Katherine Farrow (a professional singer) and Ischia Gooda (the BBC Radio Two young Chorister of the year). The audience are encouraged to join in singing some of the Christmas carols, which they do with great gusto.

The magnificent St Michaels and All Angels Church

After all Andrea has been through recently, she doesn't quite feel up to speaking at this event. However, she stands by my side as I address the audience. I run through the timeline of our cancer treatments, pausing to emphasise moments of care and compassion that we had both received from The Macclesfield NHS Trust and The Christie.

My final anecdote is about Nathan who had asked me to film him and his mother while he rang the end of treatment bell at The Christie. It is my intention to tug on the heartstrings of the many parents in attendance. I implore that for the next generation of Nathan's living in our community we should all support, and encourage our family and friends to get behind, The Christie at Macclesfield appeal.

At the end of the evening we are given a gift of a bottle of wine and a Christmas card signed by all the fund raising team.

I hadn't realized it, but the audience contained many medical staff, not just from Macclesfield Hospital. Some introduce themselves to us to thank us for our moving address and for recognising the good work that the NHS does in caring with compassion.

18 December 2019

Andrea's favourite time of the year is Christmas. The tree and decorations go up on the 1 December and the countdown to Christmas Day commences courtesy of an advent calendar.

Sadly, neither of us have found the energy to engage with our 2019 Christmas spirit. It dawns on us that we haven't even put up a Christmas tree yet. We at least manage to put that right today and Chloe, Rhys and Arianna help us decorate it. When I say "help us", I mean that we sit back and watch them. It's a good, amusing and festive time together.

There's an awkward moment when Rhys stands on the arm of the sofa to reach, and trim, the top branch and place the Christmas star on top of the tree. He wobbles momentarily and hangs onto the tree to prevent himself from falling. Although he completes his mission, the tree is left precariously leaning into the room.

It's for that reason that the tree falls over with a loud clatter later in the day. It had nothing at all to do with the way I had initially secured the tree in its stand.

No sir, not me!

19 December 2019

Andrea and I have arranged to meet Paul and Julie Bernardi in a pub in Mobberley for a meal. Paul is expecting the results of his biopsy sometime today. We arrive first and get a message that they're on their way, with no mention of the results. It's a tense moment extinguished only on the arrival of a smiling Bernardi. His biopsy has confirmed that he has prostate cancer.

So why the happy face?

The prostate is a small gland, found only in men, about the size of a walnut. It's located between the penis and the bladder and surrounds the urethra, the tube that carries urine out of the body. The main function of the prostate is to produce a thick white fluid that creates semen when mixed with sperm produced by the testicles.

Prostate cancer is the most common cancer in men in the UK. Ordinarily it develops slowly, so there may be no signs for many years. Symptoms usually appear when the prostate is large enough to press against the urethra, changing the way you urinate. However, it is also quite normal for the prostate gland to grow due to hormonal changes as a man gets older. This is known as benign prostate enlargement

For many men, as is the case with Paul, treatment is not immediately necessary. His doctor has recommended prolonged and active surveillance. Paul is more likely going to die of old age than of prostate cancer. The weeks of uncertainty and worry about his health have conclusively ended with a diagnosis completely opposed to the one that the initial fear of cancer had demanded.

The Spirit of Rooster

Bernardi 1 – 0 Cancer (final result, game over).

We planned to eat in Mobberley this evening so that we could also visit our friend Dave Clayton at The Big Hill Distillery, the home of *The Spirit of George* gin. The 'George' is a reference to George Herbert Leigh Mallory the British mountaineer born in Mobberley. He was last seen alive on 8 June 1924, about eight-hundred vertical feet from the Everest summit. On 1 May 1999 his preserved body was found with compelling evidence to suggest he had made it to the summit.

The botanical composition of this hand-crafted gin, created to honour his name and his spirit, compliments his back story. Deliciously dry with flavours from Nepal of ginger, cloves, cinnamon, cardamom and a hint of Himalayan tea.

The owners, Dave and Ben, have invested in George Mallory's never-say-die attitude to scale the heights of the highly competitive spirits production industry to successfully create this double gold multi-award winning gin. I'd recommend gin fans everywhere to visit the distillery and online at www.bighilldistillery.com.

Dave proudly provides us with a tour of his distillery with charm and the expertise of a master craftsman of his trade. As we drive away, to the sound of various gin bottles rattling in the back of the car, a thought occurs to me. Life sometimes requires us to dig deep and find the spirit, the resolve, the determination that enables us to climb mountains. Although Rooster is a fictional character, I wonder what he and George would have made of each other had they met half way up Everest.

Our planned evening not yet complete, we drive to MADS Little Theatre for the annual mulled wine jamboree. All the usual suspects are there, we are amongst the very best of friends.

I should state for the record that I am not yet able to drink alcohol beyond the odd glass of wine or a single, medicinal gin and tonic. If I do I very quickly pay the price with an uncomfortable bowel movement. Although I respect my current alcoholic limitation, I will occasionally challenge it, but only in the safety of my own home.

Despite driving to a pub, a distillery and a mulled wine event, all in one evening, I stick to the comfort of soft drinks only.

Well, maybe with the exception one small tipple of George!

20 December 2019

This afternoon we learn that Rob Copeland's father, Clive Copeland, had peacefully passed away this morning. He was eighty-five years old, suffered from Alzheimer's and recently moved into a nursing home. Although we met him a few times at MADS theatre, our thoughts instinctively turn to Rob first. To show our support we message to ask how he is and for the funeral arrangements.

This evening is a time to visit Luke, Kerry and new-born Oliver in Macclesfield hospital. Oliver is as cute in person as he appeared to be in his photograph, more so, because we get to hold and cuddle him. He's not allowed to go home just yet as his heart rate and temperature need to be monitored. I think we stay longer than visiting hours permit, but it is hard to let him go.

22 December 2019

Today is Clive Copeland's funeral and one we attend in support of our good friend Rob, Clive's son. The funeral is a Jewish funeral, the likes of which we have never attended before. Jewish burials take place as soon as possible after death, usually within twenty-four hours. but cannot take place on the Shabbat (Saturday) nor during most Jewish holidays.

Rob has a number of MADS friends in attendance today including our travelling companions Cameron and Stuart. As we drive through the Jewish entrance of Mill Lane Cemetery in Cheadle, we notice a freshly dug grave in the graveyard.

On entry to the cemetery lodge, men are directed to the right-hand side of the coffin and women to the left. The hatless men are handed a kippah, a cloth, brimless cap, to cover our heads with. I am sat next to David Bye, Rob's father-in-law. With a big grin Rob hands him a kippah, saying:

"It was my dad's."

The honour is not lost on David who takes it and places it on his head with a smile, a nod and a certain reverence.

Before the service begins a Keriah is performed and Rob's shirt is torn. This is an ancient tradition and a symbol of mourning. The Rabbi says some kind words and chants a few Jewish prayers in Hebrew.

The coffin, a simple, closed, biodegradable casket, is then wheeled down a pathway to the freshly dug grave, with the congregation following in procession.

More Hebrew words are spoken by the graveside but out of our earshot. The coffin is lowered into the grave and the men are invited to take turns to use any of the three shovels standing upright in a mound of earth. The local grave-diggers then finish the job.

The congregation forms two lines, one either side of the pathway. The mourners, immediate family members only, then walk the line between the congregation, shaking hands and offering thanks. Rob pauses to warmly kiss the back of Andrea's hand. Returning to the lodge, we offer our sympathies to the Copeland family and leave.

The mourners return to the family home, where Shiva is observed. This is a period of ritual mourning allowing individuals to express their sorrow. The MADS friends who have attended gather at the home of David and Maureen Bye for drinks and nibbles.

Upon reflection, I am struck by a number of things. The funeral was full of Jewish traditions I felt respectfully compelled to observe, despite my own atheism. Rob handled himself particularly well; burying your father is not an easy undertaking. When somebody dies the world seems different, smaller and with fewer opportunities. Then someone new arrives and the world is full of infinite possibilities again.

Renewal is constant, introducing fresh hope and unique prospects in its path. By continually seizing them, our own renewal becomes iterative.

Max returns home from Australia in the evening, where he's been traveling with Robyn these last seven weeks. It's fabulous to see him and catch up with his adventures.

23 December 2019

Despite Andrea's recovery being interrupted by other related and non-related conditions, she has powered through and is gaining strength. The distraction of recent, various people-centered celebrations has lifted us both and enabled Andrea to put her rehabilitation into perspective.

During the last few weeks, I have considered returning to work and have started to search various job sites for an appropriate IT contract. Today I am interviewed for an opportunity at Barclays and offered the position.

I had a thirty year career with Barclays and left them on good terms and with voluntary redundancy in 2009. I have been contracting ever since, but have never lost my deep respect for the company that cared for me and taught me so much over so many important and formative years. I keenly accept the offer, although I'm acutely aware that other opportunities are also starting to materialise.

The Christie fund-raising team post their online report of the Christmas concert at the St Michaels and All Angels Church. It's a good read that recalls a magical and memorable evening. I share it on Facebook asking friends to get any uncertain symptoms checked and to donate to the Christie at Macclesfield appeal.

24 December 2019

To my Andrea:

"It was Christmas eve babe
In the drunk tank
An old man said to me: won't see another one
And then they sang a song
The rare old mountain dew
I turned my face away and dreamed about you
Got on a lucky one
Came in eighteen to one
I've got a feeling
This year's for me and you
So happy Christmas
I love you baby
I can see a better time
Where all our dreams come true."

— *Fairytale of New York*
The Pogues

Andrea has a chest scan appointment at Macclesfield Hospital. It's all very routine but necessary in order to track the DVT. Since taking the blood thinning medication there's been no repeat of the symptoms that required me to call on the emergency services. She will be contacted with the results within the next week or so.

Whilst we are in the hospital we visit Kerry, Luke and baby Oliver. Sadly, the doctors want to continue monitoring Oliver's progress for a few more days. Their first family Christmas will be spent in hospital. The joy they feel at having Oliver in their lives seems to soften the blow. He is their renewal and matters the most.

We leave the hospital and make our way to the Red Willow pub for our annual Christmas Eve gathering with the MADS company. Amongst all the lively banter, I have a moment of quiet reflection and look around the room at all the happy, chattering faces.

It all began almost three years ago in *Jerusalem* and in the company of many of these giants. Their unbelievable kindness never once wavered and has helped to carry both Andrea and I to this day. This day when we can see a better time, where all our dreams come true.

25 December 2019

There is no better place for us to be on Christmas Day than at home in the company of my three sons Luke, Max and Cyrus. As is the tradition I cook the Christmas dinner with help from Andrea when called upon.

Over the last week we have stood defiantly with The Christie family against cancer, embraced the company of those friends and family who have shared in the intimacy of our last three years and we have celebrated new life. Our renewal is complete.

We have bared our souls, described every limiting nuance of our physical and emotional condition throughout our living torture. To finally be able to quote with confidence the words on the end of treatment bell:

> Ring this bell 3 times well
> Its toll to clearly say
> My treatments done
> This course is run
> And I'm on my way

May the tears you cried during the 2010's water the seeds you have planted for the 2020's.

THE EPILOGUE MONSTER

I have this vision of a horrible little monster in hell called *cancer*, a really ugly, twisted and nasty piece of work. He's been watching and manipulating my life over the last couple of years and giggling to himself at my misfortune. Somehow he's been able to send a lot of misery and suffering my way. But recently he's suddenly thought:

"Crap! Well that's not the way I planned things to turn out for him."

So, how have things turned out since I was first diagnosed and then treated for cancer? I've survived, that's pretty important. But how I've survived is also important.

Over the last two years I have changed physically. I have a shark-bite scar across my back. Mr Krysiac once said that scars are like tattoos but with better stories. Whilst I appreciate the sentiment, I doubt that a brutal, angry looking scar will be admired as much as an artistic tattoo. Does brutality lend itself to better story-telling than artistic creation?

My lower left lung and a good deal of my bowel have been removed. The loss of half a lung still gives me occasional breathing difficulties, but this will improve with time.

The partial removal of my bowel also involved cutting away the top part of my anus. This means a shorter waste disposal route and a smaller excrement loading bay, resulting in a greater urgency when needing to poo. Add to this the temporary damage that radiotherapy caused to the healthy tissue in my bowel and that sense of urgency is compounded. This will also get better with time.

The soles of my feet get sore with pins and needles, particularly when cold, due to permanent damage caused by chemotherapy. I consider this peripheral neuropathy to be a healthy reminder that my system took the maximum amount of chemotherapy it could tolerate and then it took just a little more. Unlike the elderly, terminally ill gentleman we met during my first session of chemotherapy, I can never regret not having had enough of this necessary poison.

The three tiny tattoos I carry are a permanent badge of honour which remind me of the thousands of survivors who, like me, have rung the End of Treatment Bell at The Christie.

These physical changes emanate from the great fight that my surgeons, oncologists and nurses have had against my cancer on my behalf. These amazing healers are human too and, as such, invest emotionally in their patients. I'm sure they carry internal scars from many similar fights, particularly from those whom they have lost.

So *how* have I survived?

My fight against cancer was a psychological one; it took place in my head. I resolved very early on not to let it damage my spirit. Even if cancer broke me physically, my spirit, the seat of my emotions and character, would remain intact.

The thing I didn't see coming is that my fight nourished my spirit, which not only is still whole, but has grown. Facing extreme adversity with the support of courage, love and compassion has boosted my psyche. I feel uplifted because of the experience. Caring for my courageous wife during her cancer treatment has matured my spirit even more.

"Cancer can take away all of my physical abilities. It cannot touch my mind, it cannot touch my heart and it cannot touch my soul."

– Jim Valvano

I have seen humanity at its very best and have met and been inspired by extraordinary carers and victims alike. The NHS is an institution like no other, that invests in the holistic well-being of every individual it serves. It mends us physically, but does so with a warmth and understanding that caresses our soul. People truly caring for people.

My relationship with Andrea has not only survived acute difficulties, but it has blossomed because of them. Each of us have been both cancer victim and caregiver. Together we have confronted my mortality and the uncertainty of Andrea's initial prognosis. We have discussed the real possibility of my early and painful death, to ultimately discover a deeper love that can survive almost anything.

My sons have distinguished themselves with dignity. Man for man they stood by me, armed to the teeth, in my fight, with humour and courage. In doing so, a steadfast, mutual respect has emerged that binds father and son with a new and permanent admiration.

My friends have become closer to me. They have honoured me with a friendship love that I would not have experienced without my suffering. The friends I have lost were kind enough to leave a piece of them with me. They were giants and, each day, I feel privilege and pride for the connection we once had.

My professional career has remained intact. My stubborn refusal to let cancer destroy my ability to work has resulted in my continued IT consultancy. My year-long absence in 2017 had no lasting effect. Whilst my contract with

The Spirit of Rooster

Defra fizzled out due to Brexit buffoonery, I have a number of new opportunities in the pipeline to consider. My absence has stiffened my resolve not only to continue working, but do so with more commitment and a renewed energy.

The faith that MADS had in me to continue acting in between cancer treatments gave me a healthy distraction. The 2019/20 season that lies ahead contains many exciting acting prospects for me to consider. My front-of-house duties will keep me close to a company I feel fortunate to continue serving and be an active member of.

Dealing with cancer and its treatment has made me feel more determined to enjoy both my professional career and my Theatre work whilst I can. I now value them both, more than ever.

That determination and the *Rooster* spirit that both Andrea and I have displayed in recent years has also attracted a positive notoriety that we have tried to put to good use. The many giants supporting us dug deep into their pockets resulting in thousands of pounds being donated to excellent cancer causes. The publicity, media exposure, presentations, charity events, training video and this book that followed, exposed cancer as beatable. This ugly assailant enjoys being a terrorist, but terrorists are rightly subverted when victims no longer fear them. I like to think that we have made a small contribution to making cancer appear less fearful.

For all that, I say; thank you cancer, you horrible little monster. You have served me well. I have confronted you and your repulsive provocations but it's my destiny, my future and my way. Time might fly but I am the pilot.

"It is not in the stars to hold our destiny but in ourselves."

– William Shakespeare.

I do not plan for this book to serve as a lesson to others. I want it to simply be the telling of a real-life sequence of connected events which tell a story of survival. A story that will resonate with many people who have suffered, are suffering and will suffer from this terrible plague.

Some have kindly said they have felt inspired by the way Andrea and I have handled ourselves during treatment. I have certainly felt inspired by those who have cared for me and suffered with me. So I understand *inspiration*. It is an important human reaction. It is contagious and results in distinction, greatness, glory and feeds genius. I do not claim to have any of these attributes but I have been privileged to witness them in others.

Some of you reading this book may be suffering your own cancer hell and will recognise the challenges I have encountered. Some may have cared for a cancer victim. Possibly you have just been diagnosed and are planning your own unique treatment path. If you are looking for help, remember that this book is a record of my experience. Yours will be very different.

But, for what it's worth, my top tips are:

1. Get diagnosed NOW! If only one reader does this then this book has been worth publishing.
2. Check your bumps for lumps. Mammograming your boobs is more important than instagramming them.
3. Whatever happens retain your sense of humour.
4. Do everything that the medical profession tells you to do.
5. Your fight against cancer takes place in your head, so find resilience.
6. Love conquers everything, so let it.
7. Listen to the suffering of others. Other victims, carers and medics are human too. Be ready to offer them support.
8. There is no dignity in having cancer. Get used to that quickly.
9. Accept that you are different, try to be normal.
10. Pain is weakness leaving the body. So let it.
11. Pain is temporary, quitting lasts forever. So don't.
12. Spend time thinking about your own death. It's not death that you're fighting, so befriend it.
13. Cancer and its treatment are traumatic. You may survive but you will never be the same physical specimen again. However, you will see the world through wiser eyes.
14. Communicate, communicate and communicate, how you're feeling and what you're going through.

15. Life still goes on around you. Get involved, more than ever before.
16. Meet with triumph and disaster and treat those two imposters just the same, stoically.
17. Finally, and most importantly, when things seem especially rough just ask yourself, "did I shit my pants today?" If the answer is no, you're doing alright.

I do not anticipate this book flying off the shelves. I don't mind if it doesn't, that's not why I wrote it. Cancer is a tough subject to read about and I am a novice author. However, if a miracle does happen and it wins the Nobel Literature Prize, I should warn you that I'm not planning a sequel. This will not become the first of a trilogy. This book is most definitely a one-off.

The final chapter of my cancer caper has been written, there is no more. Like Rooster, I have banged my drum and summoned up all available mythical giants who continue to stand with us. Like Rocky Balboa, we have been hit hard and done our best to stay on our feet and keep moving forward, to win.

We are fortunate to have returned to happier, healthier times.

Move along, cancer, you monster, you have no more business here.

ABOUT THE AUTHOR

Hans Keith Oldham had a thirty year career with a major financial institution leaving it in 2009. Since then he has worked as an IT consultant across many diverse industries. Always believing that there is a book in everyone, the opportunity to put pen to paper came following two years of serious illness. Diagnosed with bowel cancer in 2017 he began a colourful and challenging period in his life. One that culminated in writing this, his first book.

Hans lives in Cheshire with his wife Andrea and two dogs Alfie and Stanley. He has four grown up and departed children from a previous marriage in Alyssa, Luke, Max and Cyrus. Alyssa has a much loved son, Zachary Attenborough Newton.

Since 2014 Hans has developed a passion for Theatre, specifically the Macclesfield Amateur Dramatic Society. Storytelling through acting is a performance medium as old as civilization itself and one that he is becoming accustomed to. Storytelling through writing, however, is a new departure for him.

****

Sadly, during the proofreading of this book Andrea's bridesmaid, Mia, passed away; may she rest in peace.